What Others are Saying

"A View From the Interior" serves as a [...]
time was in Madison. It offers a behind [...]
decisions were made. More than that, [...]
in these pages is a committed, compassionate cop—human, imperfect, decent, humorous, and kind.

—Doug Moe, *Wisconsin State Journal*

* * *

This is a story that needed to be told and I am glad Chief Riseling made the effort to tell it. This book will become a reference and required reading in more than one police class. Riseling held true to her values in some pretty trying circumstances and didn't allow politics to trump her core values.

—Reggie Gauger, Associate Dean (emeritus), Sheboygan, Wisconsin

* * *

This story reads like a well-written suspense novel that I couldn't put down. The side stories help the reader understand how the influence of past events in Chief Riseling's life served her well for the challenges she faced. There are no better ways to learn than by experience and hearing directly from those who have risen to a challenge and found success.

—Francine Tompkins, Associate Professor, PhD Education

* * *

This is what democracy looks like, so we will re-visit events like this in the future and police need to be prepared to practice tolerance of freedom of speech in these kinds of populist assemblies in spite of the political pressure to do otherwise.

—David Couper, Author of *Arrested Development*,
Chief of Police Retired, City of Madison, Wisconsin 1972-1993

* * *

This is a must read, for any law enforcement leader responsible for Emergency Government plans, Homeland Security tactics and strategies, as well as managing a multitude of Police resources at critical events. This book reflects the courage, wisdom and commitment to do the right thing, protecting the U.S. Constitution, during a very tumultuous time in Wisconsin's history.

—Richard Thomas, Chief of Police, Retired
Cities of Beloit and Port Washington, Wisconsin

* * *

During an unprecedented time in Wisconsin history, the effective response by police inside the State Capitol is a testimony to the leadership. This book chronicles the achievements crafted by Chief Riseling and other law enforcement leaders and tells the story of dedication and commitment displayed by police officers who worked tirelessly to bring this extraordinary series of events to a successful conclusion.

—John Gould, Chief of Police, Retired
Village of Cottage Grove, Wisconsin

* * *

A View *is not only an interesting story, it is an excellent primer for anyone charged with protecting our freedom of speech and assembly rights. It is a must-read for Incident Commanders who may be responsible for balancing the needs of our bosses and our duty to protect Constitutional Rights.*

Chief Riseling gives insight into the complexities of handling huge protests with many conflicting needs and a large multi-agency assemblage of responders. Chief Riseling's honest first hand perspective of the Wisconsin State Capitol protests made for an interesting page turning story of a women police commander in one of the most difficult leadership challenges that I have seen.
—Chief Dwight Henninger, Vail, Colorado

* * *

This book contains the raw truth about what really went on inside the Wisconsin Capitol during the 2011 protests. Chief Susan Riseling, placed in charge of everything happening within the Capitol, stood her ground against the politicians, police administrators, and state bureaucrats, to not only keep the peace between the factions, but to be sure no one's Constitutional rights were compromised. That is the real story.
—Jerald Jansen, Chief (ret.) Village of Shorewood Hills, WI, Police Dept.

* * *

This is a fascinating book that lends new insight into the already well-documented uprising... The reader discovers just how difficult it was dealing with the frustration of a huge crowd of people who felt they weren't being heard by the politicians in Madison. Through it all, Riseling adhered to her staunch belief that law enforcement can't take sides in political disputes. Frankly, Wisconsin was lucky to have someone with her modern policing philosophy in that key position.
—Dave Zweifel, editor emeritus of the *Capitol Times*

A View from the Interior

Policing the Protests
at the Wisconsin State Capitol

A VIEW FROM THE INTERIOR

Policing the Protests
at the Wisconsin State Capitol

SUSAN RISELING

MILWAUKEE, WISCONSIN

Published by
MavenMark Books
An imprint of HenschelHAUS Publishing, Inc.
2625 S. Greeley St. Suite 201
Milwaukee, WI 53207
www.HenschelHAUSbooks.com

All HenschelHAUS titles, imprints, and distributed lines are available at
special quantity discounts for educational, institutional, fund-raising,
or sales promotion.

Publisher's Cataloging-in-Publication Data:
Riseling, Susan.
A view from the interior : policing the protests at the Wisconsin
state capitol / Susan Riseling.
p. cm.
ISBN: 978-1-59598-255-1 (pbk.)
ISBN: 978-1-59598-256-8 (e-book)
Includes bibliographical references and index.
1. Protest movements—Wisconsin—History—21st century.
2. Wisconsin—Politics and government—21st century.
3. Crowd control. 4. Police.   I. Title.
HV6474 .R57 2013
363.32`16—dc23
2013948090

Cover photograph: Joe Lynde, Capitol Connection.
Other photographs throughout the book are credited to the
appropriate photographers and used with permission.
All photos are in color in the Kindle version of this book.

Printed in the United States of America.
Third printing.

*To the women and men of law enforcement,
who often find themselves
between a rock and a hard place.*

Without debate, without criticism
no administration and no country can succeed,
and no republic can survive.
—John F. Kennedy

TABLE OF CONTENTS

List of Names i

List of Abbreviations vii

Floor Plan of the Wisconsin State Capitol viii

Acknowledgments xi

Foreword xii

Preface 1

Introduction 7

Chapter 1: The Early Days 13

Chapter 2: Growing Branches 55

Chapter 3: A Peaceful Protest 111

Chapter 4: This is What Democracy Looks Like 161

Chapter 5: Voluntary Compliance 217

Chapter 6: Trust Built, Trust Broken 239

Chapter 7: Trials and Tribulations 309

Chapter 8: Transitions 357

Chapter 9: The Lingering End 385

Index 395

About the Author 401

LIST OF NAMES

Albert, John C.: Circuit Court Judge presiding in AFSCME v Department of Administration, March 2011

Altman, Bradley (Brad): Lieutenant, Wisconsin State Patrol, Interior Branch Division Commander, occasional Operations Chief, occasional Outdoor Commander

Barca, Peter: State Assembly Member representing 64th District (Democrat) served as the Assembly Minority Leader

Barica, Sue: Lead Administrative Assistant for the Capitol Police, responsible for everything—namely logistics and purchasing

Beecraft, Kim: Police Communications Operator for the Interior Branch

Blackdeer, Daniel (Dan): Deputy Chief, Capitol Police, Incident Commander, Member of the Policy Group. Promoted to Acting Chief of the Capitol Police May 18, 2012. Returned to Deputy Chief July 2012

Blair, Ron: Assistant Director, Department of Administration, Capitol Facility Manager

Blazel, Ted: Sergeant-at-Arms for the Senate, member of the Policy Group

Bridges, Brian: Assistant Chief, University of Wisconsin Police Department. Deputy Interior Branch Director—Operations

Brooks, Karl: Assistant Chief Warden, Wisconsin Department of Natural Resources, Substitute Deputy Interior Branch Commander, Assistant to the Deputy Interior Branch Commander—Staffing, lead officer for briefing Emergency Police Services

Brunner, Clark: Lieutenant Access Control, University of Wisconsin Police Department. Interior Branch squad leader and access control specialist

Burke, Dale: Assistant Chief (ret.) University of Wisconsin Police Department, University Response Plan Emergency Operation Center Manager, Interior Branch Division Commander

Curtis, William (Bill): Emergency Services Coordinator, University of Wisconsin Police Department. Interior Branch: records management, public communications, information analysis, and logistics. Promoted to Emergency Services Supervisor in 2012

Diamante, John (Johnnie): Captain University of Wisconsin Police Department. Interior Branch Division Commander, occasionally Deputy Operations Chief in Command Post

Donovan, Tim: Lieutenant Colonel (ret.), Interior Branch Public Information Officer March 1-5, 2011

Dowling, John: Member of the University's Office of Legal Services, assisted Chief Riseling with her court appearances

Dunbar, Donald: Adjutant General (Brigadier) Wisconsin National Guard, promoted to Major General August, 2011, member of the Policy Group

Ellis, Michael: President of the Senate, State Senator, 19th Senate District (Republican)

Ewing, Ruth: Sergeant, University of Wisconsin Police Department Squad Leader, Planning Assistant—Interior Branch, promoted to Lieutenant May 2013.

Falk, Kathleen: Dane County Executive (Democrat)

Fitzgerald, Scott: State Senator 13th Senate District, Majority Leader Senate, (Republican)

Fitzgerald, Stephen (Steve): Superintendent, Wisconsin State Patrol, former US Marshal for Western District of Wisconsin, former Dodge County Sheriff, Member of the Policy Group

Fitzgerald, Jeff: State Representative 39th Assembly District, Speaker of the Assembly, (Republican)

France, Paul: Planning Section Chief or Logistics Chief Command Post, Wisconsin Emergency Management

Fuller, Patrick: Assembly Clerk

Gilkes, Keith: Chief of Staff to the Governor (Republican)

Goetsch, Byron: Captain, Wisconsin Department of Natural Resources, Interior Branch Division Commander

Gossenheimer, Carol: UW–Madison Senior Program Analyst, Assistant to the Interior Branch Director—Coordination

Hanson, Doris: State Representative 1993-1998 representing the 47th Assembly District; previously served as the first woman Secretary of the Department of Administration.

Huebsch, Michael: Secretary Department of Administration. Former State Representative 94th Assembly District (Republican)

Jansen, Jerald (Jerry): Chief Shorewood Hills Police (ret.), Assistant Chief University of Wisconsin Police Department (ret.), Assistant to the Branch Director—Planning

Jensen, Jodi: Assistant to the Secretary of Department of Administration

Kuschel, Todd: Substitute Incident Commander, Deputy Incident Commander, Assistant Chief (ret.) University of Wisconsin Police Department. Promoted to Lieutenant Capitol Police May 18, 2012. Promoted to Captain in September of 2012.

Lazzaro, Maria: Assistant Attorney General, second chair, representing the Department of Administration

Lautenschlager, Peggy A. (Peg): Plaintiff attorney representing the American Federation of State, County, and Municipal Employees (AFSCME). Former U.S. Attorney Western District. Former Wisconsin Attorney General (Democrat)

LaWall, David (Dave): Emergency Service Coordinator, University of Wisconsin Police Department. Assigned to the Interior Branch in a support role for records management, logistics

Lindgren, Craig: Sergeant, Wisconsin State Patrol, Interior Branch Squad Leader. "Field promotion" to Sergeant/Lieutenant

Lind, John: Lieutenant, University of Wisconsin Police Department. Assigned to the Capitol as night Interior Branch Director

Lyall, Katharine: President Emeritus, University of Wisconsin System

Mahoney, David (Dave): Dane County Sheriff, Member of the Policy Group—Capitol Grounds/City Streets

Marchant, Robert (Rob): Clerk for the Senate

Martin, Carolyn (Biddy): Chancellor University of Wisconsin-Madison. Became President of Amherst College July 2011

Matysik, Jerald (Jerry): Chief of Police, City of Eau Claire, Wisconsin. Author of Letter to the Editor regarding the use of the police

Matthews, David: Assistant Administrator Wisconsin Department of Justice, Division of Criminal Investigation, promoted to Administrator of DCI October 2012.

Means, Steve: Assistant Attorney General. Lead counsel representing the Department of Administration

Merdler, Scott: Sergeant, Capitol Police

Mlsna, Leslie (Les): Sergeant, Wisconsin State Patrol, Interior Branch Squad Leader. "Field promotion" to Sergeant/Lieutenant and then Lieutenant/Lieutenant

Neuman, Christopher (Chris): Lieutenant, Wisconsin State Patrol, Interior Branch Safety Officer, Division Commander. Promoted to Captain fall 2011.

Newman, Benjamin (Ben): Professional Standards Lieutenant, University of Wisconsin Police Department. Assigned to the Command Post Planning Section, Interior Branch Capacity Management, metal screening, negotiation teams , named Chief of Southern Illinois University, Oct. 2013.

Newton, Michael (Mike): Captain, University of Wisconsin Police Department, Interior Branch Division Commander

Ozanne, Ismael (Ish): District Attorney of Dane County, Wisconsin

Pfatteicher, Sarah: UW–Madison Associate Dean College of Agriculture and Life Sciences, Assistant to Interior Branch Director. Aide-de-camp

Pocan, Mark: State Assembly Representative 78th Assembly District (Democrat). Elected to the U.S. House of Representatives November 2012

Price, Darren: Major, Wisconsin State Patrol, occasionally attended Policy Group

Reilly, Kevin: President of the University of Wisconsin System

Riseling, Susan (Sue): Associate Vice Chancellor/Chief of Police University of Wisconsin Police Department. Interior Branch Director, member of the Policy Group.

Rogers, Steven (Steve): Captain, University of Wisconsin Police Department, Commanded University Police Department in absence of the Chief. Occasional Interior Branch Division Commander, promoted to Assistant Chief July 2013.

Renlund, Cari Anne: Chief Legal Counsel for the Department of Administration, returned to private practice June 2011.

Rutherford, Lisa: Lead Counsel University of Wisconsin-Madison, became Chief Policy Officer and General Counsel March, 2013 at Amherst College.

Sasso, Kari: Patrol Lieutenant, University of Wisconsin Police Department, assigned to Capitol Capacity Management, metal screening, and negotiation teams, promoted to Captain June 2013.

Schaffer, Brandi: Emergency Service Coordinator, University of Wisconsin Police Department. Served in the Interior Branch Support, logistics

Schmidt, Marc: Lieutenant, Capitol Police, Interior Branch Division Commander. "Field promotion" to Captain. Retired May 2012

Silbernagel, Mark: Lieutenant, University of Wisconsin Police Department. Night shift Interior Branch Director

Soley, Karen: Captain, University of Wisconsin Police Department. Deputy Operations Chief in Command Post, University Branch Director

Stark, Randall (Randy): Chief Warden, Wisconsin Department of Natural Resources. Deputy, Interior Branch Director. Second negotiator with the leadership of union and protest groups. Intermittently attended the Policy Group.

Teasdale, Charles (Chuck): Captain, Wisconsin State Patrol. Operations Chief, toward the end of the engagement attended Policy Group

Tonnon Byers, Anne: Sergeant-of-Arms for the Assembly

Tubbs, Charles: Chief, Capitol Police. Member of the Policy Group. He served as principal negotiator with union leadership and protest groups. He resigned June 1, 2012 to become Dane County Emergency Management Director.

Virgil, Tina: Director, Division of Criminal Investigation. State Fire Marshall. DCI liaison to Interior Branch Director

Walker, Scott: Governor of the State of Wisconsin. Elected November 2010, sworn in January 2011 (Republican)

Wall, Edward (Ed): Administrator, Wisconsin Department of Justice Division of Criminal Investigation (DCI). Became Secretary of Corrections October 2012.

Wernet, Kevin: Assistant to Interior Branch Director, aide-de-camp. Instructor at Blackhawk Technical College, firefighter, Southwest Wisconsin Incident Management Team, Emergency Management, McFarland, WI.

Whiry, Renee: Emergency Service Coordinator, University of Wisconsin Police Department. Assigned to the Interior Branch for support services, records management, and logistics.

Wray, Noble: Chief of Police, City of Madison, Wisconsin, retired October 2013.

Ystenes, Peter (Pete): Detective Lieutenant, University of Wisconsin Police Department. Assigned to the Capitol, Capacity Management, metal screening, promoted to Captain July 2013.

LIST OF ABBREVIATIONS
AND ACRONYMS

AAG: Assistant Attorney General
AG: Attorney General
ASFCME: Association of State, Federal, County, Municipal, Employees
CPD: Capitol Police Department
DA: District Attorney
DCI: Division of Criminal Investigation
DCSO: Dane County Sheriff Office
DNR: Department of Natural Resources
DOA: Department of Administration
DOJ: Department of Justice
EOC: Emergency Operations Center
EPS: Emergency Police Service
IAP: Incident Action Plan
IC: Incident Commander
ICS: Incident Command System
MFD: Madison Fire Department
MPD: Madison Police Department
NIMS: National Incident Management System
TAA: Teaching Assistants Association
URP: University of Wisconsin Response Plan
UWPD: University of Wisconsin Police Department
UWS: University of Wisconsin System
WEAC: Wisconsin Education Association Council
WLEA: Wisconsin Law Enforcement Association
WSP: Wisconsin State Patrol

Ground Floor

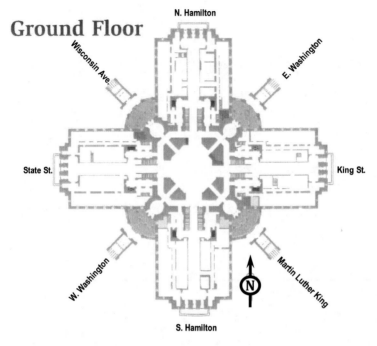

First Floor

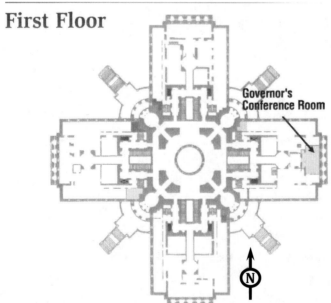

Floor plans courtesy of the Wisconsin Department of Administration

Second Floor

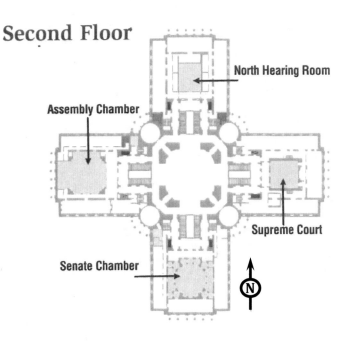

North Hearing Room

Assembly Chamber

Supreme Court

Senate Chamber

N

Fourth Floor

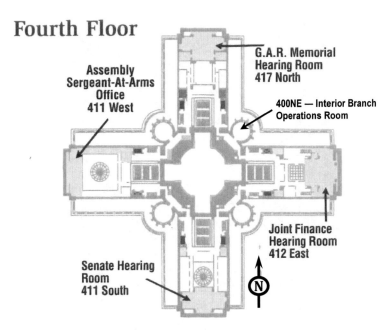

G.A.R. Memorial
Hearing Room
417 North

Assembly
Sergeant-At-Arms
Office
411 West

400NE — Interior Branch
Operations Room

Joint Finance
Hearing Room
412 East

Senate Hearing
Room
411 South

N

ACKNOWLEDGMENTS

SO FEW THINGS IN LIFE ARE ACCOMPLISHED ALONE AND THIS EFFORT IS NO different. I would like to thank my parents who raised me to believe I could do anything, ensured I received a good education, who taught me right from wrong, to be fair and that one's word is one's bond.

I would also like to thank my partner in life, Joanne E. Berg, whose support and love make me a better person. In addition, her love of the written word is extraordinary and she is a wonderful "editor."

More thanks go to my friend, retired Chief Jerald Jansen, for his wisdom, hard work, and wise council; to Mr. Dan Rosenblatt, my friend and mentor, for his willingness to "read ahead" and write the foreword for the book. Dan's years as Executive Director of the International Association of Chiefs of Police is a unique qualification to offer insight into policing; to my assistants in the operation: Brian Bridges, Randy Stark, Kevin Wernet, and Sarah Pffatteicher; to my employer, the University of Wisconsin–Madison that believes in and practices "The Wisconsin Idea," which allows me to serve in a far broader role throughout the state and country; to Mark Golbach, Joe Lynde, and Jim Escalante for the use of their photographs that capture the scene of democracy in progress; to Kira Henschel of HenschelHaus Publishing for her guidance, knowledge and savvy—thank you!

I would also like to thank former Capitol Police Chief Charles Tubbs and Deputy Chief Daniel Blackdeer, who gave me the opportunity to use my skills and ability and lead the largest contingent of law enforcement organized to deal with civil unrest in the State Capitol in over forty years.

Finally, I would also like to thank the women and men of the Interior Branch, February 11 to March 10, 2011, who came to work, stood watch, and facilitated the exercise of the First Amendment to the United States Constitution for over one and a half million of our citizens.

The Wisconsin State Capitol. Protesters gathering on the lawn.
(Photo by Mark Golbach)

FOREWORD

YEARS AGO, I SAT IN WITH A GROUP OF POLICE EXECUTIVES WHO WERE asked to help create a law enforcement research program. The conversation was helpful but wandering and needed a sharper focus. So I asked one of the more thoughtful but quiet chiefs at the table what he wanted from a research program.

"Give me a crystal ball," he said. "Tell me what my future problems will be and how I can get ready to deal with them."

We were all stunned. He was right on target and everyone in the room agreed, but we weren't sure how to create that predictive lens or the remedies that would be required from the perspective it generated.

In retrospect, though, the response to his suggestion was in hand and not so difficult to achieve. And, in many ways, the readers of this book will find that crystal ball.

There are thousands of independent police agencies in the United States and tens of thousands more operating in democratic societies around the world that confront a wide variety of challenges daily. These challenges include such variables as culture, population, size, resources and, of course, local, state and national laws. The global policing mosaic, thus, is too large and too varied to expect that anyone can tell any single agency head what will land on a department's doorstep the next day.

Reports on trends and specific crimes, however, serve to give notice to the observant chief of what's in the wind. But how can the effective police leader best prepare?

The answer can be found in the commitment of a remarkable community of police leaders who put a very high value on learning from the experience of others—both giving and receiving.

Almost every police executive is willing to share his or her own experiences and to learn from the experiences of peers. And it is in that remarkably open and giving behavior where the response to the chief on that research panel can be found. By creating and sharing a record of what happened, as well as the why and how the police agency responded to a particular event or situation, a police executive can truly help others enhance their abilities to predict and prepare. The more the presentation shares and the more candid it is, the more value there is to the practitioner.

Chief Susan Riseling is a true believer and active participant in this sharing process. In this outstanding work, she has assembled a document that delivers valuable lessons to the field. She carefully articulates how the law enforcement community responded to a remarkable series of events that occurred in Wisconsin during the first few months of 2011. This book presents a highly detailed history of the many issues and problems that arose when law enforcement agencies from around the state were required to come together to ensure the free speech and assembly rights of the people of the state, while maintaining order and protecting the peace.

A View From the Interior—Policing the Protests in the Wisconsin State Capitol, is an open, honest, and candid work. It is not a review of perfection; in fact, the best lessons learned from the Wisconsin experience presented here are where the mistakes were made— from communications failures to leadership struggles to shifting priorities to swamped personnel—and how they were creatively, intelligently and successfully overcome.

There is a message, an insight, a morsel of truth on every page of this book that provides the reader with a fresh opportunity to learn. Chief Riseling presents the whole story, going to great lengths to weave into her narrative both the professional and personal aspects of these events as part of her overall objective to provide the reader with every opportunity to learn from her experience. For me, this is as rare as it is valuable.

This publication serves as a meaningful tool for the law enforcement practitioner at any level, just as it serves to help the general public gain a better understanding of how law enforcement agencies and leaders operate in times of political uncertainty, chaos, and high tension.

Perhaps the most inspiring aspect of this book is the clear and often repeated recognition by this remarkable police chief and her colleagues that their primary role in this crisis was to protect the Constitutional rights of the people in Wisconsin.

Those citizens who assembled to engage in peaceful protest of their government's actions during this time were well served by the men and women of law enforcement in Wisconsin. They were truly extraordinary guardians of the public trust.

Dan Rosenblatt
Executive Director of the International Association
of Chiefs of Police (ret.)
Alexandria, Virginia

*The first night of the Interior Branch operation, February 17, 2011.
Looking inside at Kevin Wernet and Chief Sue Riseling.
(Photo by Tony Barnes)*

PREFACE

THE PHONE WOKE ME AT 6:10 A.M. "CHIEF RISELING, SOME GUY HAS U-locked himself to the rear axle of a U-Haul truck in the loading dock of the Primate Center," my dispatcher informed me.

"Why?"

"He's an animal rights activist and he wants to block the operations of the loading zone."

"Well, that's one way to do it, I suppose."

"Chief?"

"Yes?"

"I've just been told three more people have U-locked themselves together by their necks at the front of Primate and another woman has chained herself to the front door."

"OK. Who is there from our shop?"

"Right now, Security Officer Jim Hooker. The day shift sergeant will be here shortly."

I thought for a second. "OK, tell Hooker just to monitor and make sure they don't hurt themselves. Send the sergeant over when he arrives, page UW news service and Lieutenant Burke. I'll be there in thirty minutes. Thanks."

When you are a police chief at a Big Ten University, you can expect animal rights activists, as well as debate, discussion, dissent, protests, marches, rallies and vigils. If it isn't animal rights, it's tuition hikes, it's sweat shops, it's Regent policy, it's the war, it's "Don't Ask, Don't Tell." It is always something. At UW–Madison, it is "something" dozens and dozens of times a year. It is what democracy looks like when it meets higher education.

It was 1999 and we knew the animal rights activists were touring the country, University to University, and we had expected a visit to UW–Madison. The activists stayed for days at each of the other campuses they had visited, blocking traffic, chaining themselves to doors and to each other. So this wasn't a total surprise really.

When I arrived that morning at the Primate Center, a large one-story research facility housing hundreds of animals, sure enough, there the activist was, bike-locked to the rear axle of a truck that was backed into the loading dock. I looked under the truck. The axle was about 17 inches off the ground. The young man's neck was at an unnatural angle.

"Hello, my name is Sue Riseling. I'm the Police Chief here. What's your name?"

No response.

"Doesn't that hurt your neck?"

Nothing.

"Where's the key?"

"I don't have the key."

"You don't have the key?"

"Nope."

"OK, so you have locked yourself to the axle of a truck, which doesn't belong to you and you do not have the key. Do I have that right?"

"Yep."

"Who rented the truck?"

"Don't know."

"OK, you don't want to give me your name—I get that. What do you want me to call you?"

"Whatever."

"OK, Whatever it will be then. I am going to assign an officer to you because I don't want you to hurt yourself."

"Whatever."

His compatriot had chained herself to the front door, and three others had, U-locked themselves to each other by their necks. The threesome was on the landing just outside the front door. A crowd of about 250 had formed to see what we would do.

Security Officer Jim Hooker, who had been first on the scene, came over to me.

"Morning, Chief."

"Jim."

"They superglued all the door locks around the building perimeter. We were able to get one open. We've got a locksmith on the way for the others."

"Thanks. Keep me posted."

The loading dock had three bays available, but only one was blocked. The building had more than one entrance, so we simply redirected staff to the other bays and doors. These young adults wanted to make a point. I wanted to help them make their point. This was freedom of speech—they had picked the content, time, place and manner. As a police chief, I had learned long ago that "time, place and manner" were mine to choose—never the content. I had every legal basis to remove them. They were trespassing and blocking entrances, both illegal activities under Wisconsin law. However, the exercise of basic Constitutional rights is important; it is fundamental for Americans and, like a muscle, should be exercised periodically or it will wither away.

By choosing one of three bays, and only one of a handful of doors to the building to block for their demonstration, the activists did not keep the lab and its staff from functioning. It didn't matter what I thought of their cause. I valued their First Amendment rights and it was my role to protect their rights.

What I can manage is *time*. No need to rush in this situation.

Place—the UW Primate Center is the place to protest against the use of monkeys in research. Since we had other ways in and out the building, this didn't present any problems for us.

Manner—I wouldn't have chosen to lock myself to an axle of a truck or chain myself to a door. I have close friends, but I am not sure being locked to them by our necks was the way to go. Who was I to say the approach wouldn't work for their cause? Their manner didn't actually pose an issue for me as long as we didn't have to move them or cut them loose.

We assigned an officer to watch the four in front of the door. Another officer stayed near the young man under the truck. I didn't want "Whatever" to hang himself unintentionally. By noon, "Whatever," still under the U-Haul, had a pretty sore neck and he needed to use a rest room. The officer assigned to him radioed the Command Post we had set up for the event. The young man wanted us to cut the lock and free him. We once again suggested that he give us the key. He claimed he didn't have it. He explained to the officer that whenever he has done this before, the police had always cut him loose within a half an hour, then arrested and jailed him. *What kind of protest is that*, I wondered?

Eventually nature's call was too great, but he didn't want to be freed by his own actions, so he wet his pants. Meanwhile, the folks at the front door had worn adult diapers so when they needed to relieve themselves, they were prepared. What they hadn't come prepared for was that we were willing to let them have their day— all day in fact. We asked them repeatedly for the key to their locks, and they repeatedly told us they didn't have the keys. I was unwilling to use a saw that close to someone's neck when the disruption to the building operations was minor. So we waited.

By 5:00 p.m., the young man under the truck was screaming at the crowd to give us the key to the lock. He couldn't take it anymore. The key flew out from the crowd. We picked up the key, released his neck, had him checked by paramedics, placed him under arrest, and whisked him away to the county jail. Once the foursome at the front door realized their colleague had given up, they too called for the keys, which also came from someone in the crowd. We unlocked them, arrested them, and took them to jail. We contacted the U-Haul company and had someone come to retrieve the truck. The activists had rented it just for this purpose. The next day, they left UW–Madison; there would be no multiple-day stay.

I take the First Amendment very seriously. My responsibility to uphold the First Amendment is a supreme honor. I have studied the characteristics, moods, actions, and features of dissenters. It is my business. If you are going to exercise your First Amendment rights in my jurisdiction, be prepared to fully exercise those rights.

The protesters got creative. (Photo by Joe Lynde)

Protesters starting to gather around the Wisconsin Capitol building.
(Photo by Joe Lynde)

INTRODUCTION

ONE OF THE MOST VISIBLE SEGMENTS OF OUR GOVERNMENT IN EVERYDAY American life is law enforcement. While the complete history of law enforcement is for another book, there have been many times in American history when law enforcement personnel were used to suppress citizens' Constitutionally protected rights. In American law enforcement, our authority always falls under civilian leadership within the government. What happens when civilian leaders order law enforcement to act in a manner that may suppress the exercise of Constitutionally protected rights? Does law enforcement refuse such orders or follow the directives as the system of civilian oversight would suggest?

The 1960s were the decade of my birth and many events of that time shaped my thinking. Before I was old enough to understand anything about protest marches, demonstrations, and law enforcement, two men would become a part of a dark history of the profession to which I would dedicate my life's work.

Theophilus Eugene "Bull" Connor was the Commissioner of Public Safety in Birmingham, Alabama in 1963. A member of the Klu Klux Klan in the 1920s, he vehemently opposed ending segregation in Alabama. He became notorious across America for his actions taken against demonstrators in May of 1963. On May 2, he and his men (and they were all men back then) arrested over 950 African-Americans between the ages of 6 and 18 for participating in a march. Many more protesters turned out the next day to object to Bull Connor's actions. Bull Connor ordered that fire hoses be used

7

on the protesters. The power of water shooting from a fire hose can rip the skin and damage flesh. He also ordered the use of police dogs to attack the demonstrators. By May 7, he and his men had arrested approximately 3,000 protesters. The images horrified America.[1]

A few years later, a cattle rancher was appointed Sheriff of Selma, Alabama by his boyhood pal, Governor Jim Folsom. Sheriff Jim Clark was known for carrying his cattle prod and using it on African-Americans. It was Sheriff Clark who, along with the Alabama State Patrol, attacked marchers on the Selma Bridge on March 7, 1965 in what became "Bloody Sunday." Using a mounted posse comprising mostly KKK members, he sent them onto the bridge to beat and trample the marchers. In a second march just a few days later, 2,500 protesters were turned away from the bridge. But when the march began again on March 16, the marchers were escorted by 2,000 soldiers and 1,900 Alabama National Guard members under federal command. This time, the marchers success-fully walked across the Selma Bridge.[2]

My childhood memories of the 1960s include stories of the civil rights marches and the massive anti-war protests in the city where I was born, Washington D.C. My grandfather was night editor of the *Washington Post* and so news was a key part of my growing up.

In April of 1968, Dr. Martin Luther King Jr. was assassinated. I was seven years old. Riots and violence erupted throughout the country. In June of 1968, Bobby Kennedy was assassinated. I remember my parents' sadness over these events as absolutely palpable. Dinner conversations were heavy, with my father

---

[1] "Segregation at all costs: Bull Connor and the Civil Rights Movement," www.youtube.com/watch?v=j9T1y.04MGg).
[2] *The Encyclopedia of American Law Enforcement*

expressing that it was simply un-American to assassinate people you disagreed with politically. Americans were supposed to vote for change, not win it through violence. Yet the unrest continued.

I heard about the Democratic convention in Chicago being less about the speeches inside and more about the violence between the police and demonstrators outside. Television showed pictures day after day of violence.

Around the time of the riots, I remember my father placing a baseball bat in the car as we piled in to visit my grandfather in Washington, DC. We took longer routes to his home to avoid the riots or the burned out portions of familiar city blocks. My memories are of realizing that my parents were afraid for our country and our family's safety.

As the unrest settled down, my father made a point of driving us through the burned out sections of town. He and my mom talked about fairness and equality. I listened and learned that no matter what job you had, there was pride that came from working. I learned that it didn't matter how much money you made; it was what was in your soul that was valuable. And when things become so unfair and lopsided, some would take to the streets, to be heard and have their needs addressed. By my 8th birthday, I had seen firsthand what racism, inequity, and injustice did to a city I loved. It was that same year I decided that I was going to be a "policeman," because I felt I would treat people better.

In 1967, the findings of the President's Commission on Law Enforcement and the Administration of Justice were published. While too young to read or understand their words, these volumes would become the cornerstone of what I learned later in college about the criminal justice system.

As the years passed and I grew up, my goal of being a police "man" shifted to becoming a police officer and while in college, the goal morphed to becoming a police chief. Over my career, the methods of teaching in a rigid police academy style has given way to a more collegiate atmosphere. Policing methods have changed. The management of incidents has become far more structured, especially since September 11, 2001.

Following the horrific attack on our country, the Federal government developed the National Incident Management System (NIMS) and as a part of that system, the Incident Command System (ICS) became the response structure for all first responders to use.

As originally conceived, the Incident Command System (ICS) functions well in physical emergencies such as fires and floods. The goals are clear in those situations: preserve life and protect property. The tactics are generally agreed upon: extinguish the fire or restore the levy, dam, or flood gate. Each role in the Incident Command System is defined and has specific responsibilities. The five main functions of Command, Operations, Logistics, Planning, and Finance are spelled out. Individuals trained in the functions can be exchanged in or out at the end of an operational period. While ICS is responsive to political leadership, the tactics are left to the first responders. Fires don't decide to burn and floods don't rise because of who the Governor might be or what the mayor said in a statement to the city. One doesn't negotiate with a fire or with a flood.

Political and protest demonstrations are different. While law enforcement may use the structure of Incident Command to organize the first responders and achieve the lofty goals of preserving life and property, there are other significant goals. For example, a key goal is the preservation of Constitutionally protected rights of the people to agree or disagree with their elected leadership. Attempting to dialog or negotiate with a burning wildfire would never be considered, but negotiating and talking with demonstrators is vital in a democratic society. Who should have that dialog? What happens, for instance, when the two sides in a political

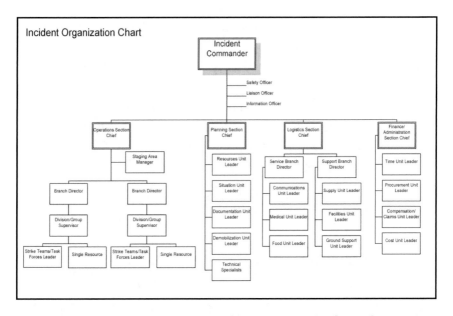

Incident Organization Chart

standoff refuse to talk and the side that controls the police wants aggressive enforcement action against their opponents, not to preserve life, but to make their political point? How much autonomy should law enforcement leaders have from their elected civilian leadership?

When politics are swirling during a demonstration and an Incident Commander's shift is over, another individual steps in to take his or her place. What if the new Incident Commander decides to follow the politician's directives and takes aggressive action? Are the hard-fought negotiations of the current day disregarded?

In November of 2010, Scott Walker, a conservative Republican was elected to be Governor of Wisconsin, following a two-term Democrat, James (Jim) E. Doyle, who had not run for re-election. Wisconsin by most accounts is a moderate state having gone "Blue" in the last several Presidential elections, yet celebrates being the birth place of the Republican Party. This is a state that has produced both "Fighting" Bob LaFollette and "Tailgunner" Joe McCarthy. The progressive movement in the state helped Wisconsin become a leader in worker's rights. Former Republican

Governor Tommy G. Thompson was a moderate by today's standards and served three and a half four-year terms before heading to Washington to serve in the George W. Bush administration as Secretary of Health and Human Services.

Wisconsin has worked progressively on welfare reform and offers BadgerCare health coverage for the uninsured. In government, industry and education, the state's motto of "Forward" is taken literally. Wisconsin has never been a state with a singular political identity, and the diversity of mindset that is so characteristic of the Badger State came into sharp focus in the early weeks of 2011 at the Capitol in Madison.

This story is one of remarkable efforts of many good people attempting to do the right things under tremendous pressure. In some respects, the story offers a case study on how not to structure a response to a massive demonstration. It is one view—an insider's view—supported by thousands of pages of documentation of one of the largest demonstrations in Wisconsin's history.

View of the Wisconsin Capitol and Square with protesters.
(Aerial photo, open record)

Chapter One

EARLY DAYS

On the 11th of February 2011, a gathering of local police chiefs took place in Madison, Wisconsin, to prepare for what was initially anticipated to be a work stoppage in response to the Governor's announcement of a "Budget Repair Bill." Significantly, most of the attendees at these early planning meetings had long-standing professional relationships with one another, going back two decades. Many had trained together; most had come up through the ranks of their organizations together and had watched one another mature into leadership positions.

This shared history would serve to help the group ramp up quickly; each knew the others' strengths and capabilities, and communication was smoothed by years of collaboration. No introductions were necessary, no exchanging of cell phone numbers or email addresses. And yet, as in any long relationship, there were times when familiarity was a burden. Old tensions did not melt away in a moment of need. If anything, conflicts were intensified with the stress of the protests, especially because the Governor's Bill would strip bargaining rights for of the some state's police forces, but not all. In addition, each agency brought its own unique style of policing appropriate to its jurisdiction and blending

*these styles into a coherent whole would prove challeng-
ing. The public may have seen a friendly, cooperative,
and unified police force, but behind the scenes there was
plenty of drama.*

FOR ME, IT ALL STARTED WITH A CALL FROM A LONGTIME POLICE
colleague, Charles Tubbs. Charlie and I go back a few years—like
twenty. A teddy bear of a man, Charles is 6 foot 5 and around 270
pounds. I, on the other hand, stand at 5 foot 5 and weigh
significantly less. When he and I stand near each other, we are like a
modern-day *Mutt and Jeff.* The man has the gift of gab and
possesses a kind and gentle soul. When I came to Wisconsin in 1991
at the ripe old age of thirty to be the Chief of the University of
Wisconsin-Madison Police Department, Charlie worked for the City
of Beloit Police Department and we met occasionally at conferences
and other training.

From day 1, I liked his pleasant personality, his desire to get
along with folks, and his personal calling to public service. After
Charles retired from Beloit, he worked for Homeland Security. He
was then appointed Administrator of the Wisconsin Division of
Juvenile Corrections. With a desire to return to law enforcement, he
had been named the Wisconsin Capitol Police Chief in 2008.

For him to call another state agency police chief was nothing
out of the ordinary. He was gathering the usual group of state,
county, and municipal law enforcement agencies to talk through
what the Budget Repair Bill might mean for work stoppages,
slowdowns, protests, and the like. "Charlie, I'll see you at your place
tomorrow at 11:00 a.m." I said as our conversation ended.

It was Thursday, February 10, 2011, and newly elected
Governor Scott Walker was about to unveil a Budget Repair Bill on
Friday, in which he proposed requiring public employees to
contribute more to their health care benefits as well as to their

pensions. In addition, the Bill called for an end to collective bargaining rights for almost all public employees including groups like teachers, snowplow operators, 911 dispatchers, school bus drivers and city workers. The Bill, however, did provide an exemption for deputy sheriffs, municipal police officers, firefighters and state troopers.

The Bill had not exempted University Police, Capitol Police, Department of Natural Resource (DNR) wardens, or Department of Justice investigators. These would be the very people who would be called upon to help with whatever the future held for work stoppages, slowdowns, or protests. This Bill's provisions fractured all law enforcement agencies because supervisors and command staff were not exempted. Only officers, troopers, and deputies who were represented by law enforcement unions were exempt. Supervisors and managers would have to begin the increased payments from their paychecks the very next month.

It took little imagination to believe that protests were likely to follow on such an announcement. Then the Governor indicated during a press conference on February 11 that he was prepared to deploy the National Guard if state correctional officers chose to strike. Tensions flared.[3] In spite of his claims that his proposal was simply a reasonable approach in a difficult budget climate, it was clear the Governor anticipated his Bill would raise objections and perhaps even violent ones. The union representing the correctional officers quickly responded that they had no plans to strike.

At the University, teaching assistants (TAs) also felt attacked by the Bill and by the Governor's actions. TAs are an integral part in how teaching is delivered at any tier one research institution, and UW–Madison is no exception. Wisconsin's TAs were among the first TAs to unionize.[4]

---

[3] http://www.jsonline.com/news/statepolitics/115911379.html
[4] The first contract was 1970, forming the first teaching assistants' union in the United States.

The University as a whole was in flux. Having seen its state-funded support decline year after year, the University had to rely on outside funding to survive and even though the state supplies just 17 percent of the overall support to run UW–Madison, it is governed, in a large part, by the state.[5] While the 17 percent is critical and necessary to continue general operations, it is far from enough to support a major educational enterprise.

It was largely understood that public employees (municipal, county and state) felt wrongly blamed for the state budget deficit that they hadn't created. State employees had just finished two years of involuntary furloughs equaling a three-percent cut in pay each year. The Governor's solution of balancing the budget was seen as unfair and punitive. While many understood the need to contribute to their health care and pension benefits, it was the attempt to silence the voices supporting collective bargaining rights that fueled the collective's contempt and anger. There were various scenarios of what people and their unions might do in reaction to the news.

During the Vietnam War era, the campus and the city experienced many large rallies, protests and marches. Whether in response to the first Gulf War, the beating of Rodney King, sweatshop labor practices, or gay rights—activism and dissent are as much part of the culture in Madison as rowdy football Saturdays. Over the forty years since the violent clashes between police and protesters, law enforcement adapted its protest-response techniques to emphasize facilitating free speech rather than controlling crowds.

In essence, the same community policing philosophy that moves 85,000 Badger fans safely in and out of Camp Randall Stadium on a football Saturday could be used to ease, guide and

---

[5] http://uwalumni.com/Backgrounder.March.2012

coordinate the movements of a crowd of protesters half that size up State Street or around the Capitol Square. To approach a crowd where there is an expectation of combat ensures conflict and the Governor's preemptive mention of the National Guard stoked a fire in the collective bargaining community.

Friday morning's meeting at the Capitol Police (CPD) head-quarters in the basement of the Capitol was like so many I had attended over my twenty years as chief. Accompanied by my right-hand man, Assistant Chief Brian Bridges, we settled into our seats around a crowded table. Brian was a 30-year veteran in law enforcement having started his career as a deputy sheriff in a northern county and arriving at the UW in 1979. He is a brilliant law enforcement tactician, who worked longer and harder than anyone I ever knew.

The relationship among law enforcement agencies within our county is very close. Our officers and deputies cooperate daily on many issues. For years, our agencies have worked large events together: from Presidential and Vice-Presidential visits, Fourth of July fireworks, and Halloween events, to Badger football games, and Ironman triathlons. We have secured dedicated space for Command Posts, enjoy radio interoperability, subscribe to the Incident Command System (ICS) and train together periodically. We share an overall philosophy of community policing and problem solving. We all quickly agreed—no National Guard. Civilian law enforcement could (and should) handle the situation.[6]

Information we had gathered from talking with various union leaders led us to believe the unions would be taking the weekend to meet and strategize their response. In fact, the Wisconsin Education

---

[6] The last time the National Guard came to campus to enforce crowd control measures was during the Vietnam protests. Tear gas and billy clubs were put to frequent use against the demonstrators; at that time the crowd was comprised of a large percentage of UW–Madison students.

Association Council (WEAC), located on the south side of Madison, was very busy organizing its leadership and members. Using Facebook, blogs, and phone calls, WEAC was rallying its 98,000 members, most of whom were teachers. Using all of its twenty-nine offices throughout the state, they made sure every member received a phone call. WEAC went on to use its influence and relationships to engage the private unions as well.

Each law enforcement agency discussed what resources it would bring to an "event," whatever that turned out to be. As we thought of how to handle the myriad possible scenarios that could occur at the Capitol over the next week, we remained mindful that State Patrol would need to assume responsibility for the prisons if corrections personnel began a job action. No one felt the need for a Command Post yet. We agreed to meet Monday, February 14th at 7:00 a.m. at the Madison Police Department (MPD).

The official residence of the Wisconsin Governor is a 1920's mansion that sits on the eastern shore of Lake Mendota in the Village of Maple Bluff, just outside the City of Madison. The white, three-story, classical Revival style, 20,777-square-foot structure, sits on 3.7 acres. It boasts a magnificent view of the Madison skyline and fabulous sunsets from most of its ten major garden areas. The state acquired the home and property in 1949 for $47,500 from Madison banker Thomas R. Hefty.

When a small group of protesters came calling at the Governor's Mansion on Sunday morning, February 13, they found the seven-bedroom, thirty-four room mansion with its thirteen bathrooms empty except for some Capitol Police, including Chief Tubbs, who were responsible for securing it. It seemed the new Governor and his family were still residing in Wauwatosa, a suburb of Milwaukee. The protesters stayed outside the wrought iron antique fence, were friendly with the police, and readily shared their plans for the week.

Capitol Police Deputy Chief Dan Blackdeer and Chief Charles Tubbs had held a planning meeting on Sunday with the Capitol Police personnel and Todd Kuschel, a part-time employee with the Department of Administration, focusing on incident management and continuity of operations planning. They discussed several scenarios and staffing strategies. Todd realized what was being discussed would take a full planning team weeks to accomplish. The Capitol Police had neither the team nor the time to manage what they might be up against.

On Sunday, with Todd facilitating, the group began to diagram a basic structure for leadership for the upcoming events. The Capitol Police Department (CPD) was a lean command organization with just the chief, a deputy chief, one lieutenant, and a number of seasoned sergeants. They needed more people to assist them— and quickly.

Many of the sergeants, while senior members of the organization, had never been responsible for the size and scope of the plans that would be needed in the coming days. Many had commanded a small number of police officers, but nothing like what they were about to face. Since Dan and Charles had held an organizational meeting on Friday, both knew several agencies would help them. Who specifically would help and in what particular positions was yet to be determined.

Todd and Dan both shared a sense of foreboding. There was so much to do but few to do the work. The process of gathering disparate staffs from differing agencies had always been the method used, but somehow it seemed less adequate this time, more nebulous. The event was being triggered by an action having a direct impact on law enforcement personnel. It was becoming less clear as to where law enforcement leaders would stand politically and how that stand might affect their decision-making.

DAY 1: MONDAY FEBRUARY 14, 2011

BY MONDAY MORNING OF VALENTINE'S DAY, THE CAST OF AGENCIES SITTING around the table had grown and even the chairs that lined the walls of the larger meeting room at MPD were filled. Deputy Chief Dan Blackdeer opened the meeting by walking us through the events of the past weekend.

Dan and Todd had worked late Sunday night preparing an Incident Action Plan (IAP)[7] for Monday's meeting. Dan explained the IAP for dealing with the anticipated crowd of 2,000 UW–Madison students and teaching assistants who now planned to march to the Capitol to deliver protest material in the form of "Valentines" to the Governor.

A small Command Post (CP) would be established in the MPD meeting room where we were sitting. We all agreed to the tried and true plan we had used for similar events. UW Police would handle the crowd on the campus, and as the crowd marched up State Street, the Madison Police Department (MPD) would join in. At the Capitol, when the group went inside, the Capitol Police Department would take over and the UW Police would join the Wisconsin State Troopers and DNR Wardens to help on the inside if the Capitol Police needed assistance. Day 1 looked pretty straight-forward.

Chief Tubbs informed us that the American Federation of State, County and Municipal Employees (AFSCME) had been granted two permits to use the Capitol Square on Tuesday, February 15 and again on Wednesday, February 16 at 11:30 a.m. each day, with a crowd estimate of 15,000 people. With crowds that large, we all felt that things were going to get interesting, but could still be handled with a variation on our usual arrangements. In a nutshell, MPD

---

7 Standard practice in what is known as incident management, an IAP documents basic facts and broad goals and serves as a common starting point for those responding to an emergency, a disaster, or any complex event requiring a coordinated response from multiple agencies.

would manage the city streets and the county sheriff's department would assist with the area of the Capitol Square itself. State law enforcement agencies would handle the inside of the Capitol building. For Tuesday and Wednesday, the decision was made to open up our customary large event Command Post, located a few blocks away at the Madison Fire Department (MFD). We would meet again at 7:00 Tuesday morning and reassess.

As we were walking out of the meeting, Chief Tubbs asked me to join him at the Masonic Center the next morning at 8:00. He was to speak to the unions' leadership about the police role in the demonstrations and about our mutual expectations. I was honored to be asked and happy to attend.

The significance of the meeting at the Masonic Center was profound and foreshadowed what was to come. During the protests in the late 1960s and early 1970s, local law enforcement was not asked to address the protest organizers and discuss expectations. The fact that in 2011, both sides thought this was an important thing to do and were willing and eager to have the meeting, set a positive tone for the cooperation to come.

Meanwhile, some 600 students and TAs were gathering in the sunshine on the UW campus in front of the Memorial Union, the largest of the two student unions on campus. They began the nine-block walk up State Street to the Capitol Square. As they went, the UW Police and MPD blocked traffic so the march wouldn't be interrupted. This kind of facilitation was another sign of how much law enforcement had changed since the Vietnam era. In essence, the police and protesters had developed an implicit (and at times explicit) agreement: as long as protesters were clear about their non-violent intentions, the police would facilitate their right to protest. The police would simultaneously work to defuse tensions.

By the time the group of students and TAs arrived at the Capitol, their numbers had grown to 1,500. They entered the

Capitol loudly with various chants aimed at their dissatisfaction with the Governor, the Repair Bill, and the Legislature. They marched to the Governor's office where, in full view of the local news cameras, the students dumped thousands of Valentines for the Governor on the security/receptionist's desk. In a party-like atmosphere, they walked around inside the building, gathering in the Rotunda cheering and chanting. Eventually the students left the building without incident.

Day 1 at the Capitol ended as we had hoped and the doors to the Capitol closed on time, promptly at 6:00 that night.

That evening, the Chancellor of the University of Wisconsin–Madison, Carolyn A. "Biddy" Martin, called a senior staff meeting at her official residence, Olin House. She wanted to discuss the situation involving the TAs, their union the Teaching Assistants Association (TAA), and other union-represented employees, and how the situation might affect campus operations. I arrived at Olin House and joined my University colleagues: the deans of the schools and colleges, the Chancellor's Cabinet, and representatives from the University Committee. All were seated around a very long table just inside the foyer. I was the only cop in the room.

Two representatives from the TAA addressed the group regarding their issues and concerns. Following their brief presentation and short question-and-answer session, they left the meeting. On their way out, I spoke with both representatives and gave them my business card. I knew over the coming week we would have a lot of contact and we needed to keep the dialogue going. They were extremely pleased with how the day went. Their Valentine drop had been a success.

> The University of Wisconsin Madison is a large, complex research University. With over 42,000 students, about 16,000 staff and faculty, the largest football stadium in the state, and a level-one trauma center on its western

border, it has a lot of moving parts. Keeping the University open and running takes considerable effort. Much of that effort is performed by people represented by unions or sympathetic to union members.

Since 1999, the University has had an extensive University Response Plan (URP) to guide campus administration, police, and a team of staff volunteers in strategies to cope with a variety of incidents ranging from tornados and blizzards to manmade crises like building fires and shootings. The plan is exercised by about 100 people twice a year. Since September 11, 2001, the plan has been exercised or actually used over fifty times.

The plan has an agreed-upon framework for institutional decision making. It has built in redundancies, a communications plan, evacuation plans, staffing plans and logistical support that often can be the key to success or the cost of failure. Roles of each participant are clearly defined with expectations, job descriptions and tasking. Everyone uses the same "playbook," working together toward the same goal.

Beyond the URP, the University has completed extensive planning for a possible pandemic flu. Pandemics differ from other emergencies in that the loss of staff and their productivity can come and go in waves. That is, not everyone is ill at the same time or to the same degree. The nuances of how to respond to such an ongoing crisis are different from a sudden emergency.

All of this structure, planning, scenario building and practice put the University on solid ground to handle whatever labor unrest might come as a result of the Governor's Budget Repair Bill.

In contrast to the well-developed and organized University Response Plan (URP) with its built-in executive group interacting with an Emergency Operations Center (EOC), relying on incident personnel to help guide decisions, strategy, and public information flow, the Command Post's functions for this event were chaotic and disconnected from the executives in leadership and the front line personnel at the Capitol. At the Capitol, no one but law enforcement seemed to be meeting with the state government staff managing the incident. Police were primarily reacting rather than planning and strategizing. No one seemed to be in charge of managing what was shaping up to be more than a routine march on the Capitol.

For now, the best I could do was manage my own University Police team of 132 employees and the needs of the entire University. In thinking about handling all of the various components, I realized I could use some veteran help. Assistant Chief Dale Burke had been a police officer when the TAA went on strike in 1980 and had retired a month earlier in January of 2011. Dale lived locally and from time to time, would stop in for lunch and to catch up on the news. I decided I would ask him if he wanted to re-engage and work for a while. He readily agreed.

Dale had thirty years of experience and was everyone's friend. His upbeat personality mixed with a bottom-line practicality was appreciated by all. He was quick with a handshake and a smile. A tremendous leader, he was well respected and loved by the members of the department. While Dale never looked for the spotlight, it found him throughout his career. The year before the protests, he had been recognized by the Chancellor for his outstanding service to the University and over his career he had accrued many department awards.

Dale loved the University of Wisconsin and was Bucky Badger's biggest fan. Dale could run any size operation, so having him back onboard was a tremendous asset. His first task would be to call together the University's EOC for an organizational meeting and to be proactive about probable assignments. We would begin by implementing the URP structure we knew well.

DAY 2: TUESDAY, FEBRUARY 15, 2011

ALL THE VARIOUS POLICE AGENCIES RETURNED TO THE MPD MEETING ROOM at 7:00 a.m. for Day 2, Tuesday, February 15. By this time, our communications with the unions led us to expect a crowd of up to 15,000, a far cry from the 1,500 students on Valentine's Day. We decided it was time to open the joint Command Post (CP) at the Madison Fire Department (MFD) headquarters, just a few blocks from the Capitol Square. We had no idea that the CP would be open for twenty-one straight days.

The CP is completely wired with pre-staged dispatch connections, video feeds from outdoor area cameras, large screens in which to view data, video, weather stations, cable television and the Internet. Off the main room are offices that can be converted to meeting rooms. One of the rooms has 24/7 video conferencing. This CP is the primary location used for large events that occur with some regularity.

Following the Tuesday morning police briefing, a group of commanders headed for the CP, while Chief Charles Tubbs and I headed for the Masonic Center located on Wisconsin Avenue two blocks away from the Capitol to meet with AFSCME Union leaders.

It was a brisk, chilly morning, yet sunny and very nice for February in Madison. We were greeted warmly.

The union, representing about 68,000 members, had identified about 200 volunteers to serve as marshals to help manage the operation of an anticipated crowd of 15,000. They were running buses from seven cities across the state to transport members to the rally. We entered the auditorium and were greeted by the marshals, many of whom I recognized from the previous day's Valentine event. After a few minutes, we were joined by Lieutenant Brian Ackeret from MPD, who was going to be responsible for the police teams who would facilitate the short march from the Masonic Center to the Capitol later that morning.

> *Police departments have a variety of tasks they must do to support their mission: maintaining order, enforcing traffic, preventing crime, and enforcing the law. Carrying out these responsibilities requires a great deal of discretionary decision making.*
>
> *In my view, adhering to and enforcing the United States Constitution is not negotiable. Law enforcement is often placed on the front lines of interpreting the Constitution on-the-spot and in the heat of the moment, without the benefit of a law degree or years on the judicial bench. It is my belief and practice, that law enforcement officers under my command will proudly facilitate and uphold the rights outlined in the U.S. Constitution.*
>
> *Exercising Constitutional rights is fundamental and foundational to what it means to be an American. There is no other country in the world that touts its Constitution as much as the United States. Yet, when some Americans wish to express their views by assem-*

bling, blocking traffic or boycotting a product, there are other Americans who may disagree with the particular view and may disagree with the method of expression.

I have often found it fascinating that there are some people in the United States who tire so quickly of the various ways people express their beliefs and exercise their rights—especially when the protest or the demonstration results in an inconvenience that affects them directly. As a practical matter, we all need to have more patience with each other when it comes to this important exercise of our Constitutional rights.

There are certain actions that inflame most Americans. One is the burning of our nation's flag. I personally find it abhorrent. My father, a World War II veteran, instilled in me a respect for what the flag symbolizes that I never let it touch the ground, and the only time I would ever set it aflame would be when it is worn and tattered and needs to be retired respectfully. To see an American flag lit on fire to make a political point is hard for me to endure. Yet I have had to do so, and will continue to defend the right of my fellow citizens to express themselves in that dramatic manner.

Chief Charles Tubbs, speaking without a microphone, greeted the group with his thundering "good morning." The response was tepid, so he thundered again. This time, the response was loud and energetic. Charles addressed the group and talked about the importance of non-violence and continuing the dialogue between the unions and the police. He also described his vision of a successful event for everyone involved. He wanted to make sure the crowd knew what to expect from the police and also what the police would expect from the crowd and the marshals. Chief Tubbs' speech was kind and gentle in tone. Listening, it reminded me of a coach prepping his team and outlining strategy before a big game.

After a few minutes, Charles finished and I stood to address the group. I covered the five components of the First Amendment of the U.S. Constitution, mentioning that I thought four of the five clauses were in play. I joked that I didn't think freedom of religion was involved, but I did acknowledge it was still early. The role of the police, I explained, was often a balancing act between opposing sides. The police are responsible to make every effort to remain neutral while working to protect everyone's rights. What we wanted to see was successful use of the First Amendment's tenets: 1) peaceful assembly, 2) petition the government for a redress of grievances, 3) freedom of speech, and 4) freedom of the press.

The three police agencies involved in the meeting at the Masonic Center believe in and practice problem-solving-policing. My involvement in problem-solving policing started twenty years ago. It is a philosophy about policing that was developed by Professor Herman Goldstein of the UW–Madison Law School. Basically, problem-solving policing entails using data and analysis, working in partnership with stakeholders and other interested parties to resolve conflict, or mediating outcomes, finding solutions, and then assessing to see if the solution truly worked. Chief Tubbs and I both encouraged the unions to exercise their Constitutional rights to the fullest and to have a successful event. There was a shared sense of confidence about how the day would progress.

As Charles and I headed out of the building, I reflected that both Charles and I grew up with the civil rights movement, the women's movement, and the Vietnam War. I knew that both Charles and I had studied the history of the civil rights movement and the tactics and teachings of Dr. Martin Luther King Jr. and that we both have strong beliefs in the use of nonviolent activities to accomplish social and legislative change. The use of night sticks, unreasonable force, fire hoses, and patrol dogs to stop an orderly and peaceful demonstration were simply not part of who Charles or I are as leaders.

When people believe their government is not listening and when faith in government is lost, serious problems, including violence, can occur. As things began to swirl in Wisconsin, the world was watching the people of Tunisia and Egypt in Tahrir Square on the daily news, YouTube, Twitter and Facebook.

As Charles walked with me to my car, I again told him I would help in any way I could. I headed off to get a hair cut and vote in the primary race. One of the contests was for the Wisconsin Supreme Court.

The Budget Repair Bill, which had been announced on Friday, moved to the Joint Finance Committee for its review, testimony, and deliberations in room 412 East of the Capitol. It had been decided that those wanting to address the Committee would be given two minutes to do so. The room quickly filled with those representing labor. Given the length of the sign-up list for those wanting to speak, it was clear the meeting would stretch late into the evening. For the moment, however, those speaking kept pace and for the most part were civil.

The crowd of 15,000 was making its way to the Square, some with children in strollers. Many people were wearing matching tee shirts with the AFSCME logo. To accommodate the crowd, large flat-screen televisions had been erected in the Rotunda so that people could watch and hear the proceedings in the already-filled-to-capacity Joint Finance Committee's hearing room. Union supporters stood along the perimeter of the Rotunda and cheer when they heard a speaker they agreed with.

So far, nothing about the protests or the committee testimony was terribly unusual. But there were hints of unrest that far exceeded normal expectations. After a rally, the crowd did not dissipate. The queue for Joint Finance continued to grow and by 1:00 p.m., the line was long enough that if all the speakers used their full two minutes, the committee would need to meet past midnight. Ordinarily, the Capitol closes at 6:00 p.m. on weeknights. Under state law, however, the Capitol must remain open when the Legislature is in session or when a committee is holding a hearing. The normal closing time would have no bearing that day.

After the Chancellor's cabinet meeting, I accompanied Assistant Chief Brian Bridges to the Capitol to check on our officers. We stopped in the University Police break room at Capitol Room 400 NE and talked to the officers there as they took their breaks. I even played a few rounds of poker with a couple of University Police detectives. I won. After ensuring the officers had been fed,

UW Police Captain Johnnie Diamante, Lieutenant Kari Sasso and Lieutenant Clark Brunner clear bridge so that TVs can be installed for the crowd to watch the Joint Finance session. (Photo by Tony Barnes)

we headed to the Command Post at the Fire Department. The Incident Commander on duty was Deputy Chief Dan Blackdeer of the Capitol Police.

> *Years before, when I served as a Vice President of the International Association of Chiefs of Police, Dan and I had worked to establish a Capitol Police Section within the IACP. Dan put a tremendous amount of energy into the development of the Section and because of his hard work the Section was established in 2008.*

Dan asked to speak to me alone. It was obvious that he was already tired and a bit frustrated. Dan had worked throughout the weekend trying to prepare for this week. He had assigned Todd Kuschel to do some planning. Todd had been an Assistant Chief for the University Police before he retired in 2005, and had gone on to become an instructor of the Incident Command System (ICS).

Todd possesses superb people skills and had tremendous knowledge of how Incident Management should be structured and function, but the number of details and sub-plans were too much for any one person to handle, and Dan had his hands full with running the CP. Dan asked if Brian and I would draft a mass arrest plan and work out the logistics for it. It was not that any of us expected to make mass arrests. Such plans are a standard part of contingency planning and I assured Dan he would have the plan before the end of the day.

The crux of the rest of the issues on Dan's mind focused on his own chain of command within the Department of Administration (DOA), which was led by a Secretary newly appointed by Governor Walker. In addition, Dan had few resources to assist him within the CP. I listened, offered some suggestions, and assured him that University Police would help wherever we could. Dan thought it was time to get some assistance from other trained Incident Command response people in the southern region of the state. I agreed.

I brought my Assistant Chief Brian Bridges up to speed. After talking through all of the developments, we decided we would divide the UW Police into two 12-hour shifts, moving two thirds of the staff to a 7:00 a.m. to 7:00 p.m. shift. UW Police could then send the maximum number of folks to the Capitol. We placed Captain Steve Rogers in charge of all University functions requiring a police presence on campus, with Lieutenant Mark Silbernagel taking the reins overnight. This would free all the rest of the commanders for assignment at the Capitol, in the Command Post, or in support of the University Response Plan if the Chancellor chose to activate it. The University Police team was well organized and trained to adapt in this way, and had a hundred URP-campus trained volunteers who could be called on to support our efforts. Our flexibility and resources stood in stark contrast to the Capitol Police (CPD), who had fewer personnel to draw on and faced bureaucracy in every decision.

Brian and I headed back to the Capitol. The building had a very large crowd inside. In fact, it seemed like there were way too many people in the building. As we entered the Capitol and toured around the various alcoves, we saw many people we knew who worked for the state or city in various capacities. The energy was high and the mood was quite festive. Writing a mass arrest plan seemed out of step with the crowd's liveliness.

We surveyed the building, the elevators, and the CPD headquarters in the basement of the Capitol, and then began to write the mass arrest plan. While police arrest alleged offenders every day, they usually do it one or two at a time. In large crowds, the potential is for many and multiple simultaneous arrests. Systems and officers can easily become overwhelmed. The plan needed to have prompts on when to activate, arrangements for where to take those in custody, and how to move from the arrest location to the processing center, as well as staff to process the arrested, and make charging decisions. Without a plan, the process would be inefficient and people could get hurt.

In addition to the plan and staffing to carry it out, we knew we would need supplies at the ready. The UW Police has pre-made mass arrest kits, ready to be pulled from a shelf and taken straight to the field. The kits include citation books, bond schedules, bond amounts, flexible hand cuffs, latex gloves, spit hoods, assorted batteries, paper bags for the contents of pockets from an arrested individual, plastic bags, labels, ties, booking sheets for the jail, and large envelopes in which to place all report items. We called for these mass arrest kits to be brought to the Capitol. We established an offsite processing center and put the finishing touches on the plan and sent it off to DC Dan Blackdeer in the Command Post.

At home that night, I received a text message from another retired UW Police Assistant Chief, Jerry Jansen. He had been watching the news and was hoping things were going all right for us at the University and downtown. He was keeping track of everything from his winter home in Mesa, Arizona. I, of course, had to inquire about the weather... One text message led to another and before we knew it, Jerry agreed to fly back to Madison on Thursday to help Dale Burke with the EOC responsibilities.

I called Chief Tubbs and talked over the events of the day with him. The Capitol would be open long into the evening. We discussed some of the frustrations from the CP and the suggestion that he reach out to Wisconsin Emergency Management (WEM). WEM had staff trained to support Command Posts. It seemed we all would benefit from their logistical, planning, and staff support. Charles agreed and said he would talk with his bosses in DOA about how to make all this happen. He informed me that Joint Finance Committee was still meeting and there was no end in sight.

While the Joint Finance Committee hearing on the Governor's proposal began at 10:00 that morning, those signed up to speak would take the Committee through the night. It was clear that things were running behind schedule. Many of those in line waiting to testify were posting regular updates to Facebook and Twitter, noting the size of the line and remarking how emotionally moving the testimony was to hear.

That evening, we also received word that the committee co-chairs (Republicans) had ordered the queue to be closed, even to those who had registered to speak. One of the people posted, "we are flooding the chamber" and closed with a plea to "RT" (retweet). The pent-up emotion of those waiting in line began to erupt, with chanting and pounding echoing in the hearing room and the waiting areas. Meanwhile, the legislators, who had been at it for nearly 12 straight hours, began arguing among themselves about how to proceed.

Senator Bob Jauch pleaded with his Republican colleagues, "This is their building, not ours." As suddenly as it had begun, the eruption settled as the speakers' queue re-opened fifteen minutes later. Things were still backed up as those who had registered at 2:00 in the afternoon were just being called to the hearing room for their turn to speak. It was shaping up to be a very long night.

An hour later, the mood changed again. Just before 10:30 p.m., a rumor began to circulate that the Joint Finance Committee co-chair Robin Vos (Republican) intended to close the hearing in the early morning hours around 2:00 by simply having the Republican committee members leave, bringing the committee below quorum. Within five minutes, Facebook and Twitter came alive in response, with one posting proposing, "If the Republicans exit, maybe we shouldn't leave at all."

By 11:15 p.m., blankets, pillows, sleeping bags, and food began to arrive at the Capitol. Signs started to be taped up on the walls.

The Governor's mention of the National Guard several days earlier had indicated he expected a fight on his budget proposal. But a fight involves interaction, debate, and discourse. The Republican legislators who served on the Joint Finance Committee suggested they preferred not to have a lengthy engagement with their opponents. The protesters were not going to give in so easily to this seemingly lopsided turn of events. Many of those testifying before Joint Finance made clear that they knew the Democrats did not have the votes to reject the Governor's proposal, and they did not fully expect to sway the Republicans.

The protesters suspected they would lose. What they wanted was a chance to be heard. The perceived disrespect of being seemingly ignored or simply "going through the motions" of a hearing incited at least as much anger as the prospect of smaller paychecks. Ironically, and not for the last time, the attempts by Republican politicians to speed the process along ensured that their opponents would strive all the harder to slow things down.

Midnight came and went. The Republicans on the committee left the hearing in the wee hours of the morning. But those members of the public in the room, still on a list to speak, would stay on and be heard by the Democrats on the committee. The meeting went on all night. People slept until it was their turn to testify. They rolled out sleeping bags and mats for some minimal level of comfort.

The Capitol's marble floors are cold in February and incredibly unforgiving. By law, the doors of the Capitol were not all locked because of the listening session. TAA members made plans to stay as long as necessary and established an operations center of their own in some Capitol offices and in a hearing room. The Democratic legislators made sure the protesters had rooms from which to operate. The crowd was energized, loud and organized.

A considerable number of people wandered the Capitol and like the students the day before, visited areas directly outside the

Governor's office to chant and sing. Sleeping in the Capitol had begun.

The homeless jumped at the chance to have a warm place to sleep and the protesters were happy to feed them as well. In fact, in the early days the protesters ate far better than the police who had received lunches made by the prisoners at Oakhill Correctional Facility!

Day 3: Wednesday, February 16

Day 3 started at 7:00 a.m. with another meeting. Following the meeting, I received a phone call from Charles. We talked over how "big" this event was getting, and no one thought today's rally would be the last.

The Madison School District had to close because many teachers did not report for work. Rumor was that more school districts would follow. Closed schools meant teachers and possibly some students would join the AFSCME crowd. The mixing of age groups was likely to prove very interesting.

Later in the day, an estimated 600 Madison East High School students would march over two miles from their high school to the Capitol. They would be joined there by a large group of Madison West High School students, who had marched to the Capitol as well.

Charles asked me to pull together a morning planning meeting. I was again honored to be asked and pleased to contribute. He would handle the meeting with labor at the Masonic Center by himself and I would facilitate the planning meeting for 9:00. I called the principals of all the key police agencies involved and asked them or a representative with decision-making authority to attend the meeting. I spoke briefly with Incident Commander, Capitol Police Deputy Chief Dan Blackdeer, whom I asked to kick off the planning meeting.

The only real newcomer to the planning meeting was Warden Captain Byron Goetsch from the DNR, but he quickly fit right in. We talked about an overall strategy in which Madison police would stay on the city streets, which included the streets surrounding the Capitol Square. The city police would take responsibility for closing the Capitol Square to vehicular traffic to accommodate the crowds. This was something the city was accustomed to as the Square routinely closes for events.

The county sheriff would assist the Capitol Police (CPD) by patrolling the area from the Square's sidewalks to the doors of the Capitol. Capitol Police, UW Police, Wisconsin State Patrol (WSP), and Department of Natural Resources (DNR) wardens would handle everything from the doors in—in other words, the entire interior of the Capitol building.

We agreed on rules of engagement that law enforcement would use when dealing with crowds. We established that we would take enforcement action for felonies and serious misdemeanors and outlined a level of tolerance regarding what may be construed as civil disobedience. The discussion was lively and as with any discussion worth having, there were a few tense moments, but overall everyone agreed with how to proceed for that day as we prepared for the next round of protests and marches.

It was agreed that an operations room would be established for the inside of the Capitol itself. We designated the conference room we were currently using, 400 NE. A lieutenant or captain from each of the four state agencies—CPD, WSP, DNR, and UWPD— would staff this room for their operational base.

Madison and Dane County representatives left to return to the Command Post. The four state agency representatives began immediately to make a list of all the plans that would be needed to secure the inside of the building. Then we divided up into work groups and started getting things organized operationally. Captain

Michael Newton, Lieutenant John Lind, and Emergency Service Coordinator (ESC) Brandi Schaffer, all from the UW Police Emergency Management Unit were present.

Within the hour, Brandi, a former navy medic and mother of four, had completed an Incident Action Plan (IAP) for the group for that operational period. Captain Newton and Lieutenant Lind had completed a staffing and post plan for any of the UW Police assigned to the building. Michael had phoned the University Police and had other staff en route with supplies that he and the other state law enforcement representatives would need in the days ahead.

Deputy Chief Blackdeer was in high demand as three of the state agencies lacked basic knowledge about the Capitol building, did not know at that time the key non-law enforcement actors, and how the Capitol worked. Dan brought in two of his senior sergeants to assist with all the planning efforts and then returned to the CP. I assured him that I would stay a while longer and then join him at the CP in the afternoon to discuss things further.

The University activated its Emergency Operations Center (EOC) to assist the University in case the teaching assistants walked out of their teaching assignments in reaction to the Budget Repair Bill. With Dale Burke in charge, the EOC quickly formed. Agreeing to meet every morning at 8:00 to assess the situation, spin-up time in the event of work slowdowns or stoppages would be held to a minimum. I checked in with Dale periodically.

When I arrived at the Command Post, the stress seemed high among some of the personnel. Incident Commander Deputy Chief Dan Blackdeer once again asked that I speak with him privately. He acknowledged he was tired, overly emotional, and frustrated. He truly felt alone in command. He hadn't spoken directly to or had any communication from Chief Tubbs all day. In fact, they couldn't seem to reach Charles by phone or on the radio. Dan needed to gather his wits about him. I encouraged him to take a break. We talked about pacing one's self. He was working 18 hours a day and not sleeping well. He agreed and then left the CP for two hours—transferring command to Captain Charles "Chuck" Teasdale of the Wisconsin State Patrol.

My experience with Chuck was very limited. His "day job" was serving as captain for District 1 of the State Patrol, which served the county in which my agency was located. I had seen him at some Dane County Chiefs' meetings where he appeared to be a squared-away young captain who seemed highly organized and professional —the trademarks of a trooper.

The next person to take me aside was Todd Kuschel, my former assistant chief. Until his retirement in 2005, Todd and I had worked together at the University Police for fifteen years. At one point in his career, he helped build our emergency management unit, which was responsible for the University Response Plan.

He said that working for DOA was nothing like working at the University. The can-do attitude of the University just didn't exist in DOA. Beyond the Capitol Police staff, the people in DOA didn't understand what was happening, or the support role they needed to play. It didn't help that many of the top officials at DOA had taken office just weeks before. Todd explained that he, too, was emotion-ally "fried." No one from their shop beside Dan and Todd would stand up and deliver plans that would actually work. Even though I had no positional authority in this situation, I sent Todd out the door for a couple of hours to clear his head.

Two hours later, Brian Bridges, Todd, Dan, and I met in Shoo, a high-end, funky shoe store at 109 State Street. Because a strong, cold wind had come up, we stepped inside to get out of the near freezing temperatures and noise of the protest group on the Square. The Shoo staff member was very accommodating and allowed the four of us to talk.

As the Incident Commander, Dan didn't feel he had adequate support. Chief Tubbs seemed to be getting pulled in different directions with differing orders from his boss, the Deputy Secretary of DOA, and the Governor's Chief of Staff, Keith Gilkes. Dan would give instructions to the field commanders, only to find the Chief was giving different directions to officers posted in the Capitol. We all advised Dan to meet face-to-face with Charles and sort out how to move forward together. Dan knew he had to face his boss to get some direction, but we recognized talking this through with his boss under this much stress would be difficult.

We agreed the planning function was especially weak. We knew how to collaborate on planned events that allowed time for coordination, and we were capable of responding to unexpected events that required only short-term response. The challenge here arose from the combination of the unexpected and long-term. We knew this would require planning, coordination and pacing, but we didn't have the luxury of time. Brian and I immediately offered Lieutenant Ben Newman from our staff to assist with planning. With that, Todd and Dan returned to the CP.

Meanwhile, a large crowd had turned up as promised—and right on time. Bolstered by the Madison teachers, the AFSCME rally was larger than the day before. When Asst. Chief Brian Bridges and I entered the Capitol via the ground floor State Street entrance, one of four main entrances to the Capitol building, we found the building was brimming with people and dozens of signs were taped to the walls. We had a hard time moving through the crowd. The ground and first floor of the Rotunda were completely jammed with people.

I turned to Brian, "This isn't good."

"No, this is trouble." He answered.

"We have got to get out of here and get up higher so we can see."

The second floor bridges and parapets were overcrowded, as were the marble grand staircases that connected all the floors. People sitting on staircases made the stairs impassable. There were lines for every women's bathroom and most of the men's bathrooms. We were relieved when we finally were able to make our way to a limited access elevator for a quick trip to the fourth floor. This crowd size and density was dangerous.

Although a certain amount of disarray is typical when any operations center or Command Post first opens, the staff would ideally have ready access to computers, printers, phones and radio, maps, and diagrams of the facility. If possible, live video feeds and news broadcasts would be available via large screens. Office supplies—paper, pens, staplers, sticky notes—would all be in abundant supply. There was nothing typical about this situation.

As we entered the Operations Room, what we found in 400 NE was beyond disarray. It was harried. Everyone was trying to use cell phones, as the room only had one wired phone line and the cell reception was spotty at best. Access to the Internet was extremely limited, and only State Patrol Lieutenant Brad Altman had consistent Internet reception. There was one set of enlarged floor plans for the Capitol, so people were working off multiple 8.5-by-11 sheets with each of the four building wings per sheet. The four state law enforcement agencies only knew their individual portion of the operation. No one seemed in charge or to have the whole picture. No one seemed to have a sense of the danger about the overcrowding in the building.

I had seen firsthand what crowds can do when momentum takes over and the density is too great. The power of a wave of human beings can bend metal, crush bones, and suffocate people. I had lived through it more than once in my career, but most memorable was on October 30, 1993, in Camp Randall Stadium.

The Wisconsin Badger football team was enjoying its best season in a long, long time. There was no doubt the Badgers would be in a bowl game and not just any bowl game, but possibly one of significance. Camp Randall, home of the Badgers, was sold out for every game. With the expansion of the Big Ten Conference to include Penn State, the Badgers hadn't played the University of Michigan Wolverines for several years. Michigan was a perennial powerhouse in college football. Beating Michigan was a strong desire for every team in the Big Ten and Wisconsin was no exception.

It was a cool day in Madison and there were light snow flurries. The game was scheduled that morning to begin at 11:00 Central Time and it was to be featured on a little known network at the time, ESPN. The atmosphere was electric.

On game day, I usually partnered with UW Police Captain Phil Dixon. But Phil was away for his annual hunting trip to Wyoming. His absence certainly changed my strategy for getting through the pregame and game. When Phil was present I never worried about a thing. With his thirty years of experience, he had every detail of the stadium memorized and every staff responsibility handled. Without him, I felt we needed to be more systematic in our preparation.

I made sure that the day before the game, much to the teasing and smirks from my remaining command staff, we were ready in the event we beat Michigan. Most believed it wouldn't happen. I asked them to humor me and to place the postgame plan on paper. At the briefing on game day, most of the officers working would also smirk at the idea of a Badger victory, but all were upbeat and wanted to see the Badgers beat the Wolverines.

The game was evenly played and as the fourth quarter was coming to a close, we realized that there was a very good chance of winning. Wisconsin needed to hold on to the football, and we needed to eat up some clock. When Wisconsin got a first down and Michigan was out of timeouts, we knew victory was ours, but time remained on the clock. Students seated in five adjoining sections began to move downward from the upper stands in a giant wave, compressing the students in the rows closest to the field. Time ticked down on the game clock.

Seventy rows of people were now compressed into forty rows. Iron railings anchored into concrete began to bend. The chain link fence with its reinforced steel 3-inch pipe inside an outer 4-inch pipe began to bend. With time still on the game clock, a portion of the railing gave way trapping screaming students beneath it. A section of the fence shot up into the air, landing and trapping more students. The entire fence line protecting the student section gave way, catching more students beneath it as if they were trapped in a cage. Where the fence didn't break or bend, students were jammed so tightly they were literally turning blue as they fought to breathe. The game finally came to an end and the teams left the field. Throughout the stadium, people sensed something was terribly wrong. Everyone outside of the students sections seemed to stop and watch quietly as if the event were occurring in slow motion.

In the Stadium Operations Center high above the field near the press box, a Command Post of sorts, the

University Police, medical director, and stadium opera-
tions staff scrambled to deal with the tragedy they saw
unfolding before them. The police in the seating sections
were attempting to actively engage the crowd—not to
keep them from the field, but instead to attempt to
rescue those trapped beneath the tangle of metal
railings and fences. The fans kept coming from the rows
above in waves jubilant, not realizing (or not caring)
that they were stepping on, walking over, or jumping on
their fellow students trapped beneath.

We initiated a city-wide mass casualty medical
response plan. We ordered 16 ambulances, twice the
entire city's complement, to respond. The county began
its county-wide medical response plan to support the
city. Ambulances were streaming toward Camp Randall
from the cities, towns, and villages that surrounded
Madison.

Police officers were performing CPR on the pulseless
and non-breathing students who were lying on the field.
Some of the crowd, thinking the officers were arresting
those on the ground, began to pull the officers away from
the stricken students. The UW Marching Band continued
to play upbeat polka-style music, and some of the
students were dancing in rings around the officers who
were performing CPR. It was surreal.

The stadium announcer tried over and over again to
alert people to the crushing and the medical emergencies
in progress but the noise level was so high, few in the
crowd rushing the field could hear him. When the
ambulances began to arrive, one after another after
another, driving directly onto the field, people finally
started believing the announcer.

We finally managed to get the band to stop playing and leave the stadium. Some of the football players had come back onto the field and were trying to assist rescue efforts. We began to re-establish order.

In the end, there were 10 pulseless non-breathers and a total of 69 people transported to local hospitals. Thankfully, no one died.

It was the largest incident of its kind in American sporting at that time. The lessons learned that day about crowd dynamics, police tactics, triage, command of incidents; protocols, stadium design, and leadership were profound for me.

After leaving the Capitol Operations Room and quickly walking outside to get a decent cell phone signal, I called the Command Post and reported what I had seen. The CP, located at the well-equipped but off-site Madison Fire Department, seemed unaware of the extent of the crowding situation. According to the Incident Action Plan (IAP), Lieutenant Brad Altman of the State Patrol was the Operations Chief; I wondered then if Brad actually knew he was "in charge."

Via phone, I explained my concerns to Incident Commander DC Dan Blackdeer. I told him that immediate action was needed to restrict access to the Capitol building. He would need a strategy to move people out to establish a safer level of capacity inside the building. He told me that he didn't think he was authorized to do what was needed.

I felt sick as I hung up the phone. At this point, AC Brian Bridges and I discussed the situation and realized that we could not do much else. We had told the Operations Chief, WSP Lieutenant Brad Altman, and Incident Commander Blackdeer of our concerns. My Assistant Chief and I had no authority to command the officers in the Capitol. We had completed the mass arrest plan and no one was suggesting or asking us to do anything more. So we checked on our staff and reluctantly headed back to our headquarters on campus to hear the latest campus information. To actually leave the Capitol was very difficult for me. When faced with what I believe to be a vacuum of leadership, I am genetically programmed to step up and lead. Frustratingly it took all the self-discipline I could muster and a lot of deep breathing to walk away.

The University EOC was opened that afternoon for a face-to-face meeting of the members. Brian and I stopped in and found EOC Manager Dale Burke in charge with things humming right along. Plans for potential class closures were being discussed, using part of the University's Pandemic Flu Plan as a template lessened the burden on the staff. Backup instructors were being considered. Combining classes was discussed. Drafts of possible press releases and informational pieces for the web were being written. Compared to what I had just left downtown, the University's EOC was extraordinarily ordered and methodical.

The TAA was attempting to stage a walkout for 10:00 the next morning. The EOC had quickly compiled planning data and we knew that Thursday, 815 teaching assistants accounted for how 1,345 classes would be taught, affecting 17,416 students. In addition, some faculty teaching other classes that day had stated they would not cross a picket line to teach. So the actual number of classes and students affected was not something we could accurately predict because we didn't know which faculty would side with the TAA.

By Wednesday afternoon, it was clear that protests at the Capitol were going to get larger—and fast. School districts around the state were facing the same reality the Madison School District had faced. Their teachers would be missing from classrooms and districts would have to close. Wisconsin Education Association Council (WEAC) was organizing dozens of buses to transport teachers to Madison.

Bus schedules for Thursday had also been set: six buses from Milwaukee, two from Racine, three from Eau Claire, two from

LaCrosse, two from Wausau, two from Green Bay, Manitowoc, Prairie du Chien, River Falls, Superior (that bus would depart Superior at 3:45 a.m. to make the 6-hour trip to Madison), Whitewater, Jefferson, Dodge County, Stevens Point, and Platteville. As the afternoon went on into the evening, the number of school districts closed on Thursday continued to grow.

Watching the 10 o'clock news at home, I saw the names of the closed districts scroll by, reminding me of the closed school postings during severe winter weather. The weather wasn't the story tonight; in fact, despite a strong wind, today the weather had been mild for February. With good weather forecasts, it was likely that the 30,000 person crowd we had seen would grow much larger by Thursday. The unions were fully mobilizing. Law enforcement would need to find a way to do the same.

DAY 4: THURSDAY, FEBRUARY 17, 2011

WE REPORTED IN AGAIN AT 7:00 A.M. TO LISTEN TO THE CP BRIEFING. AS expected, the crowd would be larger and there was a very good chance the Square would need to be closed to traffic for much longer than the previous days. People continued to sleep overnight in the Capitol as the legislative committees continued to meet.

The building hadn't been closed at all overnight and people were allowed to come and go freely. People had brought even more mattresses into the building. Some were real inner-spring mattresses, not just the inflatable mattresses you would see on a camping trip. With the mattresses came blankets, pillows and sheets. The protesters were setting up house.

The University's EOC also reopened as the University braced for the TA walkout. The EOC polled the academic departments to see if absenteeism was high and if there were critical services in jeopardy. With local schools closed, staffing issues at the University became more complicated as some employees with children had to remain home.

A half hour into the CP briefing, help arrived in the form of Kevin Wernet, an instructor in ICS at Blackhawk Technical College in Janesville. Kevin was also a fire fighter, and he was tasked to the Planning Section working for the Planning Section Chief, Paul France.

By 9:00 a.m., Incident Commander DC Dan Blackdeer was reassigning Kevin to be the Logistics Section Chief, so Kevin got to work on finding parking for the police officers who would be arriving from outside Madison to assist with the overall effort. At 9:30, Dan asked Kevin to go to the Capitol itself.

As Kevin left the Command Post and walked the three blocks to the Square, he met up with a large crowd headed up State Street to the Capitol, including a group of bagpipers who had come to play. The crowd was very interested in the bagpipers and cleared the sidewalk to watch the happenings. Thanks to the bagpipers, Kevin was able to glide right by to arrive in the Operations Room 400 NE around 10:00.

UW–Madison Chancellor Biddy Martin and UW System President Kevin Reilly were scheduled to meet with the Governor at 9:00 that morning in the Governor's conference room. This meeting had been set before the announcement of the Budget Repair Bill and prior to the reaction that came with it. In the meeting, they would hear directly from the Governor about the University System's budget and the UW–Madison budget in particular. Everyone knew that with the sagging economy and the deep cuts in the state budget over the past two years, more cuts were coming. How big, how deep, and with what conditions was uncertain.

The other twelve UW campus chancellors would join Chancellor Martin and President Reilly at 9:30 to hear from the Governor about the budget and how it would affect their campuses. My staff was told to make sure that Chancellor Martin, President Reilly, and the other chancellors were able to gain safe entrance to the Capitol.

As the chancellors arrived at the Capitol, they met up with a protester who, believing the chancellors were legislators, began yelling "You assholes. You should stand with the working man." The UW Police asked the man to move on, but he didn't and instead approached the chancellors, getting very close to them. "Fuck you, you elite morons." Again he was asked politely by the officers to step back and leave the chancellors alone.

The protester persisted and then poked one of the chancellors in the chest with the sign on a stick he was carrying. "Hey, I'm talking to you. You need to listen." A UW Police officer arrested the obviously intoxicated man while other UW Police escorted the chancellors inside without further incident. It was the first arrest made during the protests. There would be surprisingly few to follow.

I met up with UW Lieutenant Pete Ystenes while the chancellors were meeting inside. Pete explained the repeated warnings, the obvious intoxication, and then the poke. He said with a chuckle that he would be curious to know what the guy's blood alcohol content would measure on a breath test at 9:30 in the morning.

I then connected with the chancellors and the University President as they left their meeting. Some of the chancellors wanted to visit their legislators, while others were headed to Olin House to meet with Chancellor Martin. President Reilly seemed preoccupied as I led him out of the building.

With the departure of the chancellors and President, AC Brian Bridges and I breathed a little easier. Inside, the Senate was attempting to go into session to debate the Budget Repair Bill. The Republicans had the votes to get the Bill passed, but the Democrats wanted to be heard before a vote would be taken. In a bold and unusual move, the Democratic senators decided to leave the state and head to Illinois to deny the Republicans a quorum. For their plan to work, all Democratic senators needed to leave.

Earlier in the day, Democratic Senator Tim Cullen from the 15th District wanted to inform the Capitol press corps about the death of his close friend, former Supreme Court Justice Bill Bablitch. For the strategy of "escaping" to Illinois to be successful, Senator Cullen had to be out of the Capitol by 10:45 a.m. to avoid being detained. His colleague and President of the Senate, Mike Ellis (Republican), knew of Cullen's press conference and agreed not to convene the Senate until 11, giving his friend time to leave the Capitol and the state.

During the course of the proceedings, a group of citizens in the viewing galleries became disruptive. Efforts to suppress the disruption only added fuel to dissent. Law enforcement was called in and nine people were removed and arrested. The arrested were transported out of the Capitol to the offsite processing center that had been designated the day before in the mass arrest plan.

To get a feel for the crowd, AC Brian Bridges and I walked the entire Capitol square. It felt colder today, but the crowd was bigger than ever. We went back inside the Capitol and again commented on the density of the throng of people. They were everywhere. We exchanged greetings with many in the crowd. People were determined, yet remarkably upbeat. There was a sense of purpose, and they possessed an intense energy. The crowd was so dense we gave up trying to get to the Rotunda. Instead we decided to head to the Command Post three blocks away. On our way, we saw Sheriff David Mahoney outside the East Washington entrance of the Capitol.

Dave had served for 26 years in the Dane County Sheriff's office before being first elected sheriff in 2006. He had just been re-elected the in the fall of 2010. Dave had been President of the deputy sheriff's union during his time as a detective. He was also a member of the bomb squad.

Dave had worked many Wisconsin home football games in Camp Randall for me over the years. When he was first elected sheriff, he called me to make sure it was still okay for him to work for me on game days. I was glad to have him, though I wondered if he wanted a new assignment given his newly elected office. He said he would work wherever I told him to work, but if it were all the same to me, he would like to keep his spot on the sideline and his duties with the marching band. That was an easy request to grant.

Over his four-plus years as Dane County sheriff, Dave and I had grown even closer. We would call each other periodically for advice. As with his two predecessors, I offered to send a detective from my staff to work any homicide county-wide that his office would be investigating. I knew in turn that I could count on his department for expertise that we lacked. Periodically he would ask me to send him a lieutenant or captain when he had an internal matter or incident occur that needed an "outside" view. In short, we knew how to be good neighbors.

Dave and I were exchanging information about crowd size and crowd temperament when I heard someone about a block away yelling my name. He was walking quickly toward us and it took a few seconds to realize it was my next-door neighbor, Ted. It seems that in the earlier disruption of the proceedings in which nine individuals had been arrested, one of those arrested had been Ted.

Beaming with pride, he told us the whole story of how he and a small group had decided to yell and holler to disrupt the "steamrolling" by the Republicans. According to the officers involved while they were taking Ted out, he kept hollering that he was my neighbor. Ted was pumped and headed back to the crowd.

As I bid the Sheriff good-bye, a group of cops standing nearby called me over. "Hey, Chief, is that guy really your neighbor?"

"Yes, he really is my next-door neighbor."

"Geez, where do you live?" and there were laughs all around, implying that I could not live near such a rabble rouser.

"In a really nice neighborhood on the near West Side of Madison," I replied. "By the way, he's a lawyer." I left them laughing as Brian and I continued to the CP.

When we arrived at the CP, Incident Commander DC Dan Blackdeer was holding a briefing. As Dan finished up, Chief Tubbs entered the Command Post for the first time that day. Dan asked to speak to me and Charles in a nearby office. When we were all seated, Dan gently tried to persuade Charles to more broadly share the information he was getting from the Governor's Chief of Staff and the Secretary's office in the Department of Administration (DOA). As Incident Commander, Dan knew he was on a very short leash. He had very little decision-making authority, as everything had to be vetted by DOA. These restrictions are counter to the principles of the Incident Command System.

If Chief Tubbs was going to insist on being the only connection to civilian authority, then he had to be more accessible to the Command Post and to Dan in particular. The tension was thick and I was extremely uncomfortable. I suggested I leave, but both of them asked me to stay.

Chief Tubbs was under tremendous pressure. He had been hired in 2008 under a Democratic Governor. Here we were six weeks into a new Republican administration. With the new Governor's arrival came a new cabinet and new staffers. Charles was still adjusting to the new administration and of course, they to him.

The Capitol Chief of Police serves all branches of the government, regardless of party affiliation. Chief Tubbs' DOA supervisors were obviously (and necessarily) in support of their boss, Governor Walker. The protesters were clearly not in support of the Governor.

Yet the Governor's staff and the Secretary of DOA's staff were in a position to strongly influence, if not decide on, the actions of the Capitol Police. What was not clear was the level of control the Capitol Police could exert over the other state, county, and municipal law enforcement agencies. Undeniably, Charles was between the proverbial rock and a hard place. To top it off, his number-two guy was questioning his direction and leadership.

Dan made his points and Charles listened, but tired and frustrated himself, his patience was wearing thin. Dan needed some reassurances only Charles could give to him. Conversely, Charles sought reassurances from his leaders, but as it appeared to some, political calculation was all they offered. Their job was to help the Governor get his Bill passed, not to facilitate the actions of those opposed to it. I suggested Charles try to check in more often with Dan, even if by text message. Charles said the state cell phones he and Dan were issued did not allow for texting.

Incredible. I was beginning to get a glimpse of the world Dan and Charles inhabited.

I asked Dan to give Charles and me a minute. Dan quickly left. I was concerned for Charles. The stress of the situation was growing more serious and there was no end in sight. People were calling Charles to meetings for constant updates, but from where I sat, there was no structure or process being used by anyone. It was chaos. There was no workable executive structure for crisis management. There was no streamlined method for gathering information, vetting it, and then communicating it to others. There was virtually no staff for logistical support or purchasing needed items. There was no financial support and no planning support.

Charles promised he would email and call in more often. In a sad bit of irony, he noted that because he needed his phone with him all the time, he could never re-charge it and he didn't even have a spare battery.

Too many people—crowds in the Capitol on every level. February 18, 2011. (Photo by Kevin Wernet)

Chapter Two
Growing Branches

IT SEEMED LIKE FEBRUARY 17, 2011 WAS LASTING A LONG TIME, AND IT was just after 1:30 in the afternoon when AC Brian Bridges and I left the CP and headed for the Operations Room. Once again we found the Capitol overcrowded, dangerously jammed with people. We shuffled in the crowd for a while on the ground, first, and second floors. Moving among the many bodies was difficult and slow. It felt a bit like the Camp Randall stadium concourses at half-time with everyone trying to get to restrooms and concessions. No one was moving about easily. The difference, of course, is that half-time eventually ends, people retake their seats, and the crowd melts away. Both Brian and I still thought there were far too many people in the Capitol.

Eventually we entered 400 NE to find a lot happening without any obvious structure. I called the University EOC and asked them to send coolers with ice and bottled water up to Room 400 Northeast (NE) and Room 300 Southeast (SE), which served as a break room for the police. The loaded coolers arrived in less than 30 minutes. Room 400 NE still had only one phone and a single, wired Internet connection.

There were people in the room I hadn't seen before; one of them was Kevin Wernet from Blackhawk Tech. Kevin was trying to draw out the ICS organizational structure and identify some accountability. To exemplify the lack of structure, Kevin was currently struggling to get an accurate count for the number of lunches he needed to order; it was long past lunch time and officers were more than hungry.

UW Police Captain Mike Newton asked to speak with me outside the room. Mike (37 at the time) is a hard-charging-living-life-as-if-he-is-double-parked-get-it-done guy. Mike can find success regardless of the circumstances, and even when lacking resources, he finds a way to make things work. I hired Mike as a police officer in 1998, and I've since promoted him to sergeant, lieutenant, and captain. He is married and the father of two delightful little girls. He works like a fiend and has earned his Master's degree while working full-time; he is now working on a PhD.

Mike explained that the operation inside the Capitol was a "cluster." No one was leading, people were confused about what needed doing and who should do it. The CP, located three blocks away, didn't seem in touch with what was happening inside the Capitol. Chief Tubbs was in the building, but he would reassign staff without letting the operations folks or the CP know of the changes. No one seemed to have the big picture. Food was late in arriving for the officers, and there was an inadequate supply of liquids. The building was exceptionally dry and dehydration was a significant issue. Mike thanked me for the coolers and the water.

When I returned to the Ops Room, Chief Warden Randy Stark from the DNR was there. Through various police associations, I had known Randy for years, but never worked an actual operation with him. I quickly learned he was a very organized, strategic thinker. He possessed a wonderful demeanor and a droll sense of humor. I asked him what he thought of the situation. "Somebody needs to lead," was his response.

I then spoke with WSP Lieutenant Brad Altman. Brad was another guy I had known for twenty years. Brad worked many UW football games over the years, and we had a great relationship. He explained to us that the support wasn't there for the operation—

phones, camera feeds, Internet, food—none of those resources were there, although he knew they had been promised. Every agency was doing the best it could, but was acting independently from one another.

Next I talked to Lieutenant Marc Schmidt of the Capitol Police. He described not knowing who to listen to—Chief Tubbs, DC Blackdeer, or WSP Lieutenant Brad Altman. Marc was a lieutenant, but he had captains from UW and DNR in the room. This morning, they had been joined by the Chief Warden. Marc felt uncomfortable. He knew the Capitol like the back of his hand, but this operation was completely different from anything he had ever been a part of before.

I discussed the situation with AC Brian Bridges. We knew we had no formal role, and we could simply report in and leave once again. All start-ups are chaotic; this would sort itself out eventually. Yet this start-up phase was already into Day 4—far too long in my book for this much chaos.

Using the hard-wired phone, I called Incident Commander DC Dan Blackdeer and reported on the situation once again. While he thought it was clear on paper who was in charge of what, the enormous crowds and lengthy shifts were beginning to be trouble-some. More police were needed, and he informed me of the city police department's decision not to come onto state property, and the county's decision not to come inside the building. The state resources were no longer adequate.

Dane County Sheriff Dave Mahoney had started to reach out to other sheriff's departments in Rock, Iowa, Dodge, and Walworth counties for assistance. Those sheriffs were willing to start sending resources beginning Friday and to have their deputies work inside the Capitol.

Dan Blackdeer wanted to discuss activating the Emergency Police Service (EPS) through Wisconsin Emergency Management

(WEM). He was thinking ahead and realized with the Governor's Budget Address scheduled for February 22, we needed to, at the very least, sustain staffing levels. We might even need to increase law enforcement staffing until that date.

Information gathered on the street indicated that the weekend protests were going to involve even larger crowds then the ones we had seen so far. We concluded it was a sound idea to activate EPS. This was a significant step and one not to be taken lightly, as EPS had not been activated for an event this large since 1989.

The last time Wisconsin's Emergency Police Service was operational in a significant way was for protests against Native Americans spearfishing at various boat landings all over the state. Police were called up and sent to various armories throughout the state, where they slept when off duty and lived for days. Each morning, they would head to the boat landings to keep peace between the Native American tribes and the fisherman (overwhelmingly Caucasian) protesting the Native American rights to spearfish in the lakes.

Divided by regions of the state, the EPS system is well designed to gather disparate resources into workable teams and deliver those teams to the staging area for an event. In each region, there is a sheriff who acts as the Area Director. Each Area Director has a deputy, who is a police chief in the same region.

When the request comes from Wisconsin Emergency Management (WEM) to the sheriffs, they notify all of the agencies in their region and request available staff to assist. Once the sheriff (or chief) has the number of available officers for his or her region, WEM is informed.

If more resources are needed, another region is activated. Regions closest to the event are tapped first, to keep travel time and potential lodging needs to a minimum.

The current level of staffing in the CP was no match for this new deployment of officers. The Logistics Section was struggling to keep the number of resources they currently had deployed, fed, and equipped. The Planning Section was struggling as well. None of these struggles were from a lack of effort or dedication. The challenges came from a lack of resources and clear leadership.

As the conversation continued, I not so gently reminded Dan that Brian and I had offered over and over again to help, but had not been given any particular job. While the other senior leaders—the Sheriff, State Patrol Superintendent, City Police Chief, and the Administrator of the Division of Criminal Investigation—had been just playing advisory roles, DNR Chief Warden Randy Stark and I were spending time in the Operations Room. Dan hesitated. It was one thing for him to have assistant chiefs and captains under his command in ICS, but to have potentially two chiefs in Randy and me, that was a different matter.

Dan was silent for about thirty seconds as he thought about it and then asked if I would run the interior operations. This is where I thought I could help the most, so I quickly agreed and told him I would have Assistant Chief Brian Bridges and Chief Warden Randy Stark as my principal deputies. We agreed he should inform Capitol Police Lieutenant Marc Schmidt and WSP Captain Chuck Teasdale should inform WSP Lieutenant Brad Altman. Once that was done, I would take command of the interior operations.

I called UW Chancellor Biddy Martin to discuss the developments. Since the Budget Repair Bill had been introduced, she and I had contact via email, texts, phone calls, or meetings nearly every day. Working where I do, I get a lot of opportunity to meet and work with incredibly intelligent people. She is among the best intellects, seasoned with a heavy dose of common sense, that I have ever met. I explained the division of labor and how we were addressing the campus needs while simultaneously assisting at the Capitol. She was completely supportive and was pleased to have us at the Capitol—especially with the involvement of our TAs and some of our students, staff, and faculty. We agreed we would keep in touch.

My next call was to the Vice Chancellor for Administration, Darrell Bazzell. I again explained the situation. He pledged his support.

I huddled up with Randy and Brian to fill them in. Once Brad and Marc had received their calls and hung up their phones, I stood up and asked for everyone's attention. It was 3:00 p.m. on Thursday, February 17, Day 4. I explained the change in leadership and command. I asked the group how we were going to fix the current situation. There was silence. Then Kevin Wernet suggested we run it like a fire scene. Since none of us were firefighters and nothing was burning, we began the usual good-natured ribbing that happens between the fire service and police. We had a few laughs. We really had little or no clue what Kevin was talking about.

I asked Kevin to talk a little more about what he meant by running the event like a fire scene. He explained that at a fire scene, people quickly grasp they are there to extinguish a fire, save lives, and save property. While things appear chaotic, the management of the situation was structured. Kevin was trying to sort through applying the Incident Command System used on fire scenes to this protest, but with no law enforcement in his background, he struggled to make all the pieces fit.

I suggested we turn our attention to the Incident Command System (ICS) chart and together, we established a new branch under the ICS model. The Incident Command System has five major components: Command, Operations, Logistics, Planning, and Finance. The University Police was the first law enforcement agency in Wisconsin to adopt the Incident Command System in 1994. We have used it routinely for football games, protests, and rallies.

Within ICS, there is supposed to be one leader, the Incident Commander. Within Incident Command, you can use a Unified Command, in which multiple commanders from multiple agencies collaborate to make joint decisions. It was unclear at this point if we were using Unified Command or a single Incident Commander. While DC Blackdeer had the title of Incident Commander, it didn't seem he had the authority.

For now, in our chart, which may have differed from the chart at the CP, the title of Incident Commander went to Deputy Chief of the Capitol Police, Dan Blackdeer; Operations Chief would be Wisconsin State Patrol Captain Charles "Chuck" Teasdale. Both men were in the Command Post inside the Fire Administration building. Chuck would have deputy operations chiefs from the University Police and DNR.

As Branch Director, I would report to the operations chief, Chuck. University Police Assistant Chief Brian Bridges and DNR Chief Warden Randy Stark would serve as my deputies inside the Capitol. WSP Lieutenant Brad Altman, CPD Lieutenant Marc Schmidt, University Police Captain Mike Newton, and DNR Captain Byron Goetsch would be division commanders in the Capitol.

In the Interior Branch, we would organize by geography and not by agency. We would establish a reasonable span of control for supervisors within the Capitol. We were not sure of the city police or county sheriff's department role in this ICS structure, so we left them out. It was also unclear how Chief Tubbs fit into the structure. It seemed that Charles wanted to be a part of some decisions, but

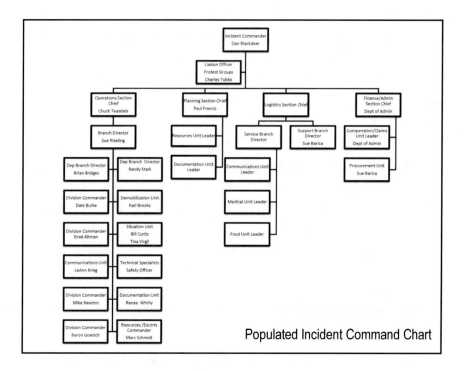

Populated Incident Command Chart

had largely delegated the functions to Dan; it appeared he had done so without granting Dan the authority to make decisions and lead the operation.

Wondering what a firefighter was doing in the middle of a police operation, I sat down and asked Kevin Wernet what his role was here. He explained that the Southwest Incident Management Team (SW-IMT) had been activated to assist.

The SW-IMT is comprised of approximately forty professionals from police, fire, emergency medical personnel, public works, and emergency management, with extensive incident management experience using the National Incident Management System, Incident Command System (ICS) model. Team members' employers agree to allow team members to deploy for up to 72

*hours on short notice. The team's purpose is to assist
community leaders by providing personnel to fill critical
management functions within the organization during
an incident, or to augment and assist agencies with
management tasks. Team members are required to
complete many ICS courses and have experience using
the system. It's important to note that the team does not
take over leadership of the incident, it merely provides
depth to the requesting agency that is typically stretched
thin when there is an event that exceeds its day-to-day
capacity.*

Kevin had spent a brief time in Planning and Logistics at the CP, and
had been sent to the Operations Room in 400 NE to help in any way
he could. He suggested he become my aide. After that, we were an
inseparable team.

With that settled, the group made a quick organizational chart
of what was to be in each division. We listed all the supplies and
items we needed for the room itself. We had learned from Brad that
if we needed anything, we should figure out how to get it ourselves,
since the CP hadn't really been able to assist with logistics to date.

Marc started using his contacts within the Capitol to get us the
immediate items we needed: more phones, Internet hook-ups, and
tables. Captain Michael Newton activated all four of the University's
Emergency Service Coordinators at my direction. They loaded vans
with equipment: computers, printers, flip charts, office supplies,
radios, batteries, power strips, air cards, and then reported into the
Capitol. With little direction, they set up the room, captured notes,
began to organize the records we were making, and handled
incoming issues as problems seemingly poured into the room.

Room 400 NE was normally an Assembly hearing room. The
room was round in shape, approximately 700 square feet, with one

By 4:55 p.m. on February 17, 2011, the Interior Branch was forming. (L to R, standing): The original Branch leaders, Byron Goetsch, Randy Stark, Kevin Wernet, Sue Riseling, Johnnie Diamante, and Brian Bridges. (L to R, seated): John Lind, Brad Altman, Marc Schmidt, and Michael Newton. (Photo by Bill Curtis)

Protesters in the Capitol. (Photos by Jim Escalante)

long conference table in the middle, surrounded by oversized executive chairs. Circling the walls were two rows of non-folding chairs that were stackable. Over the first few days, some of the chairs had been stacked, but they still took up a lot of space. There was an antique credenza that although empty, weighed a ton, and when four capable men tried to move it, they thought better of it and left it where it stood. We filled it with office supplies.

Any chairs not in use were moved to the hallway. All the food was moved into the hallway, as well as the coolers that held water and soda. Other tables were brought in and placed against the circular wall or facing out toward the center of the room.

Having access to a printer large enough to print big floor plans had been an issue. In University Police emergency management and infrastructure security units, we had such a printer, known as "BAP," which affectionately means Big Ass Printer. It was capable of printing large, oversized documents. Using email, we sent the images to the University, where a staff member printed the documents, and a University Police officer delivered them to us. What the group had been waiting on for days had now been completed in about 30 minutes.

Large sized ground-to-fourth floor plans, by directional wing with over-arching headers (Assembly, Senate, Executive, Supreme Court), plus aerial photographs of the building and the streets surrounding it, also went up on the walls with masking tape. (Little did we know then what controversy tape would cause.) We posted a floor plan for the room, designating who was where, along with the table configuration to be created. Eventually, a chart of events for each day would be posted along with a deployment chart. A formal mission statement for the Interior Branch was to be drafted and hung for all to see.

Brad had accessed camera feeds on his computer. These showed him four cameras from the outside of the Capitol. Efforts to get a screen and a projector for everyone to see the feeds had failed. His efforts to get a TV in the room had also been unsuccessful. Brad was to act as our camera monitor until we could get this addressed. We did manage to acquire 75 radios with earpieces from University Police and another 25 from the CP. These would help greatly with interoperability when we brought in other police agencies from around the state.

The Command Post was working hard on communications issues and things were taking shape. There were dispatchers assigned to handle the radio communications for the inside and outside of the Capitol. Patching us all together from various frequencies was necessary and done with great skill. The other communications issue the CP was working on was to connect us to the CP by video conferencing. At the time, I needed to go to DC Blackdeer's office in the basement of the Capitol to connect via video.

A major concern to the division commanders was that preparations for the Madison Winter Festival were to start the next day, Friday, February 18, 2011. This was an event where the streets surrounding the Capitol are deliberately covered in snow for various winter sporting events to occur on Saturday. To prepare the streets, trucks filled with snow would dump load after load of the white stuff onto the streets. They planned to start this dumping operation on Friday evening around 5:00.

An extremely large protest rally of 50,000 people was also scheduled for Saturday. The two events clearly would not mix well. I called the CP. Chuck was aware of the situation so he and Dan, along with Chief Tubbs, were working with the organizers to get the Festival changed or cancelled.

While getting things organized, I was introduced to the sergeant-at-arms of the Assembly, Ann Tonnon Byers. The Assembly and the Senate each has its own sergeant-at-arms. The sergeant

is elected every two years and executes directives from the leadership for whichever house they are working. Two specific responsibilities were in play tonight:

1. Maintain order and quiet in and about the chamber,
   remove disorderly persons, or clear the galleries or other
   areas of the chamber when directed to do so by the
   presiding officer in relation to any disturbance which may
   occur in or near the chamber.
2. Carry out the instruction of the presiding officer in
   compelling the attendance of absent members.

Ann, dressed in a business suit, blonde hair in a bun, was cordial yet
business-like. Along with her was Patrick Fuller, the Assembly
Clerk. He possessed a striking shaved head and piercing eyes, and
the Marine Corps emblem on his tie told me all I needed to know.

Patrick and Ann came across as serious and no nonsense. Our
Operations Room was one of the many Assembly rooms they
controlled, and I was hoping to use it and another of their rooms as
a meeting/briefing room. I explained the new organizational
structure we were attempting to put in place. They shared the
schedule for the Assembly and what they thought would happen
when and where. They were very helpful in understanding the
dynamic of the political situation. We exchanged cards. If they
needed anything, they would call me or come to room 400 NE.

Next up was Senate Sergeant-at-Arms, Ted Blazel, who was
in a hurry about one thing or another, so our first meeting
occurred quickly.

Earlier in the day, fourteen Democratic senators had left the
state in an effort to delay the vote on the Budget Bill. It was
rumored they had traveled about an hour away to Rockford,
Illinois. Ted Blazel was ready to fill me in and gain my help with all

he needed. He and Senate Clerk Rob Marchant were professional and courteous, but were obviously distracted.

The Capitol Police and staffers, such as the chief clerks and sergeants-at-arms brought with them a familiarity of the Capitol building, as well as the political process. University Police brought experience managing large-scale events. Now we needed to merge our knowledge and skills to navigate this unprecedented historical event together.

I turned my attention to what tomorrow morning would bring. By 7:30 a.m., 62 police officers and deputies would be arriving from outside the Dane County area. They would arrive via squad car and would not be able to park at the Capitol or in the densely populated isthmus of downtown Madison. Kevin was still working with the CP to locate offsite parking and arrange for transportation to the Capitol. We wanted to bring in the 62 officers without alarming anyone about the sudden appearance of four to five dozen police vehicles in a downtown neighborhood.

The officers would need an unobtrusive way into the Capitol; we understood their appearance at the main doors would likely raise tensions in the still calm and sleeping crowd in the Rotunda. The officers were to provide security, as much for the protesters as for anyone or anything else, but their arrival might easily be taken as a sign we meant to clear and then close the building. We chose to use an underground tunnel connecting the Risser Justice Building across the Square with the basement of the Capitol. As long as the protesters were peaceful and the government continued to operate, we had no immediate need to interfere with their continued presence.

These 62 officers coming from outside the county did not have the benefit of knowing the city, the Capitol, or the protesters, and would need to be thoroughly briefed before heading to their posts.

Madison is known for its liberal politics, and the University brings a population far more international than anywhere else in the state. Much of the rest of Wisconsin is considered rural and socially conservative. Those in the northern sections of the state tend to view Madison with a certain amount of suspicion and disdain regarding Madisonians, who live in an Ivory Tower fantasy land believed to be populated by aging hippies. Given this disconnect between Madison and the surrounding areas, we thought it necessary to brief the officers with care. We certainly respected their professionalism, yet we wanted to dispel any possible preconceived notions about the Madison protesters.

When bringing in this many officers and deputies from around the region, we couldn't be sure about the level of crowd control training or experience they possessed. In Wisconsin, law enforcement, for the most part, is deployed with a collection of weapons at their individual sides. While trained when and how to use these tools, they choose which one best suits the situation using their own discretion.

When police are brought together and have to work as a team, they can no longer make individual decisions based on their own discretion as they do when they are on their own. For example, a police line must act as a coordinated team. An established police line cannot have an officer break that formation because she thinks she needs to take some action—that kind of independence weakens the line. Similarly, an officer who makes an individual arrest without other officers knowing can fracture a truce or escalate a situation dangerously.

The concept of working as a team does not come easily to the police. Police officers are taught to operate independently, establish control, use their best judgment and discretion. They are taught not to trust but to verify, to establish facts, to be skeptical, and to keep their professional distance. Each step of the way an officer must be prepared to justify actions, response, and decision making. As a result, when individual police officers are placed into a group, they may be members of that group without it being a well-functioning team.

University Police's strategy for dynamic crowd situations is to use officers in pairs. Two pairs can easily coalesce into what is known as a "mini-team" of four with one person acting as leader. Two mini-teams can merge into an eight-person team, with one person acting as the leader. Two teams of eight can join, and an additional leader is added for a squad of seventeen.

The Wisconsin State Patrol only uses squads of seventeen. I quickly learned that troopers come in groups of just two sizes—and always wear their campaign hats (think "Smokey the Bear")—even inside. They either arrive individually, alone in a car on a highway, or in groups of seventeen. No number smaller than seventeen was to be used for a state trooper crowd control response. Really?

In the ensuing days, when I asked for the troopers to do a particular job that might require four staff, they would send 17. Periodically, the silliness of this inflexibility would make me laugh out loud. When I asked for a job that might take 25, they would send 34. There were moments when sending 17 to do the job of four was overkill and I was concerned that the additional troopers would cause an unnecessary escalation of tension and show of force. So I wasn't laughing anymore.

We had to be prepared to blend law enforcement into different groupings depending on the action of the crowd and how we wanted to engage them. These tactical differences had to be carefully ironed out during the daily briefing. Most of the agencies divided into whatever sized groups we needed. The state troopers, on the other hand, remained in their squads of 17 and refused to integrate with other agencies or break into smaller operational units.

Officers or deputies needed to be instructed on their assignments, and each branch division commander was responsible for compiling a post plan for the division. My job was to review these plans and agree on the number of personnel to assign. Each detail needed quick decisions.

Protesters continued to gather at the Capitol, having gained momentum as a result of the 14 Democratic senators leaving the state. The building interior once again became overcrowded. We knew it was going to be a busy night. By about 9:30 that evening, all of us were too tired to function effectively, so we wrapped up for the day.

We all agreed we would need to be back in the Operations Room by 6:30 the next morning. We would brief officers from state agencies at 7:15 and the other agencies when they arrived. Briefings would occur in 412 East, another Assembly meeting room, thanks to permission given by Anne Tonnon Byers, the Assembly Sergeant–at-Arms.

As we turned command over to the night shift and headed out, the Capitol was buzzing with people chanting and drumming. The Capitol building was allowed to remain open because hearings, listening sessions, and meetings were continuing with Democratic assembly members. People sat on the ground floor of the Rotunda drumming, which was sporadically joined by dancing and singing. There was a party atmosphere of several thousand folks in very festive moods.

On average, about 500 protesters were spending the night in the Capitol this week—a facility not designed as a hotel. In the space of three days, they had established themselves, if not comfortably, with at least all the conveniences they could muster. There were Nesco® roasters lined up on tables with hot food and lots of boxed pizzas. Cases of water were stacked in the alcoves. There was a first aid station and several information tables. It seemed that the protesters were better organized and supplied than the police.

By 10 p.m., I was home watching the local news. The Capitol rallies were the big story of the day. I was curious to see how the story was being told, when on the screen appeared an interview of a friend, Nancy Evans. In the interview, Nancy was standing inside the Capitol, protesters all around her, and she was explaining why she, as a teacher in the Monona Grove school district, felt it was important to be there. I turned up the volume and listened carefully.

Nancy had been teaching elementary general music, kindergarten through 5th grade, for 22 years in the public schools. A mother of three grown children and grandmother of one, Nancy had also taught music for ten years outside the public school system. She had never protested anything before yesterday. This was an historic moment for her, as she rarely missed work.

Nancy had carefully weighed her decision not to go to work yesterday and to call in to say she wouldn't be there. She never claimed to be sick and she knew she would take what is referred to as "pay deduct." Using personal email, she had communicated with other teachers while contemplating her own decision. She hated to be away from the school children. Nancy truly loves teaching and felt terribly guilty whenever she couldn't attend to her classes.

On Wednesday, her first day of missing work, she had headed to the WEAC parking lot. There she had taken the shuttle the union had provided and got to the Capitol early. She and some co-workers went into the Capitol and found a spot near the second floor railing. She stayed at the railing the whole day, listening to speakers, singing, and talking to folks she knew and others she had just met.

When I talked to Nancy later, she told me that she and her co-workers felt proud that they were standing up for their beliefs and making a difference for Wisconsin teachers. Originally, she was just going to stay until noon. But she stayed later because it was such a powerful and affirming experience.

Her school district was closed on Thursday, so she went off to the Capitol again. This time, she met some teachers from Janesville. The Capitol was crowded and hot inside. The noise was intense. She had never been a part of a crowd that large, yet she never felt threatened or unsafe. Everyone was incredibly supportive and helpful. Nancy saw the police all around and found them to be reassuring and even helpful in facilitating directions and answering other logistical questions.

Nancy believed that it was necessary to be a part of the protests to make a statement. She did not want to stay out of work so long that parents would become angry about teachers not teaching. She acknowledged the strain parents go through when their kids are not in school, particularly when parents cannot go to work themselves.

Sitting in the comfort of my own home, I paused and thought about my next door neighbor Ted getting arrested, my friend Nancy protesting, and my staff (and me) not being exempted from the increases in pension and health care contributions. I wondered how many protesters were just like Nancy, gainfully employed, never having protested anything before. I figured it had to be thousands. I thought of folks who worked in the Republican offices in the Capitol and were feeling scared, harassed, and threatened by the crowds. Regardless of political view, everyone was affected by what was happening.

As I continued to check the local news, the list of school districts closing continued to grow: Baraboo, Belleville, Cross Plains, Deerfield, Evansville, Janesville, Mauston, Middleton, Monona Grove, New Lisbon, Pardeeville, Randolph, River Valley, and Wisconsin Dells.

DAY 5: FRIDAY, FEBRUARY 18, 2011

"MORNING PERSON" IS NOT HOW PEOPLE DESCRIBE ME. LUCKY FOR ME, working in law enforcement for so many years, I rarely have to think about what I am going to wear to work. Occasionally, I will wear a suit or blazer, blouse and slacks. But mainly I have multiple sets of navy blue uniforms for each season of the year. I have hats, coats, sweaters, jackets, shoes, boots, and all the accessories to add to the basic uniform pants and shirts. I have a dress uniform and ceremonial hat, and I have a crowd control uniform and gear.

Having worked so many days in a row, I was thankful to have so many sets of uniforms. In a normal week, I had enough sets to get me through until I could handle the weekend laundry. Working day after day nonstop—even with multiple sets—it wasn't enough. Thank goodness, I had a lot of support on the home front.

I arrived by the skin of my teeth at 6:15 at the backdoor of my department headquarters. AC Brian Bridges, who *is* a morning person, was there to greet me along with Captain Johnnie Diamante and Captain Karen Soley. We all jumped in one car together. Captain Soley was headed to the Command Post, while the rest of us were off to 400 NE for another day.

We weren't the only ones at work early. Governor Walker had already arrived in the Capitol and was preparing for a press conference. By 6:30, I was wishing everyone in 400 NE of the Capitol a good morning. Being the last one in the door myself, I found a crew of chiefs, captains, and lieutenants ready to roll.

Establishing a routine reflects one of the ironies of emergency planning—that planning for what you can predict frees you to better react to the unexpected and unanticipated. I stood up at one of the flip charts and asked what we needed to do in the next thirty minutes before the first wave of police arrived for the day shift. In order to brief people appropriately, we had to name ourselves. We debated between "Capitol Branch" and "Interior Branch." Quickly, "Interior Branch" was chosen.

We expected 62 deputies from outside of Dane County to arrive at the offsite parking area at 7:00 to then be transported to the Capitol via bus. We went over the previous night's events and all the events scheduled for the day, which was now officially named by us "Day 5, February 18, 2011."

Over 500 people had spent the night in the Capitol. There had been no arrests.

We were relieved to learn that the Winter Festival scheduled for that evening had been cancelled. It was almost impossible to envision all that snow being dumped on the streets where 50,000 people were expected to amass and march.

The Teaching Assistants Association (TAA) had sent Chancellor Martin a letter requesting that she cancel all classes so the University could stand in solidarity with other public employees across the state. I doubted the University would cancel classes. AC (ret) Dale Burke would start his day in the University's EOC. He would let me know if I had to be concerned.

Radio communications among the four state law enforcement agencies were fully integrated and functioning. Finally, everyone could talk to and hear everyone else. We established two break rooms for the police officers and deputies.

The media room was in 235 Southwest, and the reporters could go there to get a daily pass. Passes were color coded, which enabled officers to quickly tell a current pass from an old one.

We finished up with a discussion of the rules of engagement for the police and how arrests should be handled. DNR Chief Warden Randy Stark, my deputy branch director, and all division commanders were expected to accompany me to the briefing. Kevin Wernet, my aide, was one step behind me with a bottle of water at the ready. AC Brian Bridges, my other deputy branch director of operations and the University Police Emergency Service Coordinators would stay behind in the Interior Branch Operations Room in 400 NE.

The room we were using that morning for the law enforcement briefing was the Joint Finance Committee Hearing Room, 412 East. This was the room in which the Budget Repair Bill had been discussed and earlier in the week, public testimony had been taken through the night. One of the largest hearing rooms in the Capitol, it has a raised dais complete with microphones. The room has three seating areas with a capacity of more than a hundred and includes a smaller conference room off to one side.

Randy and I headed to the dais and sat in the middle of the raised semi-circle. The room, filled with DNR, State Patrol, Capitol Police, and University Police, became very quiet. I began with the usual introductions and explained the overall ICS structure and the Interior Branch. Our branch would have four divisions that day: basement and ground floor headed by the DNR; first and second floors headed by the State Patrol, third and fourth floors headed by the University Police, and response and information teams headed by the Capitol Police.

Break rooms, media room, and radio protocols were reviewed, along with the events of the day. We covered restricted areas and various access plans, including which elevators and stairwells would be off limits to the public and staffed by police. We shared the media pass color for the day and reminded everyone to allow the janitorial staff, wearing blue T-shirts, to be allowed to go wherever they needed to keep the building as clean as possible.

I also made it clear that the custodial staff be allowed access to our food and beverages. People had been sleeping in the building overnight since Tuesday and the place was getting dirty. The custodians were working hard, but it was difficult for them to keep up. Feeding them was one way for us to support their efforts.

It was important to share the rules of engagement with the entire team. The group in 400 NE had worked to develop these rules and we didn't consider it necessary to gain anyone's approval.

Based on my own experience in dealing with protests, large crowds, and policing in those crowds, I was comfortable with the rules of engagement. Buy-in by those on the front-line is key to whether the rules will be followed with the intent and spirit in which they are established. We have all seen the "by the book" type of enforcement and the Interior Branch rules were to be applied with some common sense, respect, compassion and a touch of professional discretion.

Key to these rules was having a high tolerance for unruly behavior, behavior we all agree would not be tolerated under normal circumstances. Tasers could be used with a supervisor's approval, but only in the drive-stun mode, since shooting the projectiles in a crowd was deemed unwise. There would be no use of pepper spray inside the building. The use of pepper spray in such a structure, given the crowd size and density, would cause panic and likely cause more problems than it would solve. Since there were enough police ready to respond, we could get to the officer in need quickly.

OUR RULES OF ENGAGEMENT:

1. Communicate, communicate, communicate
2. Educate, explain, reframe.
3. De-escalate tension.
4. Problem solve, work with the marshals.
5. Very high degree of tolerance for disruptive behavior
6. No Taser use without a supervisor's approval, and then only used in a drive-stun mode.
7. Pepper spray is not to be used inside.
8. Arrests should be limited to serious misdemeanors or felonies.

There was one exception to the pepper spray rule. I told the officers that if they were in the bathroom backed into a stall and their pants were down around their ankles when a large group of whack-a-doodles attacked them, they could spray them like bugs. It got the laugh I was going for. We covered all sorts of other seemingly endless, yet important, details.

The Senate and Assembly were scheduled to go into session at 9:00 that morning but around here, we had learned that times are always subject to change. It was unclear how the fourteen senators' leaving the state would affect the Senate's start time. We were informed that the sergeant-at-arms of the Senate, Ted Blazel, accompanied by a single state trooper, followed a rumor and went to the Monona, Wisconsin, home of Democratic Senator Mark Miller to see if he was there. Unfortunately for Ted, the rumor turned out false and he returned to the Capitol empty-handed. The action made every local and some national news shows.

With the four-day "veteran" staff heading to their assignments, Randy and I turned our attention toward the 62 coming from the surrounding counties. It would be this next group to be briefed that was truly new. I had never met most of these deputies. There was no way to know how they would react to the circumstances or my command.

While women had been a part of policing in all aspects of the job since the early 1970s, some of the reporting deputies would be looking at a female police chief for the first time in their careers—and a University chief as well. Of course, I had faced many similar audiences in the past. Cops want to be led, fed, and cared about, and I could do those things and more. What I didn't know then but found out later, was that many of them had "Googled" me to determine who I was and what my police department was all about.

To our earlier briefing, we shared some basic geography of the area and the building itself. We suggested they walk the building before they went on post so they would have an understanding of where important landmarks were located as far as cops were concerned: bathroom, break room, and arrest processing. I was rewarded with another round of laughs.

We shared some details about the fantastic crowd demeanor and friendliness. While the Capitol's marble floors would tire their legs, the people's energy would raise their spirits. We spent a lot of time sharing examples of the assistance given to the police by the union marshals. The marshals were wearing traffic vests so they were easy to spot. The custodians were in their blue T-shirts. We were quick to note that if a custodian or marshal couldn't handle whatever came up, we would be surprised.

I was blunt and told the "newbies" that they had to check their politics at the door. Whether they agreed with the Governor or the protesters, we couldn't engage in the political theatre that surrounded us. This was about the United States Constitution and the oath we had all taken to uphold it. We were to facilitate the exercise of the First Amendment and to keep the elected government functioning. It was the law of the land, and we were to enforce it.

My job was to shield them from the political back-and-forth and not allow the police to become an arm of either political party or ideology. Those in the room who were in unions were exempted from the Governor's action, while others with supervisory rank were not shielded from the proposed changes in the benefit packages. I made it clear that we all had to be on the same team.

We shared the start-up issues that the event had suffered. Going from a crowd of 1,500 to close to 30,000 in four days meant that our spin-up had increased each day. Today, we were expecting 50,000. We were having trouble getting police fed on time. So I promised them that if the food did not arrive by 12 noon sharp, I would personally pay for their lunches. More laughs.

I then assigned my new aide-de-camp, Kevin Wernet, to call the CP repeatedly to ensure the food was delivered. In fact, Todd Kuschel, who had been trying to jump-start logistics was so tired of receiving calls about the food, he phoned AC Brian Bridges and told him to stop Kevin's calls. Brian retorted, "Just deliver once on time what you promised and we will stop." Fortunately Todd came through; the food arrived at 11:45 and Kevin stopped calling.

Finally, I told the deputies to meet as many other cops as they could. This would be something they would remember for a long time. Whenever possible, I told them to have fun, because there would be nothing quite like this again. With that, Randy took over and discussed the radio communications plan. He did a head count on the fly and made assignments to various locations, trying to keep members of the same department or area together. It took a while, but eventually we got them to their posts, on the same radio frequency, and introduced them to their supervisors.

As I prepared to leave the podium, I noticed a sergeant from a neighboring county sheriff's department staring at me. He had the look of a Marine. I greeted him and he was enthusiastic in his response. I asked him if he was a Marine.

He replied, "Affirmative. Steve Allerman, Dodge County."

"I thought so," I said. He smiled and asked if I was a Marine.

"No," I said. "The only regret I have in my life is that I never served as a Marine." I joked with him and guessed he had been a sergeant major. He answered in the affirmative. He was highly complementary about my briefing. He said he had heard good things about me from the officers who had escorted them in this morning. I told him he could stop blowing smoke. We laughed out loud and shook hands. He gathered up his crew and headed out.

I walked into the Rotunda and a young deputy was standing wide-eyed, staring down at the crowd. I inquired if he was all right. He turned toward me and with a thousand-yard stare still on his face, he acknowledged there were more people in the post to which he had been assigned than were in his home town. I told him my guess was he would not see anything like this again in his career. I asked him to try not to do anything to dampen the mood and we shared a laugh. As I left him to his work, I reassured him that things would be okay on his post and if I was wrong, help was close at hand.

* * * * *

IT WAS VITAL FOR ME TO UNDERSTAND FIRST AND FOREMOST THE THREATS the police could face in the Capitol. I was concerned about having to evacuate this crowd, especially if they became panicked. I needed to obtain a copy of the Capitol evacuation plans. Fortunately, Capitol Police Lieutenant Marc Schmidt was able to obtain a copy of the plan quickly.

I suggested to Brian that we modify the fire response plan to look like the one we use for the Kohl Center basketball and hockey arena on campus. He agreed. This meant the pull stations were to be silenced, which meant if someone in the crowd thought it would be clever to pull the alarm to cause confusion and panic, the klaxons would not sound. Instead, the dispatcher in the Capitol Police center would receive the alarm and send someone to check out the situation before the horns would activate. While a false sounding would be avoided, the down side is if there is a real fire, precious time could be lost. This was just another balancing act we faced.

Certainly another threat that could cause mass casualties and panic would be a bomb detonation. We again looked at the Capitol Police policy and made some modifications. At the University, we had available explosive ordnance detection canines, a.k.a. "bomb dogs." One worked days and the other at night. The WSP also had an ordnance canine. We would ask University Police Captain Soley at the Command Post to put together the canine staffing plan. We could use the canines to check out suspicious packages, backpacks, and containers. Given the volume of people and the number of items they had brought into the building, the dogs and their handlers were valuable assets for us to deploy.

Of course, while all of our planning was going on inside the Capitol, outside on the lawn, the major unions were organizing for the day's events. Some people were making their way from the Labor Center; others were walking up State Street. People were crowded into the nearby Starbucks and milling around the sidewalks on the Capitol Square. There was anticipation in the air and the mood continued to be upbeat. Capitol staff members were busy reporting to work and other folks were gathering outside the entrances.

About the time all the doors were opening fully for the day, more deputies and police showed up and had to be briefed. Thirty minutes later, another group showed up. By this time, we had added the fire response to the briefing.

Randy quickly figured out why new officers kept coming. The EPS coordinators had told departments the shift was 7:00 a.m. to 7:00 p.m. Depending on where the police were coming from, they would leave their station at 7:00 a.m., drive to Madison, park, and be transported to the Capitol. Some had driven an hour, some two from their departments. They also expected to be relieved from their shift at the Capitol in time to be back at their home stations by 7:00 p.m., which meant we would have to release them starting at 4:00 p.m. What we thought was a 12-hour on-site shift turned out to be more like an 8- or 9-hour shift.

Emergency Police Services (EPS) was designed to bolster the number of police in an area of the state, with each responding jurisdiction paying its own costs. It was believed to be a temporary measure that any law enforcement agency could activate and use, so there was no sense billing each other for it. Most sheriffs and chiefs were willing to send staff for a day or two on their own jurisdiction's dime, but as the calls went out for help on Saturday, Sunday, Monday, and Tuesday, the agencies began to hesitate.

Wisconsin Emergency Management reached out to the next EPS region. But the further out they reached, the more travel time was involved. Without being able to house officers, we were going to have to deal with longer shifts for some and reduced on-site hours for others. This presented a significant scheduling challenge. The Planning and Logistics sections in the Command Post and the EPS coordinators worked on this difficult challenge for days.

After returning to the Interior Branch room 400 NE from all the various briefings and assignments, I gathered the division commanders together, along with the support staff and the two deputy branch directors.

Our Interior Branch Operations Room was shaping up. Internet connections had been obtained, along with fourteen phone lines. AC Brian Bridges had a screen in front of him that showed the same camera display Lieutenant Brad Altman could see. We went around the room with issues and questions needing to be addressed.

The methods used by University Police during UW Badger football games with about 150 police per game, who mostly hailed from different jurisdictions, was coming in handy. I talked about the post assignment card system and numbering system we used at Camp Randall Stadium. Each post received a three-by-five card with his or her post name and number, supervisor's name, radio protocol, and the assignment directions for their post.

The division commanders needed to meet with every supervisor to find out where the supervisors had posted their people and what instructions were needed. After the information was all on paper, they would email it to Sue Langner, University Police Records Manager. Sue completed these cards for every football game, so she was well equipped to handle manufacturing the Interior Branch cards.

It would have been nice to have the layout of the Capitol on the back of each card, to help officers find their way and when asked, to assist the public. Unfortunately, we couldn't get that to work, so we printed a sheet with the outline of the Capitol, along with restroom locations. Each officer was be given a copy of the Capitol outline with his or her post assignment card.

AC Dale Burke had arrived from the University's EOC. Everything was working at UW–Madison. The TAA did not get the walkout support they had hoped. I pulled Dale aside, along with AC Brian Bridges, to share a concern I was having about Incident Commander DC Dan Blackdeer and his Deputy Incident Commander, Todd Kuschel. I explained to Dale the chaos, tension, indecision, and exhaustion Brian and I had seen earlier in the week at the Command Post. I wanted Dale to go to the CP to determine how to relieve Dan and Todd so that they could get some rest. Dale and Todd had worked together for over 25 years at University Police. I knew that both Todd and Dan respected Dale and were likely to listen to his request.

Brian summarized the issues and problems with Planning and Logistics at the Command Post. He noted we had sent University Police Lieutenant Ben Newman to the CP to assist with planning. University Police Captain Karen Soley was there as well and from what she said, she was underutilized. We wanted Dale to shore up some of the CP processes and get things operational.

As Dale headed off to the CP, we received word that the Reverend Jesse Jackson would be arriving for the noon rally. We were very conscious that the protests at the Wisconsin Capitol were not just state-wide news, but were fast becoming national, and even international news stories on CNN, FOX, MSNBC, and all the major networks. Depending on which outlet you viewed, and depending on the station and reporter's political bias, you were likely to hear entirely different stories about the event.

Wisconsin Congresswoman Tammy Baldwin escorts Rev. Jesse Jackson into the Capitol on February 18, 2011. (Photo by Tony Barnes)

At 11:52 a.m., Reverend Jackson arrived.

I had met Rev. Jackson years before when he came to the campus to speak, and again when he ran for President. The gathering crowd welcomed him and took inspiration from his words. We saw no security risk in his visit and speech. Chief Tubbs was in charge of ensuring the Reverend could move about freely through the large crowds. Chief Tubbs took a contingent of officers to facilitate the Reverend's visit. Things went very smoothly.

One of the key issues Dan had put forward directly to Chief Tubbs in previous days was that Charles needed to stay in touch with the Command Post. Nevertheless, that day, Dan still was unable to reach Charles via phone or radio. Dan didn't know where Chief Tubbs was at any time beyond the noon rally with Reverend Jackson. He even called the Interior Branch looking for Chief Tubbs.

Meanwhile Dale arrived at the CP to convince Dan and Todd to go home. That wasn't happening, despite their admitting they were exhausted and functioning on too little sleep. Instead, Dale was asked to locate Chief Tubbs. That was to no avail.

It appeared to Dale and others that Dan had no authority to decide anything without Chief Tubbs' and the DOA's approval. The problem was that Dan reported through Chief Tubbs to the Department of Administration (DOA), and Dan couldn't get through to Charles. Dan felt it was too risky if he made any decisions. He felt he lacked the authority to command the city police, the sheriff deputies, and the State Patrol. Decision-making in the CP ground to a near halt. The Incident Command System had been put into place to avoid these delays and layers of "approvals." While the CP believed what they were doing was in accordance with the ICS, it was really in name only—the spirit, the strategy, and the authority were missing.

At one point, Dan called me at the Interior Branch to discuss his lack of authority. I suggested Dan call National Guard Adjutant General Don Dunbar for advice. The general knew all the players and could provide Dan with insightful leadership. The general is respected by law enforcement, not only for his role in commanding the National Guard, but also for his leadership of Wisconsin Emergency Management. Dan said he would consider it.

My focus returned to Interior Branch operations, which would now need to pivot yet again for Day 6, Saturday, February 19. Two opposing rallies were set to occur on opposite exterior sides of the Capitol. We needed to facilitate both rallies and maintain order inside the building.

Senators and representatives, mainly from the Republican party, plus several agency heads, had raised concerns over the crowding we had seen—and continued to see—within the Capitol building itself. I asked CPD Lieutenant Marc Schmidt for the building capacity and any rules or regulations for the building's operation. He said there wasn't a building capacity. How, I asked, could that be?

I was incredulous to learn that the Capitol is not governed by the state fire codes or capacity limits. Checking with Incident Commander DC Blackdeer, he confirmed there was no official capacity or even an unofficial capacity. I asked him to request that the Madison Fire Department assist me in calculating the safe capacity of the Capitol.

Much to my surprise and anger, Dan told me Fire Chief Debra Amesqua would not allow her staff to assist because the fire codes did not apply. I hung up the phone in disbelief. I asked Marc to call the State Fire Marshall, Tina Virgil. Tina and I go back to my transitional police academy days—1991 to be exact. We were defense and arrest partners.

> *Wisconsin had a requirement in 1991, when I began as Chief of the University of Wisconsin-Madison Police, that called for law enforcement officials coming from out of state to attend a 120-hour transition academy. Constitutional law, first responder, and defense and arrests tactics comprised the 120 hours. So as a brand-new chief, I headed out to the Madison Area Technical College (now known as Madison College), where the police academy was held. There, I was partnered with a young African-American woman who had been hired by the State Division of Narcotics Enforcement (DNE). I felt for her immediately.*
>
> *Wisconsin is a wonderful place to live, but it lacks racial diversity. Tina was the only African-American in her class and now was being paired with a chief. While I was in student status, even the instructors referred and addressed me as "Chief," as they should, but I told Tina right up front to call me Sue. Tina and I tossed each*

other around like rag dolls. Without any major damage, just a few black and blue marks, we both passed arrest and defense tactics.

During the twenty years since, I watched Tina's career grow. DNE merged with the Division of Criminal Investigation (DCI) and Tina had risen through the ranks, eventually taking on the role of State Fire Marshall, in addition to all the other criminal investigation responsibilities she held.

Tina and her boss Ed Wall, the Administrator of the Division of Criminal Investigation (DCI), arrived in Room 400 NE to see me. They were also very worried about the crowding and capacity. *Terrific*, I thought. We will work this out together. However, Ed was reluctant to weigh in on giving an official opinion about the Capitol capacity. He didn't feel he had the authority to do so and directed Tina not to assist or give an official opinion.

I was astounded. Code or no code, common sense and my experience told me there was a capacity that was safe, given the structure and the exit capacity of the Capitol. I asked Marc Schmidt to arrange for me to meet with some of the state engineers or architects. He started making calls.

Next, I placed a call to my headquarters and asked them to send a wheel tape measure up that we use to mark distances at car accidents and crime scenes. I asked Wisconsin State Patrol Lieutenant Brad Altman if I could have the troopers handle the measurements I needed. Brad looked a bit puzzled. He wanted to be sure I wanted to use a squad of troopers (17 in all) to be involved with one measurement device. Couldn't I just have four troopers, one to measure, one to record, and two to run interference and move the crowd if necessary? No, but I could have seventeen...

Not believing my ears, I said, "Seriously, Brad? Seriously?"

"Yes, Chief. Seriously."

"Bradley, come on."

"Chief, in crowds, it is a squad of 17."

Turning to Marc Schmidt, I asked him to send a mini-team of four officers, led by a Capitol Police officer, to measure the common space of the Capitol inside and out. He made it happen and "Operation Floor Space" was underway.

The sergeant-at-arms for the Senate, Ted Blazel, came into the Operations Room in 400 NE and wondered if I could brief the Republican senators on the overall security situation and then facilitate a safe exit for them. Kevin and I made our way down to the second floor with Ted and entered a meeting in a room just off the Senate floor. There I met the President of the Senate, Mike Ellis. Some of the other senators I had met before. The senators offered me lunch, which I politely declined.

During my security briefing, they were very apprehensive and edgy. For the most part, they listened intently, asking just a few questions and were extremely grateful and supportive of the police. We made arrangements for them to leave within thirty minutes, as they were ready to depart for the weekend.

On the way out, one senator approached me and asked if we would be using the tunnel as part of our exit plan. When I explained the plan to get them out of the Capitol while avoiding the crowds, the senator shared a fear about the air-handling units and the concern that someone could put poison in the vents and injure them all in the tunnel. I listened intently and assured the senator we would check for that before we used the tunnel. Kevin was standing off to the side and nodded; he had already made a note to follow up.

Ted and Senate Clerk Rob Marchant looked relieved and thanked me. I asked Ted and Rob if they could arrange for me to meet with Senator Scott Fitzgerald, the majority leader. They had me stand by while they went to ask Senator Fitzgerald, who was just finishing up an on-camera interview. When he was finished, he invited me back to his office, and when an aide moved to join us, he waved him off.

I appreciated Senator Fitzgerald's willingness to meet with me one on one. I explained how I knew his dad, the newly appointed Superintendent of the Wisconsin State Patrol, and that I was here speaking to him on my own. I didn't represent the Capitol Police or the University. I was just speaking for myself. Then I got right down to the reason I wanted to meet with him.

Briefly, I explained the EPS system and the fact that for short events, no agency was reimbursed for the costs of helping out. However, unless there was reimbursement for the officers' time for this longer term event, our police support would quickly dry up. I explained the challenge of bringing people in from distant regions of the state without lodging or other logistical support. I explained that I wasn't sure how anything worked "under the dome," but it seemed to me that if we didn't straighten this out quickly, we would be in trouble.

Senator Fitzgerald took notes and my card, my cell number, and then summarized what I had said and what I needed. He thanked me for letting him know. He promised to follow up with the Governor's office, walked me out, where we met up with Senator Mike Ellis. They conversed about senate business and thanked me again for the briefing as I headed back to Operations.

The senators' police escort was arranged. The tunnel underwent a thorough security check, and the senators' departure from the Senate Chambers went as scheduled. There was a problem when the vehicles we requested from the CP were not in place on the other end of the tunnel. The Republican senators were left standing in the tunnel waiting for the ride to their cars. This was not good. I had given them my word that things would be secure and precise. It seemed nothing was going to be easy.

I jogged down and through the tunnel and met up with the senators, who were standing around wondering what was going on. I apologized and explained the glitch. They again were very kind. Several of them told me to be careful and safe this weekend. I assured them that we would all be fine. We parted there. I jogged back through the tunnel and into the Capitol. Within a few minutes, the transport vans arrived and the legislators were delivered to their cars.

By 2:30 that afternoon, we were back to considering the plans for the two conflicting rallies to be held the next day. WEAC and AFSCME were scheduled to hold a rally on the State Street side of the Capitol, where they had been rallying all week long. The State Street entrance to the Capitol was on the western side of the building.

> *The State Street entrance takes its name from the diagonal street that runs off one of the corners of the Square. The street is largely a pedestrian area that stretches some nine blocks ending on the State Street Mall at the base of the University of Wisconsin-Madison, with traffic limited to buses, delivery, and emergency vehicles. At each block, there is vehicle cross traffic. Nevertheless, foot traffic flows on the nine-block stretch daily.*
>
> *The Overture Center for the Performing Arts, restaurants, bars and stores give State Street a uniquely eclectic and festive Madison feel. It is a destination in downtown Madison, a common place for crowds to gather and makes for a convenient arterial to march from the campus to the Capitol.*
>
> *The State Street entrance to the Capitol is raised above street level and offers a natural vantage point for speakers to be seen by members in the crowd and for sound systems to be effective.*

Another group, organized by the Americans for Prosperity with support from local Tea Party members, was there to support the Governor's Budget Repair Bill and to rally in support of the Governor. They were to use the King Street entrance to the East of the Capitol, directly opposite the State Street entrance. While the King Street entrance is the same size as the entrance at State Street, it is geographically flat.

The Command Post and the units working outside would keep the groups physically separated with snow fencing. The fence line would be staffed with troopers and local deputies. The Interior Branch would have to staff inside the Capitol Saturday without the troopers. While physical barriers could be erected outside, on the Capitol grounds, inside the Capitol, the two groups would be able to mix without any separation. With tensions running high, the Interior Branch needed to plan for a potential flashpoint.

The Interior Branch division commanders were working well together. With the anticipated reassignment of the State Patrol to the exterior of the Capitol, we needed to structure the divisions of the interior differently.

DNR wardens would take responsibility for half of the State Patrol areas, while UW Police took the other half. We would heavily staff the response and information teams with the Capitol Police, and they would supplement where needed. Taking a page from the home football stadium playbook, we formed arrest teams of six officers, who would retrieve arrested persons from the posted officers. No post officers would leave their assignment. In this way, the "line" or presence would not be diminished when someone needed to be arrested and detained. The reason the arrest teams were staffed with six officers instead of the usual two was so that in the event someone went limp and had to be carried, or was extremely combative, four officers would be available to carry the individual, one on each limb, and two officers to move the team through the crowd successfully.

I gave the division commanders one hour to write up their plans, calculate their post assignments, and develop their resource needs. Then one by one, starting with the basement, ground and first floor division, the commanders outlined and briefed me on their plans. To put together plans within an hour was an extremely tight timeframe. I knew it, they knew it, but no one groused; they just started in.

While the commanders were busy planning, AC Bridges brought me up to speed on the day's events. I in turn briefed the Command Post on the day's event. Just a little after 3:00, Assembly Sergeant-at-Arms Anne Tonnon Byers informed me that she thought the Assembly would be meeting at 5:00 that evening to vote on the Budget Repair Bill. Unlike the Senate, the Assembly had enough Republican members joined by independents to have a quorum and a likely majority to pass the Bill. I appreciated the heads-up.

As the Assembly information became public via Facebook, Twitter, blogs, and the traditional media, the crowds began to swell. The unions had wanted a 5:00 rally, so the number of people on the Square and inside the building was the greatest we had seen to date. The din inside the Rotunda was deafening. An estimated 26,000 people packed themselves into the Capitol. On the ground floor, first, and second floors, people could barely move. Every grand staircase was impassable, and every balcony, parapet, and bridge was jammed.

Although the Capitol had a public address system, it could not be heard over the noise of the crowd. The drumming, chanting, and pounding continued unabated bouncing off the marble walls, Rotunda, and floors. Radio transmissions couldn't be heard by the

On February 18, 2011, the Capitol is filled to capacity, and more. (Photo by Mark Golbach)

Dangerously crowded. Protesters filling the Rotunda of the Wisconsin State Capitol. (Photo by Joe Lynde)

officers and the CP couldn't understand the officers' transmissions with all the background noise. In the Interior Branch, we used a physical "runner" system for information flow, but with the crowding, that was spotty at best.

With the division commanders planning for the next day, AC Bridges and the civilian staff worked hard to keep information coming in about the crowd, its demeanor, or any issues needing immediate attention. They also tried to push information to the CP, which didn't have a decent view of the interior of the Capitol, and could not know how jammed the building was.

I again called the CP to speak with the Incident Commander DC Dan Blackdeer. I again stated my concern about the overcrowding. Something must be done. I asked Dan what the Capitol Police normally did when the building got crowded. He said things never got this crowded. We needed to act. At the very least, I asked about limiting ingress at some entrances until the crowd thinned out. I wasn't suggesting that people be asked to leave, but we had to stop the inflow. Dan wouldn't decide. He needed instructions from a higher authority. We ended the phone call.

These were public safety tactical decisions that an Incident Commander should be empowered to make. The fact that Dan didn't have that authority would add unnecessary complexity to the challenges we would face in the upcoming weeks.

I decided to act in the interests of safety and ordered two of the major entrances (North and South Hamilton) closed to ingress. If Dan learned of this later and didn't like it, he could remove me from command. But for now, all I cared about was public safety.

At 3:30 p.m., I began our afternoon briefing by meeting individually with each division commander. One at a time, we went to the conference room off of 412 East. Each one presented his or her well-organized—and sometimes heavily staffed—plan. Given the clashes that could occur between demonstrators on opposing sides of the issue, the reasoning and staffing levels were logical and intelligently designed. As they finished, I gave feedback and then sent them to assist AC Brian Bridges with the current situation.

Brian had his hands full trying to manage the large crowd in the building. The inability of the Command Post to support planning efforts for the operation meant the division commanders and my deputy branch directors were taken away from active management and critical operations to do planning instead.

I went to check the scene in the Rotunda. The overcrowding persisted and the noise was deafening as the drum beating continued. The organizers led the crowd in chanting. Using several bullhorns or using a microphone and sound system, they would call out half the chant and the crowd would scream back the answer. The marble walls and the dome of the Rotunda reverberated with every chant. I watched and listened for just a few moments and then headed back into 400 NE. It was a just after 4:00; we had a little under an hour to go before the Assembly went into session for a possible vote.

Stopping by at Operations in 400 NE, was the newly named Superintendent of the Wisconsin State Patrol, Stephen Fitzgerald. Steve's appointment by Governor Walker to the position had created some controversy. Stephen's son, Senator Scott Fitzgerald (Republican), was the majority leader in the Senate, the person I had met with earlier in the day. His other son, Jeff Fitzgerald (Republican), was the Speaker of the Assembly. Papa Fitz, as he is affectionately called, was 68 years old at the time and his appointment to superintendent was thought by some to be cronyism.

Having had a previous working relationship with Steve Fitzgerald came in handy. We met many years before when he was the Dodge County Sheriff. He had also served as the U.S. Marshal for the Western District of

Wisconsin during the Bush Administration. He and I worked very closely with State Representative Doris Hanson (Democrat) who wanted to ban all police pursuits.

Representative Hanson had suffered a personal tragedy following an abandoned chase by a Dane County deputy. Even though the deputy had stopped chasing the fleeing offender, the offender didn't slowdown. The offender T-boned Doris' vehicle while she was on her way to vote, killing her longtime friend, Ursula Schmitt, who was in the passenger seat.

Doris was a formidable politician with friends on both sides of the aisle. This Pursuit Bill was important to her, and she wanted to see it pass and become law. The draft of the legislation was something law enforcement could not agree with. At the time, I served on the legislative committee for the Wisconsin Chiefs of Police Association. I was young, energetic and naïve.

When I saw Representative Hanson at a University softball game, I approached her and introduced myself. She curtly replied "I know who you are. I have checked you out. What's on your mind?" The fact that she was ten steps ahead of me shouldn't have come as a surprise. Every red flag went up, and I decided to just say I was looking forward to working with her on the Pursuit Bill and I hoped to have the opportunity to talk through some of the specifics with her.

"Like what?" was her response.

While I gave it my best shot, Doris didn't yield an inch or even acknowledge a single point I was making. I returned to my seat in the stands and tried to concentrate on the game, but knew I had just been thrashed.

Despite my less-than-stellar opening, the Chiefs' Association sent me to represent them at a hearing on the Bill. Outside the hearing room 415 NW, I met Steve Fitzgerald, then the Dodge County Sheriff. The Sheriff's Association had sent him as their representative.

Steve is eighteen years older than I am and had lots of experience politically, as well as in law enforcement. I bet he thought the chiefs sent me as a joke. We sat next to each other for the hearing and directly across the table from Representative Hanson.

We each said our piece and Doris listened intently. She asked tough, but fair questions. We answered as best we could. It was clear Doris wanted a good solid law, with teeth, but she was so emotionally engaged yielding an inch felt somehow like she was selling out her friend.

At one point, in attempting to answer a question Doris asked of me and annoying Doris in the process, I felt Steve step on my foot. At first I thought nothing of it, we were sitting very close. I continued speaking, not having the sense to know when to shut up. His heel pressed further and further into my foot and I was in some serious pain. I finally stopped talking. Instantly, the pressure was released. Having stopped my losing argument, Doris was gracious, summarized what I had said, actually better than I had said it. Steve had been looking out for me and I never forgot it.

The Bill passed several months later in a form that law enforcement could be proud to enforce and follow. Doris had listened and had taken our suggestions to heart. When Governor Tommy G. Thompson (Republican), signed the Bill into law, I received one of the pens he used to sign the Bill. It was my first guberna-

torial pen. All thanks to the cooperation between
Democrats and Republicans. I also gained two mentors
from the experience, Doris Hanson and Steve Fitzgerald.

I welcomed Superintendent Fitzgerald to the room and gave him a quick briefing on the set-up, and what we were planning for tomorrow. He was warm and friendly, listened intently, and then took a seat on the side and observed.

Within the Capitol, the officers on post reported feeling the tension and volume rise in the crowd. The Governor was scheduled for a press conference in the East wing. The Assembly was due to reconvene at 5:00 p.m. In Operations, we were able to hear the audio of the proceedings going on in the Assembly Chamber through the overhead sound system. At 4:55, we listened as the Assembly was being gaveled into session. Chief Clerk Patrick Fuller was calling the roll.

The Republicans were present but when a Democrat's name was called, there was silence. When the roll was complete, not one Democrat was in the chamber. It wasn't yet 5:00 p.m. and the Democrats were still in caucus. Within seconds of hearing the gavel, the Assembly Republicans began to conduct voice votes on the reading of the Budget Repair Bill and possible amendments.

The Democrats literally ran into the Assembly Chamber, many wearing their newly acquired matching orange T-shirts, shouting to be recognized. Heated procedural debate ensued. The galleries to the Assembly eventually filled, while one Democrat after another rose to lambast the Republican actions.

Representative Gordon Hintz, a Democrat from Oshkosh, representing the 54th district, rose and screamed at the Republicans to be recognized and about the manner in which this week's discussion had gone. He was upset about the way the introduction of the 144-page Budget Repair Bill had been handled, from cutting off testimony in front of Joint Finance to this new attempt to cut off dissent by beginning the session before the 5:00 p.m. start time. Other Democrats rose and shouted and pleaded for the Republicans to stop trying to ram the Bill through. A few Democrats acknowledged the Republicans had the votes to pass what they wanted, but to cut off discussion or debate and to stop the amendment process, was not in keeping with the rules of the Assembly. It was a tense and emotional 35 minutes in the Assembly Chamber.

Within the crowd in the Capitol, the texts and tweets were flying. More people began swarming toward the Capitol from State Street. The building was already dangerously overcrowded. Finally, the Speaker gaveled the Assembly into adjournment until Tuesday, at which time they would begin the process of hearing amendments to the Bill. The Governor's prediction that the Bill would pass in a week was not to be.

The Assembly Democrats and the crowd were treating this delay as a victory. Cheers erupted from the Rotunda. And I wondered out loud, "What the hell just happened?"

I shook my head and thought that if the Republicans had just started on time at 5:00 p.m., how might this have been different? Their desire once again to rush and cut things off had just led to further delay.

At about 5:40, the WSP superintendent wished us all well and left the room. As he left, I could not help reflecting on his timing. The superintendent had joined us just before all the Assembly arguments started and was leaving right after the Republicans "stunt" failed.

My cell phone rang. It was Noble Wray, Chief of the City of Madison Police. He explained that Incident Commander DC Dan Blackdeer had just informed him that the Governor's office wanted the Capitol closed tonight at its regular 6:00 p.m. closing time. I glanced at my watch, realizing it was already close to 6:00. He told

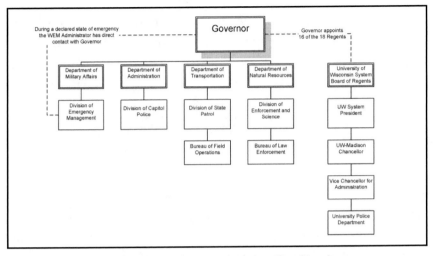

State of Wisconsin Agency Reporting Structure

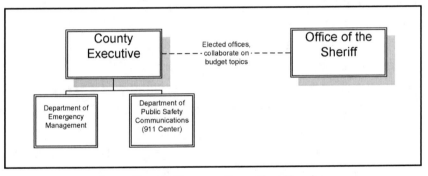

Dane County Agency Reporting Structure

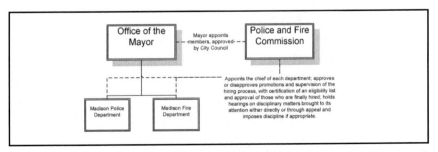

City of Madison Reporting Structure

me that he and Sheriff Mahoney both thought it was a mistake to close the building, and neither would allow his staff to enter the building to assist. He asked me if my chain of command for the state involved the Department of Administration, which is the civilian authority over the Capitol Police Department.

Theoretically, I didn't believe I had to answer to DOA, but I certainly couldn't argue that I wouldn't answer to the Governor. Under ICS, I answered to the Incident Commander, who was DC Blackdeer. Our conversation had come full circle. I was glad Noble had called me directly and that I knew where he and the Sheriff stood. However, they were not state employees, but I was. Essentially, Chief Wray, staying on city property, had no skin in the game.

In this structure as Branch Director, I reported to the Operations Chief and ultimately to the Incident Commander. Or did I? As chief of a contributing department, I retained my place on the law enforcement leadership group within Unified Command. How were all these pieces supposed to come together?

I quickly asked the division commanders if they thought closing the Capitol at 6:00 was a reasonable directive or assignment. They all agreed it would be a mistake to close the building, essentially without warning, given what had just transpired in the last hour in the Assembly. The enormous crowd was revved up and tense.

In the door came Chief Charles Tubbs, looking as stressed as ever. He had instructions from the Governor's Chief of Staff (COS), Keith Gilkes, that the Governor wanted the building to close as normal. In other words, the Governor wanted everyone out by 6:00 tonight. Charles took a seat across the table from me and the room grew quiet. Charles wanted to get a plan together and get it done. The look on WSP Lieutenant Brad Altman's face was a mix of dread and a hint of fear. I nodded slightly at Brad.

I asked Charles if he wanted to close the building. He responded that if the Governor wanted the building closed, that's what he was going to do. With the room still quietly listening to our exchange, I asked a few more questions. What did "close" the building actually mean? Did it mean not letting any more people in? Did it mean getting people out? What about all of their belongings and the supplies? Would we evacuate everyone? Staff too, including those who had the permission from a representative or senator to be inside and in those offices?

I continued with the questions. How did he envision closing the building given that thousands of people had just arrived for a 5:00 rally and with emotions stirred up by the quick pre-5:00 maneuver of the Republicans in the Assembly? Had he considered the fact that the police were already demobilizing for the day and that we hadn't vetted a plan on how to handle resistance? Our mass arrest plan was in place, thanks to Brian and my planning earlier in the week, but mass arrests took staff and time. Calmly, I continued posing question after question.

Charles just shook his head. The Governor's Chief of Staff's instructions were clear: the building should be closed and Charles reiterated that he was determined to close it.

I switched tactics and questioned the authority of the individual issuing the directive. I had never met the Governor's COS. As I explained to Charles, a Chief of Staff, in my experience, is not in the chain of command for law enforcement. The Governor certainly was, but not staff. Was this directive from the Governor, or was it from his Chief of Staff, inferring it was from the Governor? Given he had no response to my questions, I informed Chief Tubbs that the division commanders and I were not in support of the closing and emptying the building in this manner, at this time.

I offered to go with him to talk to the Chief of Staff. He declined my offer, but said he would meet with the COS again and be back to tell us the result. I called the CP and talked with Incident Commander DC Dan Blackdeer. Not sure where he stood on all this, I stepped lightly and filled him in. Dan completely disagreed with closing and emptying the building. When he had received the call an hour before from Chief Tubbs, it was Dan who had involved Chief Wray and Sheriff Mahoney. While talking to Dan, he informed me that from the cameras located on State Street, the CP could see a crowd of about 5,000 walking up State Street toward the Capitol. The building was going to get busier and even more crowded.

Reverend Jesse Jackson was in the approaching crowd and by 6:40, was leading the group inside. In my mind, the additional 5,000 people sealed the debate about closing the building. The crowd was simply too large. Sheriff Dave Mahoney walked into 400 NE. He wanted to be sure I knew he didn't favor the building closing and he wouldn't let his staff assist in carrying out the directive. He was staffing the exterior, not the interior.

My aide Kevin, AC (ret.) Jerry Jansen, Sheriff Mahoney, and I headed to the Governor's suite of offices to find Charles Tubbs and whoever Chief of Staff Keith Gilkes was. The troopers and Capitol Police stationed in front of the Governor's office saw us coming and unlocked the doors to the Governor's suite (known as "the Rock") without questioning our mission. We walked into a large, but empty, staff bullpen; the office staff had left for the day. With no one to direct us, I listened for Charles' voice. He and the Chief of Staff were standing up inside an inner office facing each other. Our group walked right into the inner office of the COS, startling both men. Charles immediately stopped speaking to Keith, excused himself, and ushered us out of the office. He asked us to wait outside in an alcove. He said he would be with us in a minute. He was clearly rattled.

We waited and very shortly, Charles came out to the alcove. He was furious with us. He slammed his leather portfolio on the desk and told me how out of line we were for walking in on his meeting. He was embarrassed by our boldness. He said, "*These* people don't like people just walking in on them." He was right.

Our move was rash and I apologized. The Sheriff just set his jaw more firmly. Charles took his portfolio, shook his head, and sat down heavily on the bench. I sat next to him. I explained the new information about the crowd size and noted that whatever decision about closing might have been made with the COS, the reality of the circumstances was law enforcement couldn't carry it out even if we were in favor of it, which we were not. He said he had heard that a large crowd was approaching and said that the COS had backed away from his directive.

Charles apologized to me for getting mad at us. It wasn't necessary, but I appreciated it. We were in the wrong. We talked briefly about the pressure and the politics. The Sheriff, Jerry, and I all suggested that Charles bring us along to his meetings with the Chief of Staff and DOA, so that he didn't have to handle these conversations alone. Charles explained that things don't work like that up here.

With that, the Sheriff left and Jerry, Kevin, and I went back to Room 400 NE. On the way, I called the CP on my cell. They could barely hear me because of the crowd noise, but I managed to let them know the building was not closing tonight. The division commanders were relieved.

* * * * *

THE MEASUREMENTS WERE COMING IN ON THE 'UNASSIGNED' OPEN FLOOR space of the Capitol. The exterior measurements from the sidewalks, terraces, and plazas were also arriving. I had a brief conversation with Ron Blair, Capitol Building Manager, about capacity and his thoughts about the crowding. Marc informed me that Gary Stults from DOA and a member of the Capitol engineering staff were on their way. When they arrived, I took them aside and explained my concerns and what needed to be resolved.

I wanted to understand the capacity of the Capitol. It was a complex set of calculations, since there are a lot of places for people to be, so an absolute number without measuring crowd density would be meaningless. We also had to consider the number of exits, as well as the number of stairways. Crowd demeanor was an unpredictable element. It is one thing to have people sitting next to each other all around the Rotunda; it is another to have them on a Rotunda bridge jumping up and down. Of course, we had all of this here, and then some.

According to a Capitol Statistics and Fact Sheet furnished by the DOA building operations on February 18, 2011, the current Wisconsin State Capitol resembles the United States Capitol and was built between 1906 to 1917. The West wing was occupied first in 1909.

In 2001, it was valued at over $246 million. Whoever calculated that amount did not understand the meaning of priceless. The Wisconsin State Capitol is an historic landmark and is an absolutely beautiful facility. It has 8,369,665 gross cubic feet and 448,297 gross square feet. The assignable space is 245,282 square feet, and the "public use space" is 161,255 square feet.

There are 43 different types of marble within the building from all over the U.S. It boasts mosaics, paintings and portraits, busts of famous justices and governors. It contains gold leaf on its carvings and spectacular plaster relief.

The Wisconsin Capitol is home to all three branches of government: the Executive, Legislative and Judicial. The Executive and Judicial branches each has a primary wing. The Legislative branch occupies two wings, one for

*the Senate and one for the Assembly. The Attorney
General's Office is located inside the Executive wing.*

*The Capitol's basement comprises a cafeteria, a small
auditorium, offices, the Capitol Police Department,
maintenance offices, and countless storage areas. The
level above the basement is the ground floor. From the
Ground Floor, you can stand in the Rotunda and look
clear to the top of the dome some fourteen stories
above.[8]*

The men from DOA understood what I was looking for and
requested access to the building archive. A CPD information team
escorted them. After looking at some records, they said they would
return to discuss their findings.

With the chanting, periodic cheering, drumming, and dancing,
the building was rocking. It was Friday night in Madison, and the
protesters felt they had struck a blow to the Governor's plan of
passing the Budget Repair Bill. Tomorrow they were planning the
largest protest to date, and they knew there would be a crowd
opposing them. Signs reading "This is a peaceful protest" began
going up on the walls, placed there by protest organizers who
wanted a successful rally without physical rancor. The signs were
posted using blue "painter's" tape to avoid damaging the walls.

Chief Warden Randy Stark and I needed to brief the incoming
officers who would work through the evening. On the way to the
briefing room, Randy told me that he had a new plan for briefing
the officers in the morning. He had also worked to clear up the
reporting times for the EPS staff. He filled me in and his ideas were
solid improvements to the process.

The DOA architect and engineer confirmed our concerns about
the number of people allowed in the building at one time. According
to them, the Rotunda bridges on the second floor were vulnerable,

---

[8] DOA Fact Sheet, February 2011.

along with the grand staircases. Not surprisingly, the staircases had been built for people to pass up and down, but not for the static weight of people packed on them all at one time. Inside the marble façade was a steel and concrete structure. The structure was bearing the weight of all the marble, in addition to the building furnishings and now the weight of thousands of people. I began to think about the strain the structure of the building must be under with the packed crowds we were seeing.

I asked them what they thought about a capacity number. They hemmed and hawed; apparently, capacity numbers were not theirs to set. I explained I would take responsibility for the determination and would leave them with plausible deniability.

They talked it over and agreed on a number: 4,000 people. I was skeptical. At least 1,000 people worked in the building. Add to that people visiting offices, hearing rooms, the legislative galleries, and court chambers; the number could easily exceed 4,000. Nor did the figure even begin to calculate the number of people who could fit into the Rotunda. My own criteria of behavior, floor calculations, crowd psychology, coupled with my training, and experience would have to suffice.

I appreciated their efforts for staying late on a Friday to assist me, then sat down to begin my own equations. As I delved deeper and deeper into this challenge, the more frustrated I became that the so-called "experts" in the fire profession wouldn't assist. I settled on a capacity number for a peaceful crowd that would gather on the ground, first, second and third floors. I knew that my number was achieved using accurate measurements, was well reasoned, and based on known criteria and not politics. I hoped it was correct and that no one got injured. Randy and I developed a "Decision Matrix" to aid with capacity management.

Essentially, we would take the data collected at the entrances, along with the exiting numbers, make a visual inspection of the various floors to see the density of the crowd at any one spot. Then we would judge whether or not we could provide an emergency pathway through the crowd in the event of a medical emergency. In addition, we had to take into consideration how the people in the crowd were acting toward one another and toward us at any one time. We also needed to include the many people in the building who had nothing to do with the protests. Finally, we balanced all that with the number of police personnel in the building who would assist in the event of an emergency.

* * * * *

AS THE DAY SHIFT EMPTIED OUT OF THE OPERATIONS ROOM, I MADE another calculation that evening, one I had never made before. It was February 18, 2011, and I was eligible to retire on March 11, 2011. On that date, it would have been 20 years since I started with the state and I was now 50 years old. I met the minimum requirements in protective service to retire. I love my job and can't conceive of the fact that I am old enough and eligible to retire. Nonetheless, I counted the days. It was "Time plus twenty-one days (T+21)" I got a sheet of copier paper and I wrote "Freedom Date T+21" and stuck it up on the wall of the Operations Room near the sign with our room number, 400 NE. With that, I headed home.

Close to midnight, the CPD quietly locked most of the entrances to the Capitol for safety reasons and to reduce their monitoring responsibilities. Two doors were left open and people could leave from any exit. As the 2:30 a.m., State Street bar closing time approached and the CPD locked the remaining doors. Officers felt that keeping the bar crowd out made it safer for the people inside the Capitol, who were now settling down to sleep in the building. About 500 people bedded down in the Rotunda area for the night. It was the calm before the storm.

Protesters walking around the Square at the Capitol. (Photo by Jim Escalante)

High school students marching on the Capitol. (Photo by Mark Golbach)

Protesters with sleeping bags and signs, preparing for the long haul. (Photo by Joe Lynde)

CHAPTER THREE
A PEACEFUL PROTEST

AS OUR FIRST WEEK AT THE CAPITOL CAME TO A CLOSE, OUR efforts gradually transitioned from the urgent scramble of first reactions to the deliberate bustle of sustained response. The determination of the protesters to keep the gathering peaceful certainly aided our work, but the size and duration of the protests created complications. Our work was shifting from simply responding to planning and anticipating what might be coming next. Unfortunately, due to politics and rancor between the Democrats and Republicans, much of what was to come caught us by surprise. Outside the echoing walls of the Rotunda, life in all its facets, continued on with birthdays, illnesses and the never ending household chores vying for our attention.

DAY 6: SATURDAY, FEBRUARY 19, 2011

When my alarm sounded at 5:00, I uncharacteristically flew out of bed ready to get to work on the next challenge. In addition to the Capitol operations, I was scheduled to celebrate Chancellor Biddy Martin's 60th birthday that night. It wasn't her actual birthday, but everyone's schedule required a bit of juggling to get folks together. Although I had helped organize the party earlier in the month, I had to turn the reins over to others. With my schedule ever-evolving and wildly fluid, I just hoped to be able to make it to the party.

I had developed an early morning routine with several of my staff. I would pull into the University Police Department parking lot at 6:15, where three or four colleagues would meet me at the back door. With our duty bags tossed in the trunk and freshly charged radios clipped to our belts, we would pile in for the short carpool up to the Capitol in the eerie dark of a winter morning in Wisconsin. The quiet of these early mornings stood in stark contrast to the chanting and drumming and constant radio chatter that would fill the dome over the coming hours.

On Saturday, February 19, I arrived early at my department at 6:00. My staff was also beginning to report and commented on my "early" arrival. I took the teasing in stride. I deserved it. I picked up my radio from its charger on my desk, looked over some notes my assistant, Cathryn, had left me, and quickly took off for the Capitol with Brian Bridges and Johnnie Diamante.

The walls inside the Capitol, especially the Rotunda, were covered with banners, signs, and slogans. It was quite an attraction to walk around and read the different posters. There was everything from bed sheets draped over the railings to professional banners and signs from the various unions. As I rounded a corner, I noticed another hand-written sign proclaiming, "The Tea Party is here to provoke us! Don't fight back! Keep this rally peaceful." Today, the principle of "peaceful" protest might get its first real test.

The previous night I had been told by the DOA representative that the second floor bridges shouldn't be allowed to become overcrowded. The bridges were a great place to stand to look down to the first and ground floors of the Rotunda, making them a favorite gathering spot. I had mentioned this to the evening crew of officers, and they had spoken to the volunteer marshals. The marshals had printed and posted signs stating "Please avoid congregating on the bridge." No doubt this was just another example of how meeting with the marshals at the Masonic Center earlier in the week was paying off. We kept an open and fair relationship with the protest groups.

Overnight, about five hundred people had slept in the "public" portion of the Capitol. This number didn't count those who had slept in hearing rooms or offices scattered throughout the building. Regardless of where they had slept in the building, they were all awake now or would be shortly.

I came across a mother sleeping on a queen-size mattress with three of her daughters, ages 3 to 12. Two of the girls were beginning to stir and I whispered a "hello" to them. One of them got up, slipped on her shoes, walked over to the food table, snatched two pieces of cold pizza and returned, handing one to her sister. I couldn't help but smile. What a unique experience to have at her age. In addition to the political "nurturing," cold pizza was the breakfast of many a college student—this young girl was ahead of her time.

In Room 400 NE, at our now daily 6:30 a.m. Interior Branch meeting, I pointed to my own 8½ x 11 hand-lettered sign and explained what "T+21" meant. Then I asked that someone change it to T+20. I was one day closer. CPD Lieutenant Marc Schmidt responded that he could have retired years ago using my criteria. We all started the day with a laugh and turned to catching up on the events of the last twelve hours.

Our plan was to open only the North and South Hamilton Street entrances for ingress. The other entrances, at State and King Streets, were going to be the sites of the day's rallies. Those entrances served a bit like "backstage" and limiting movement through them was operationally important. It appeared the event organizers were glad to have those entrances shut down for the day. In an effort to avoid overcrowding and crushing, we also maintained closures for the Martin Luther King, Jr., East and West Washington Avenue, and the Wisconsin Avenue entrances.

This would allow us to monitor and count the ingress into the Capitol. The Interior Branch staff went over the events and plans for the day. We reminded ourselves that it was particularly important that law enforcement remain neutral. Randy talked us through the new components of the briefing for the officers who would be stationed throughout the Capitol that day.

The first round of officer briefings occurred at 7:00 in 412 East, in the Joint Finance Committee hearing room we had commandeered, just around the corner from the Interior Branch Operations Room. We had rearranged the furniture to allow for storage of officers' gear and equipment that might be needed at some point during the day. The new configuration improved the comings and goings of the officers and deputies as they moved from the briefing to their posts.

Things were going well until Randy slipped me a note and said the CP had reassigned our sole communications channel to the Exterior. We didn't have another option. He excused himself to work on the problem. I continued talking about use of force, demeanor, crowd behavior, and an explanation of the new capacity management plan that we had just developed.

Another new wrinkle for the day was that an "open carry" firearms group was likely to attend the rally on the King Street side of the Capitol. At the time, in Wisconsin, the carrying of a concealed weapon by non-law enforcement was illegal. However, carrying firearms openly was allowed across the state, though prohibited in government buildings. Therefore, we cautioned the officers and deputies that people may be in the crowd carrying firearms openly and legally, but they could not carry legally inside the Capitol building itself. Though the open-carry law had been well-established in Wisconsin for years, it was highly controversial. Supporters carrying openly were often challenged by the police, and the "carriers" often video-recorded those encounters.

We talked through the relevant statute with the officers and the protocol we wanted them to use. Later in the day, our officers spotted a few open-carry folks appearing at the rally, but none attempted to enter the Capitol. (The legalization of citizens carrying concealed weapons was months away, which meant that anyone who was not active law enforcement and carried a concealed weapon could be arrested.)

With the officers briefed, we started the head count and the department count of the disparate group of officers from around the state. Assignments were beginning to be made and the matching of supervisors to staff, then division commanders to supervisors. Randy reappeared with the new communications plan and with his efforts, as well as those of the CP and the technical staff, we once again had radio interoperability within the Interior Branch.

It was getting close to 8:30, the time we wanted all officers on their posts. At each briefing, we asked the new officers to familiarize themselves with the interior of the Capitol. The doors would be opening at 9:00 with a new capacity management and crowd monitoring plan. While I didn't know the exact legal citation, I was confident that as Interior Branch Director and law enforcement, I had the authority to limit access for safety reasons.

In anticipation of the day's crowds, the staffing levels for the day shift increased dramatically to 228 officers and deputies reporting to the Interior Branch. Meals, radios, and break rotations all had to be reassessed. Kevin Wernet and I laughed that we actually were going to need a meal distribution plan. I joked that the firefighter in Kevin should be able to handle that.

Radio communications was becoming a larger issue. The Interior Branch was assigned a communications specialist to deal with all the technical aspects of keeping all of these units afloat while patching together three tactical radio channels. Dispatching was also becoming an issue. The CP had two dispatchers and the

Capitol Police, one. None were in the Interior Branch Operations Room. Technically, every time we needed a unit, we should have requested one via the CP, but that wasn't very practical, given they were off-site and not tracking our units closely.

The CPD dispatcher located in the basement of the Capitol had neither knowledge of the unit assignments or a clear understanding of what was happening above. For every call received, a Capitol Police officer would be dispatched, even though there might have been another officer, deputy, or trooper already there. This was inefficient.

Lieutenant Marc Schmidt called down to his Capitol Police headquarters and told the dispatcher not to send anyone directly, but to instead contact the Interior Branch, where we would manage the units. Marc and AC Brian Bridges would cover dispatching the operations units. I called the CP and told them that they had to track our units or stop dispatching because it was creating problems. They stopped dispatching, but did not send us any dispatchers to handle our needs.

Marc's knowledge of the Capitol and its operations was invaluable. As a good-natured practical joke, I gave Marc a "field promotion" to captain. I even gave him a set of collar brass befitting his rank. He gave me the biggest smile I had seen from him in days. He accepted the promotion and binder clipped his collar brass, still in its wrapping, to the side of his laptop. We kidded that I might be able to give him the rank, but I couldn't give him any money to go with it.

At 7:30, AC Brian Bridges received a call from Senate Chief Clerk Rob Marchant about threats that had come in overnight to two Republican senators. Marc reported the Capitol Police were investigating the threats. Senate Leader Fitzgerald now required an escort into the building at 8:00 a.m. Brian also reported that WEAC wanted to have a rally at 10:30 inside the Rotunda.

We needed to keep a headcount of building occupants. Officers from Green Bay staffed the North Hamilton entrance, while officers from the city of Fond du Lac watched over South Hamilton. Their job was to count the people coming in and estimate the flow of people going out. Because we had counted 500 sleepers in the Rotunda, we started the count at 500. As the doors opened, a small cluster of protesters entered. By 10:20, close to 4,000 people were inside the building. If the engineer and architect were correct, I should stop ingress at this level. I left the Interior Branch Ops Room to eyeball the situation. The place looked rather empty and the behavior of the crowd was fine. I decided I was going with my capacity number of 9,000, instead of trying to hold the crowd at the 4,000 level. I predicted the crowd would lessen after the WEAC Rotunda rally was over.

Protesters and the "just curious" were wandering about, eventually leaving a space for others to replace them. The sleepers rolled up their beds, blankets, mattresses, and sleeping bags and stuffed them into alcoves. Many folks could be seen using phones to snap pictures of the banners and crowds, taking turns posing at this prolonged event in the beautiful building. Speakers were taking turns presenting their views at the public microphone. Whenever the speaking stopped, the drummers began again their incessant rhythm. We ordered more ear plugs from Logistics.

Ed Wall, the Administrator of the Division of Criminal Investigation (DCI), stopped in with Assistant State Attorney General (AAG), Kevin St. John. The DCI is a unit within the Wisconsin Department of Justice that reports to the Attorney General. I was glad to explain the new capacity management plan to them and also discuss an issue that had arisen on Friday concerning statutory police powers and authority, versus the power and rights of legislators.

Usually a branch doesn't have to develop its own legal footing or research legal questions, but that was where I found myself. We needed to resolve the level of assistance we could legally give to the Senate or Assembly sergeant–at–arms in maintaining order when it involved members' behaviors. It was clear we could handle the galleries with all of our usual law enforcement practices. Yet, when the Legislature is in session, there are special rules that govern the arrest, restraint, or detention of an elected member of the Legislature. AAG St. John promised he would take a look at the statutes and send a quick note to Ed Wall later in the day. Although he wouldn't be issuing an official opinion, he wanted to help as best he could. At 12:41 p.m., he sent an email to Ed and ten minutes later, I was reviewing it with the division commanders.

What we learned from Mr. St. John was essentially that the sergeant-at-arms is responsible for keeping order. Law enforcement could intervene in the case of a physical altercation, separate the parties and if necessary, escort one or the other from the floor at the direction of the leadership of the House we are in at the time. Once outside the chamber, unless it was a felony, law enforcement would release the representative or senator, at which point they could return to the chamber if they so desired. We hoped it wouldn't come to any type of hands-on situation, but it was clear that we needed to be prepared for the unexpected.

If we had to arrest a member of the Legislature, we would send that case to the Dane County Courts. To cover my bases, I decided to call the relatively new Dane County District Attorney Ismael Ozanne. Once I explained the situation along with my concerns, he summed up his understanding of the law and gave me his advice. Essentially, we should intervene only if a legislator's physical safety was at risk or if there was an actual physical assault. We should separate the parties and stand by. Ozanne was not in favor of escorting members of the Legislature from the respective chamber, because he considered that decision and enforcement the responsibility of the sergeant–at-arms.

This conversation with DA Ozanne was a great help and would make it much easier to explain to the officers or troopers who might actually be called upon if a situation occurred. We were not looking to arrest anyone, but we also didn't want to do something at the behest of leadership or a member that was politically motivated.

Next in the door was Brigadier General Donald Dunbar, the Adjutant General of Wisconsin. General Dunbar was responsible for the National Guard, Wisconsin Emergency Management, and the state's Homeland Security efforts. I had met him a few times before, but it took me a minute to recognize him, as he was wearing jeans, a sweater, and a baseball cap, instead of his usual crisp uniform. He had been intentionally keeping a low profile since the dust-up over the Governor's comments the previous week about calling in the Guard.

I gave him a quick situational briefing, and he talked with me about how the Guard was assisting with a special unit, the 54th Civil Support Team. Their specialty was detecting any airborne threats: pathogens, toxic chemicals, biological, radiation and the like. Members of the unit had already been in the Capitol, out of uniform, had taken readings and, finding no problems, established a baseline. The University Police has radiation detectors that our officers wear in Camp Randall during the Badger home football games, but the Guard's equipment is more sophisticated and covers threats other than radiation. It was good to see the general and talk things over with him. He was a straight shooter, nonpartisan and seemed engaged, thoughtful, and kind. I knew I could count on him. He asked good questions and pledged his support.

By mid-morning, both rallies had begun outside while inside, the crowd was growing and estimated to be about 9,000. I ordered

The Americans for Prosperity began to gather in support of Governor Walker's Repair Bill outside the King Street entrance. Their numbers would grow to 2,500 (9:42 a.m., Feb. 19, 2011). (Photo by Kevin Wernet)

Protesters began to gather on the opposite side of the Capitol near State Street. Their numbers would grow to 50,000 (9:42 a.m., Feb. 19, 2011). (Photo by Kevin Wernet)

the police at each entrance door to begin a queue outside the two entrances. When someone came out, someone else would be allowed in, one to one. Periodically, the folks in 400 NE would radio to the officers working the doors to get an exit count. As the exiting increased, we allowed more people inside, trying to achieve a balance of safety while still allowing peaceful assembly.

As the main speakers at the rallies took the stage, many of the people gathered inside the Capitol moved outside to listen. Within twenty minutes, the population inside dropped to around 3,000. Eerily, it seemed like a ghost town although the drumming continued, echoing even more loudly, without the crowd to absorb the sounds.

Outside, a group of physicians dressed in their white coats was interviewing people who were seeking sick notes for missing work. After a brief conversation that often covered the stress of the events and the anxiety the protester was feeling, the doctors would write out a note giving the individual an excuse for missing work. I wouldn't learn until later that two of my friends would be among the doctors giving out the notes.[9]

The relative pause in the action within the Capitol gave me a chance to catch up by phone with University Police AC (ret) Dale Burke, whom I had sent to the Command Post to convince Capitol Police DC Dan Blackdeer and his aide Todd Kuschel to get some rest. Dale reported that the people in logistics and planning were working hard trying to get what was needed, but there was little support beyond those few people to actually carry out filling the orders.

The Incident Commander role that Dan was tasked with was still without authority; therefore, he was reluctant to act. The CP told Dale that they were once again unable to reach Chief Tubbs.

---

[9] www.youtube.com/watch?v=zjFbMDp5Pg8

Dale let me know that if I was waiting on guidance and direction from the CP, I would not be receiving any, anytime soon.

After that frustrating report, I needed some air. With the crowd inside still reduced because of the outdoor rallies, I wanted to gauge the size of the outdoor crowd. There is an observation deck, some 90 feet up, on the outside of the Capitol's massive granite dome. I thought that would be a solid vantage point to view the outside crowd and get an estimate of the entire Capitol Square and all the activity. However, that deck had some obstructed views of the crowd so I had to go higher. Accompanied by an information team led by a Capitol Police officer, my aide Kevin and I climbed the tight circular staircase to the smaller observation deck, huffing and puffing as we went.

When we opened the door to the outside, the breeze was stiff. However, the day was quite mild for mid-February in Wisconsin. From this vantage point, we could see the crowd walking the Capitol Square in the customary counter-clockwise rotation (as is the tradition for events on the Square, whether it was the Farmer's Market, Cows on the Concourse, Art Fair on the Square, or a protest march).

The view of the Madison from the deck is stunning. We took photos that we could analyze later and got a sense of the crowd on the State Street side and the King Street side. The other two sides were virtually empty. We could see all of the sidewalks and streets below on the Square, plus the streets leading away from the Square. Kevin and I talked over what we were seeing and the current density of the crowd. With the measurements from the day before, we estimated that around 50,000 people were on the State Street side and 2,000-2,500 on the King Street side. With another 500 or so milling about in between, we called it at 53,000.

When we returned to the Operations Room, State Fire Marshall Tina Virgil was there. We didn't mention our crowd estimate to her. Instead, we asked her to go up and make a crowd estimate of the whole square. She agreed and off she went. We shared our estimate with the room and were curious to see what Tina would say.

At 1:40 p.m. I received a call from Rob Marchant, the Chief Clerk for the Senate. He wanted to talk through the threats that had been received, as well as the plans he would like to see in place by Tuesday when the Senators was scheduled to be in session.

It appeared that members of both political parties had been threatened. Senator Tim Carpenter (Democrat) and Senator Leah Vukmir (Republican) had received death threats. Another threat had been made toward the teenage daughter of Senator Jon Erpenbach (Democrat). There had been at least one threat against the Governor (Republican), the First Lady, and their two sons. Rob wanted something sent to the police in the home jurisdictions of all of the senators. I told him that I would draft a bulletin if he would email me the home addresses of the senators so we could match those with the proper police jurisdiction.

Rob then shared with me the security measures he would like to have in place by Tuesday for the senators. We discussed the shooting in Arizona that had killed six people and seriously wounded United States Representative Gabby Giffords in January, just six weeks earlier. He wanted the entire south wing of the Capitol closed off to the general public from the basement to the fourth floor. He wanted to institute metal detector screening in the Senate galleries and would need remote offsite parking with shuttle service for the senators. He wanted to confirm we had taken care of the senators' concerns regarding the tunnel security and safety. I told him that we would start planning for Tuesday and inform him of the strategy as soon as possible. I contacted the CP and asked if the planning section could assist and was informed they could not.

Throughout the day, DNR Chief Warden Randy Stark continued to make adjustments to the officer briefing process. Officers would now work 13.5 hours a day for us to effectively cover a "12-hour" shift. Briefings would continue in room 412 East. We knew eventually we would have to find another room for briefing, as Sergeant-at-Arms Anne Tonnon Byers would need her room back for Assembly business. We were expecting 72 officers to arrive at 6:00 for the evening shift. Because it was Saturday, we expected sleeper numbers to increase.

Common sense dictated that in order to bring all these officers together, a mobilization plan would be necessary. What wasn't obvious is how to demobilize the officers. Some officers would work several days in a row, while others worked just one shift and never returned. It was essential to ensure that equipment was returned and issues were addressed daily.

Randy was busy working on a demobilization plan to allow for a smooth transition from the 228 officers we had working until 7:00 p.m., to the 72 who were going to be here overnight. First on the planning agenda was to manage bus transportation for the 228 officers, deputies, and troopers back to their vehicles.

* * * * *

Social media played a large part in these events. Someone would tweet a rumor and we would spend valuable time attempting to address it. Because DOA wanted to approve all communication to the public, we lacked an efficient way to address the public and quash rumors quickly.

A rumor that gained the most traction involved the Governor cancelling the furlough day and ordering all state employees back to work on Monday. We knew the furlough day was not observed by all state employees so we didn't give this rumor a whole lot of merit. The University was not on furlough and classes would be in session. What would be the point of the Governor ordering the rest of state government back to work? However, planning for all contingencies—even rumors—we had to consider what would happen if state employees were coming back to work. I reached out to the CP and then tracked Chief Tubbs down to have him run the rumor to ground. After a few hours, the CP had determined it was indeed a rumor, so our original plans remained in place.

Fire Marshall Tina Virgil returned from her picture-taking and crowd-estimating duties. She estimated the crowd to be about 50,000 people. It was good to know we were close in our estimates. Other agencies had estimated the crowd at 80,000. The Interior Branch division commanders and I thought 80,000 was too high, so we used our numbers. After a brief discussion, we decided that having various agencies estimate the crowd size was becoming comical. We joked that the DNR's inflated deer herd count was looking more accurate when compared to the way some agencies were estimating the crowd.

As the day progressed, Tina and I sat down to review every measurement on the entire Square and Capitol grounds. We independently assessed the crowd size and afterward compared our numbers. We took photos to document our estimates. We knew that both sides of the political aisle wanted crowd estimates. The Republicans would want the size to appear smaller than it was, while the Democrats would want the size to be greater than it was. I was determined to base our numbers on solid measurements.

By all accounts, the outdoor rallies were exciting. The largest group of people gathered near the State Street side of the Capitol Square. Because the crowd near State Street was so much larger than the Tea Party assemblage near King Street, the county sheriff and the city police met the incoming Tea Party buses and escorted the Tea Party through the marching crowds to the King Street entrance of the Capitol. While there was yelling back and forth between the Tea Party rally and the anti-bill protesters, there were no physical confrontations. Once the Tea Party folks had arrived at the King Street entrance, they held their rally from the balustrade in front of a crowd of 2,500. The rally was held without incident.

As the rallies ended, the number of people wanting to enter the Capitol increased. Within a matter of minutes, the count rose from 1,000 to over 4,500. By 5:00 p.m., we were seeing more than 8,000. The sparks we thought might occur when the two sides mixed inside the building never materialized. The opposing sides were able to mix, but to their credit, they did not goad one another. The large number of police standing post and milling about deterred any overly aggressive behavior.

We received word that Representative Peter Barca (Democrat) wanted to hold a hearing or listening session in room 328 NW. We assigned some officers to accommodate his request and to ensure the room didn't become overly crowded. The session went on for many hours without incident. This listening session would allow the building to remain open, heading off any potential of Chief Tubb's repeating his closing order from the night before.

I brought State Fire Marshall Tina Virgil up to speed on the capacity management plan and explained the counts to her. She thought all sounded good and agreed that things inside were much improved over the previous days this week. We switched gears, and I briefed her on the information Senate Clerk Rob Marchant had shared about the threats. Tina confirmed the information with her colleagues in Department of Criminal Investigation.

Many of the threats were being investigated by DCI, along with the Capitol Police. Together, she and I drafted an informational notice and a request for increased patrols to the police agencies in the Senators' home communities. After a quick review from a few others, we realized that because we didn't have email addresses, the notice would have to be placed in the U.S. Mail, which meant it wouldn't actually get to the agencies until Tuesday or Wednesday.

As we were pondering the inefficiencies of not having email addresses, I sent the draft memo to the Command Post. To our surprise, they were against sending the information to all of the police agencies responsible for the senators' home residences, as they did not believe the threats were substantial or widespread enough to warrant it. They also shared that DOA would have to approve the memo before it went out as official information.

This was new territory for me. I had never encountered the need for law enforcement to have civilian authorization before sharing threat information with fellow law enforcement. This seemed absurd to me. Everyday law enforcement receives pages and pages of information about threats originating from all over the country (and in some cases, the world) as part of the information-sharing we participate in with all levels of law enforcement and Homeland Security. In our communiqué, law enforcement had relevant, timely and potentially useful information, yet it was not allowed to be sent.

Once again, I had to shake my head and thank my lucky stars I worked for the University. Since almost all of the University's active community has email accounts, cell phones, Twitter, Facebook, blogs, and websites, we tend to communicate often. If we had to run through the number of seemingly bureaucratic approvals the Capitol Police had to deal with, the University would likely be in a state of utter disorder (though I'm sure there are those at the Capitol who believed that's the case!) Nevertheless, I wasn't working at the University at the moment and the Capitol regulations were in effect.

I called Senate Clerk Rob Marchant to inform him of the CP's decision not to communicate to the police jurisdictions as he had requested. I apologized for not being able to deliver. As the after-noon passed, I thought the lack of public information, along with the lack of sharing information with law enforcement colleagues, was a mistake.

The forecast for overnight was for eight to nine inches of snow. The nice break in the usually harsh Wisconsin winter weather was coming to an end. So on top of the crowds, threats, and managing hundreds of new officers daily, we had to consider the impact of the snow.

A few of my UW Police commanders wanted to meet with me off to the side. We huddled together in a private conversation. The Governor's Repair Bill had not exempted the UW Police, the Capitol Police, and some other state law enforcement from the increases in the health care and retirement costs. The Bill treated these officers very differently from their municipal counterparts and the state troopers. Ironically, my officers and the state troopers were together in the same union, yet were separated by the Governor in his budget plan.

My staff reported that the president of the union local had sent an email to all members, telling them that the CPD and UW Police would be eliminated altogether as part of the Governor's upcoming budget. They were to be replaced by a contracted service, namely Wackenhut Security (now G4S). Wackenhut Security is a private, for-profit, security company that furnishes personnel for many private businesses. Within the law enforcement field, it is common knowledge that some contract security staff are not as well trained or supervised as their public counterparts or the police.

I laughed out loud.

Unfortunately, it wasn't so funny. My top managers were dead serious and said that this was somehow linked to the Governor's plan to make the University of Wisconsin-Madison a "public authority."

Basically, a public authority model represents a break from the bureaucratic state agency system. Public authority would allow UW

–Madison to have a governing board that was concerned only about what was best for UW–Madison, a world-renowned research University with a significant global impact. Public authority status would also allow UW–Madison to set its own tuition, and allow it to deposit and invest its own funds. Finally, it would allow UW–Madison to create its own personnel system. Having a world-class University tied to a state civil service system is cumbersome at best.

I was positive Chancellor Martin would never allow contract security to take over policing UW–Madison. My staff implored me to do something as our officers were really feeling down after getting this information from their union.

I decided to check first with the chief legal counsel for the University, Lisa Rutherford. She would know what was or wasn't a component of the public authority model the Governor had proposed. Lisa assured me that the UW Police, as currently constituted, were part of the new public authority model.

Then I called the lead University lobbyist, Don Nelson. I told him about the correspondence. He assured me the union would not have information about what was in the Republican-proposed budget at this point. Don understood the stir this had caused so he used his contacts in the government to check it out. One of the people he called had helped draft the budget, and assured Don that the Wackenhut rumor was completely false.

It had been a long day and it was fast approaching 6:30. The birthday dinner for the chancellor I was originally supposed to be hosting had started at 6:00. I checked in with the party crew to let them know that I hoped to make it soon. I had the University Police commanders gather as many of our UW officers together as they could so I could address and quell the Wackenhut rumor. We gathered in a hallway on the third floor, where I addressed the rumor directly. I let them know the results of my check-in with legal counsel and with the lobbyist. I explained that we had the support of the University and there was no intention to eliminate us, with or without a public authority.

Not surprisingly, my folks asked good questions and I answered them as well as I could. Because I knew they should have had a union representative present for this discussion, I told them they were free to file an unfair labor practice or grievance against me if they wished. They laughed and wished me a good night. Even though they were still a bit unsettled, they had appreciated the fact that I would check the facts and talk directly to them.

This side drama was just one more example of the difficult spot many police were experiencing. As they were working to protect the policy-makers and the protesters, they were also having to grapple with what the proposed budget meant for their own future.

I escaped the Capitol and rushed home to change clothes and head to the birthday gathering at Olin House.

> Olin House was built in 1912 by John and Helen Olin, he an attorney and University regent. The 11,000-square-foot mansion was donated to the University of Wisconsin in 1924. It has been renovated several times, most recently in 2006-2008. The house is located in the University Heights neighborhood just west of the campus. In the latest renovation, the basement was converted to a service level. The first floor is used for public entertaining, and the second and third floors are the chancellor's private residence.

The dinner was held in the first floor dining room. I joined the partygoers just as they were finishing their salads. Several deans and some of the chancellor's friends were gathered around the table. It was warming to be welcomed like a conquering heroine, the group aware of my Capitol assignment. Everyone had brought something fabulous to eat and after days of eating cold pizza, I thought I had died and gone to heaven. The chancellor appeared very happy with her birthday celebration, and the laughter flowed easily for the rest of the evening.

Following dinner and dessert, the chancellor had the idea of playing charades. We divided ourselves into two teams. The chancellor is known for her competitive nature, a trait I possess as well...and we were on opposing teams. Game on!

Unfortunately, my team was getting trounced. When it was my turn, I pulled "The Immortal Life of Henrietta Lacks" as the book title to act out. This book was the current title for the University's "Go Big Read" initiative but at that point, I was so exhausted I couldn't have acted out my own name. How the hell?

OK, symbol for book, six words, and the first word, little... "the." OK, third word sounds like... I pointed to my partner Joanne, and somebody thankfully said "wife" and got life." OK, now I was lost. How in the world would I act out the rest? The opposing team was howling at my feeble efforts, when all of a sudden someone shouted "The Immortal Life of Henrietta Lacks."

We were stunned, especially because it came from a member of the opposing team. We burst out laughing, I was saved. I took my seat on a large ottoman and even though it was only 9:30, I promptly fell asleep as the party continued around me. Some host I had been.

DAY 7: SUNDAY, FEBRUARY 20, 2011

OVERNIGHT, ROCK COUNTY SHERIFF CAPTAIN JUDE MAURER HELPED TO serve as the Incident Commander, giving some relief to the over-taxed CPD sergeants who had been on point for too many nights in a row. A snow and icy mix came in the wee hours of the morning and the bad weather was expected to continue throughout the day. At times, it was freezing rain, intermittently changed into what we Wisconsinites lovingly refer to as "thunder snow." The Capitol was quiet when we arrived around 6:25 a.m. About 400 people had stayed overnight, and most were still asleep in the Rotunda.

I quietly walked into the Rotunda and greeted the few who were awake. We chatted briefly, and I asked them how they felt things were going. Many said they were truly grateful and appreciative for the police presence, for it helped them know they were safe, letting them get some sleep without worrying about their safety.

The Capitol had been locked at midnight last night without arrests or disturbances. People were free to go, but were not allowed to return after midnight. A few of the officers attempted some basic cleanup, including taking down a few signs, but some of the protesters had asked them to stop and so they discontinued the effort. The Interior Branch had reduced numbers to just 25 officers on the inside and six on the outside. The state troopers would be back on the inside today staffing the entrance doors. We were not expecting large crowds given the weather, but people still came.

For the Interior Branch, it was a good day to plan for what lay ahead. We started the morning off as usual. A quick overnight update and then off to brief the incoming shift. After the briefing, the members of the Operations Room met to make three "To Do" lists, one each for Sunday (today), Monday, and Tuesday. There were a thousand details to organize.

Chief Warden Randy Stark wasn't satisfied with the mobilization and demobilization plans. He vowed to get it resolved today. Randy also wanted to nail down procedures for Section 941.235(1) of the statute governing the prohibition of carrying weapons inside of government buildings. It was necessary for us to get all of these matters in writing because we didn't know if or when we would be "tapped out" and someone else would have to step into our roles.

Jerry Jansen, my retired Assistant Chief who had arrived Thursday from Arizona, would be a significant help with this task. Today he and Lieutenant Marc Schmidt were going to write up the responsibilities of the information teams, the Intel teams, and the response teams. Jerry and Marc would draft instructions and descriptions so that the teams could be independent or blended together if necessary. We once again used a modular approach of adding only the number of resources needed at one time. We found this approach far more flexible.

We needed a series of plans to prepare for the Governor's budget address scheduled to occur on Tuesday, February 22, when the Assembly would be in session. (No one had informed us the address would be delayed a week.) We already had the request from Chief Clerk of the Senate Rob Marchant to clear and hold the South Wing because of the threats to the senators.

Since the South Wing would be off limits, I assigned Assistant Chief (ret.) Jerry Jansen to review our capacity plan and change the ingress and egress doors as needed. South Hamilton could not be used because it was off limits to protect the wings from public access.

As things were continuing to heat up and the rhetoric was increasing, we developed a plan to have metal screening at the entrance to the Senate Gallery. Logic followed that if we had all branches of government in the Assembly chambers for the Governor's Budget Address, we should metal screen the visitors there as well. It was decided to have the UW Police handle the metal screening. We arranged for our hand-held detectors (wands) to be brought to the Capitol. The walk-through magnetometers we owned would have been more people-friendly; however, the limited space outside the galleries made wand screening more practical.

We relied upon the DCI folks to give us a daily intelligence briefing. The DCI representative or the administrator would review the threats with us each day, but beyond that, there wasn't much. In the Branch, we were growing frustrated with only receiving limited information. It hampered our planning efforts. I made a mental note to have a talk about the issue with DCI Administrator Ed Wall. In the meantime, I decided to call Todd Kuschel, who was the Incident Commander as DC Dan Blackdeer was on his first day off since before this all began. Todd listened to my issue and promised he would look into the flow of information. I knew I could count on Todd to be straight with me.

We had created a mass arrest plan, but we didn't have a well-defined civil disturbance plan. AC Brian Bridges was going to meet to develop a civil disturbance plan on Monday, since the Madison and Dane County commanders had decided to take Sunday off. Therefore, the development of that plan would have to wait another day.

Two days earlier, the Interior Branch had requested better signage for the restrooms, which by and large, were hidden in obscure corners of the building. I called to ask the CP for the signs and wondered out loud what the hold-up might be. There seemed to be a problem with not having a printer on contract and, by the way, the credit cards for the Capitol Police were again at their limit. The CP explained that a rush order for printing from DOA was usually completed within three business days. Logistics had requested rush orders but we would have to continue our wait. We could have had an Interior Branch staffer whip up the necessary signs in the space of 15 minutes, but instead we were at the mercy of government red tape.

Speaking of red tape, we had offloaded an explosive ordnance disposal (EOD) plan to the CP for assignment and follow through—again, we didn't expect to need this plan, but protocol suggested that having one in place would be wise. Follow-up was scheduled for today. We also needed to make sure we were assigned a new offsite location for briefings because we were about to lose access to the large Assembly room.

We suggested that the CP consider establishing an Investigative Branch for all the threats and information being collected and we asked the CP to work with the MFD to establish, or dust off, the catastrophic event plan. Todd agreed to work things from the CP end. I was grateful. It seemed like a wild ride in the Land of Oz—*Lions and Tigers and Bears*—explosive ordnance plans, threats, and catastrophes. Oh, my!

With the new configurations of building wing closures and the two parties needing to caucus separately, we needed another movement plan to get them from one area to another through the crowds on Tuesday. In addition, we had to plan safe passageways in the event of an emergency. Some of this was second nature for the Capitol Police, but there just weren't enough Capitol officers to go around. We had to get the knowledge of the Capitol Police written down so that others could be trained to handle the routes and situations as needed. An emergency evacuation plan from the Assembly Chamber was also put to paper. This was old hat to CPD Sergeant Scott Merdler, who took the floor plans and pointed out the routes and other considerations.

The Capitol has had police patrolling it since 1881, though it officially became the Capitol Police sometime in 1970s.[10] In 1969, "welfare mothers" marching to protest welfare cuts, led by a Catholic activist priest,

---

[10] Daniel Blackdeer, "Wisconsin Capitol Police," *Capitol Beat: A Publication of the IACP Capitol Police Section*, Vol. 2, No. 1, February 2010. Accessed at http://www.theiacp.org/LinkClick.aspx?fileticket=zaQJrOghRYA%3D&tabid=392.)

Father James Groppi, had gotten into the Capitol. They took over the floor of the Assembly for a week. Following that incident, an internal review called for the Capitol to have its own police department.

In some states, the Capitol Police are linked to the State Patrol or State Police. This is not the case in Wisconsin. The State Patrol reports to the Department of Transportation. The Capitol Police force reports to the Department of Administration.

Although the Capitol is oriented geographically (north, east, south, and west) it is easy to get turned around (literally and figuratively) standing in the Rotunda. When problems are reported, people often give their location in descriptive terms as in Representative So and So's office, in the GAR room (Grand Army of the Republic), or in the clerk's offices, but rarely state a room number. Capitol Police officers are worth their weight in gold in helping to decipher where things are in relation to everything else!

The Capitol Police had some very seasoned people who had lots of years of experience in the Capitol. They knew the building nooks, crannies, storage areas, back offices, basement, and tunnels like the backs of their hands. We were deliberate in placing a member of the Capitol Police, equipped with master keys, with officers from out of the area who didn't know anything about the Capitol. These response teams were great at providing protective escorts. While one led the way, the other members of the team could surround the protectee and get the person through the crowds to his or her destination. These teams would also handle the movement of arrested *persons. Finally, these teams were wonderful to have for crowd counts and crowd observation. They often escorted me to the viewing levels inside and out so I could complete crowd estimates.*

Each day, we typically had a new safety officer from a visiting jurisdiction. Incident Command protocol requires at least one officer to be in charge of officer safety. As the assignments at the Capitol lengthened, the safety officers would become much busier overseeing food safety, health checks, and fire prevention issues. The safety officer also kept an eye on weather conditions and made sure that the entrance and exits were clear as the snow continued to fall. The marble floors of the Capitol became slippery as people dragged in the snow and we had a few people slip and fall.

There would be plenty to keep us busy as the snow fell and the incessant drumming continued. Given the inclement weather, AFSCME was planning a noon rally inside. We would carefully monitor capacity as we tried to accommodate getting everyone out of the weather, while not over-packing the building.

Given the nasty weather outside and the crowd's gentle behavior inside, we had too many police officers staffing the building. One of the challenges of the Emergency Police Services (EPS) process is that you can't increase or decrease large numbers of police quickly. While we tried to obtain as much info as possible in advance, often we found ourselves dealing with events, incidents, and issues on the fly. The sergeants-at-arms shared plans for the upcoming week as best they could. Everything was up in the air. The Assembly would continue to meet. With the fourteen senators still out of state, senate proceedings were in flux. We continually did our best to make educated guesses regarding staffing needs. It wasn't easy.

Five days after Brad requested a TV for the Interior Branch Operations Room, one was delivered with a set of "rabbit ears." We laughed when it was set up, and the staff tried everything they could to pick up any station, including placing an antenna outside the window. It continued to snow. I called Todd and asked him in his role as Incident Commander if we could have a cable hook-up so that we could at least receive the *Weather Channel* and *Wisconsin Eye* (the television feed for much of what went on in the Capitol.) He agreed to have it installed that week.

We developed the "Assembly Caucus Movement Plan." With the temperament of the crowds being largely anti-Republican, we were more concerned about the movement of the Republican representatives than the Democrats. So far, whenever the Assembly Democrats mixed with the crowd, they were treated like rock stars.

The Republican senators caucused within the office complex off the Senate Floor. Moving them in and out didn't require a law enforcement presence beyond the officers and troopers already assigned to the chambers and floor. And as noted, the Democratic senators were still out of state. In fact, the Sunday *Wisconsin State Journal* reported on an interview with Senator Jon Erpenbach (Democrat) who was holed up in a Chicago hotel. Senator Erpenbach shared that all the senators were united in this tactic of leaving the state in an effort to slow down the Bill. The same article claimed the Governor was not interested in negotiating.

Our focus had to be to maintain the safety and security inside the Capitol. Regardless of the political situation, it was back to planning for us. The Senate evacuation plan was captured in writing for the Chambers and adjacent floor, and a plan was drafted for security escorts to evacuate people from the Capitol through the underground tunnel to the Risser Justice Center across the street. This plan would also be in place for Tuesday's Joint Address on the Budget. We would use it for the Legislature, the executive branch, and for the Supreme Court, if necessary. We had to ensure the tunnel would be secure and safe. While we had the inside secured, we needed the Command Post to secure the outside, including where the tunnel connects with the parking garage. All transportation needs of those being escorted were the responsibility of the CP.

There was so much going on that I had no organized way to learn about the building, politics, events, history, back-office deals, and hallway meetings, so each day, I learned to make quick adjustments. For instance, as part of the current planning process, I learned there were other tunnels into the Capitol. I asked for a briefing on these tunnels to understand where they went and who might know about them. The Capitol Police believed a number of the protesters would know about the tunnels because many of them worked for the state or had worked as contractors who helped build or run utilities through the tunnels. In other words, we realized the existence of these tunnels was not necessarily a well-guarded secret.

With all this planning occurring in the Branch instead of the CP, which included organizing documents, files and action items, we needed more staff. We had already increased the number of Emergency Service Coordinators, drawing from the UW Police emergency management unit. The University Response Plan had a robust planning group. One of its leaders is Carol Gosenheimer, who was one of my main assistants during President Obama's visit in the fall of 2010. She was worth her weight in gold. When I called Carol, she agreed to come to the Capitol to start on Monday.

The operations and events in the building didn't pause while we planned. The Sunday rally went off without a hitch, and the capacity count showed that about 4,900 people had turned out for the event when it peaked at 2:00 that afternoon. Given the weather, the protest turnout was significant, especially since every television and radio station was urging people to stay home and not drive.

Meanwhile, Incident Commander Todd Kuschel had received a call from Chief Tubbs indicating that the police needed to close the Capitol at 4:00 p.m. Everyone was to be removed. This was either a bad case of déjà vu or a repeat of Friday night. Unfortunately, it was a repeat. Todd opposed the idea and got a message through to Capitol Police Deputy Chief Dan Blackdeer, who, despite being on his much-needed day off, headed back to the Command Post.

When Dan arrived at the CP, he met with his team, Todd Kuschel, and the Planning and Operation Sections chiefs. Everyone was extremely frustrated. Who was behind the decision to close the Capitol? Certainly Chief Tubbs wouldn't decide that on his own. The members of the CP had many questions: How could this actually occur? Were the police going to open a processing center on a Sunday for those arrested or just toss people into the snow? Of course, there wasn't even time to give notice to people who might actually want to leave before being tossed out or arrested. If notice was given, would that cause more people to come to try to defend the protesters? The idea of calling extra police in from around the state at this point was deemed not viable as the roads were ice covered and slippery.

Once again, the CP team agreed that closing the building at 4:00 p.m. and evicting people was not something that could be tactically successful. Dan and Todd tried to figure out who they should call for assistance with how to deal with the political side of things. They chose to contact Adjutant General Don Dunbar of the National Guard.

The general and the Director of Wisconsin Emergency Management (WEM) arrived at the CP. Dan Blackdeer explained the situation and the back-and-forth orders to clear the building. He also described the lack of logistical support, the lack of direct contact with the political leaders, and the absence of any real authority for him to act upon. He described the city and county law enforcement stance on being unwilling to assist the Capitol Police inside the building. He asked the general to hold an organizing meeting of the leaders of all local and state law enforcement agencies involved to this point. The general agreed to do so and set the meeting for the following day.

Having no idea this was all transpiring at the CP, I was surprised to receive a call from DC Dan Blackdeer on his day off. He had gotten some sleep he said, but had been called back to duty to deal with another move to close the Capitol and evict the protesters. Dan made it clear that he was a bit fed up with this on-again, off-again closing and directing of police resources. We both felt our mission was being undercut. I agreed not to close the Capitol.

Given the weather and the fact that no warning had been given to the people who had been peaceful and cooperative, forcing them out into the snow was not a reasonable tactic. In my experience, not communicating such a decision with those involved was a fundamental mistake that could lead to violence and injuries. We had every reason to believe that if we had adequate time to communicate with the protesters, and we were reasonable in how we went about the closing of the Capitol, the majority would cooperate.

The building would reopen tomorrow at 8:00 a.m. and because it was a furlough day for state workers, we could see larger crowds. If we needlessly angered the crowd today, the crowd would no doubt redouble its efforts and numbers tomorrow. Clearing everyone out today would cause a potential battle every day at closing time. It also meant we would have to do battle every day until this ended.

The Interior Branch agreed to give Dan some professional cover; he should send Charles to see me. It would be my turn to talk Charles through why this wasn't a good tactical idea to close today at 4:00. Once again the worst that could happen to me is I would be sent back to the University. At this point, that didn't seem much of a penalty!

Charles never came by the Operations Room. The Capitol did not close, nor were the people evicted at 4:00 p.m. Joe the Plumber, from the McCain/Palin campaign days, was on the Square at 5:30. We all wondered how much he had been paid to appear. Other than Joe, things outside were beginning to look like a Currier and Ives scene on an old-fashion Christmas card.

Not long afterwards, I received a call from General Dunbar, who was gathering together several law enforcement leaders on Monday morning at the Dane County Public Safety Building to talk over how operations were going. He asked me to attend. AC Brian Bridges would follow that meeting with the civil disturbance planning meeting in the same location at 10:00.

While all this planning going on, we would periodically brief the Interior Branch group during the day. Over the course of several of these briefings, I called on State Patrol Lieutenant Brad Altman for an update, who would more times than not, turn immediately to his sergeants to report out. I half-joked with the lieutenant that I wasn't sure what I needed him for, as the sergeants were doing all the work. With that remark, I made my second field promotion of Sgt. Les Mlsna to Sergeant/Lieutenant. The other State Patrol Lieutenant Neuman, with a flourish, turned his portion of the briefing over to the same sergeant. I howled with laughter and gave my third field promotion. The Sergeant/Lieutenant became Lieutenant/Lieutenant. For the rest of the protests, that was how Les was addressed.

As activities surrounding the Capitol protests continued, faculty in the School of Education back on campus had organized two teach-ins for students who wanted to participate in learning in a different style. The teach-ins were to be held at the College Library, with more being planned for later in the week.

Also on campus, the Teaching Assistants' Association (TAA) was calling for a teach-out[11] on Tuesday to keep the pressure on the Republicans and to allow teaching to go on (in their view), but at the Capitol instead of in the classroom. Contrary to popular belief, not all UW–Madison students are liberals. Some students didn't want to be part of the Capitol experience, and complained about being forced to go there or miss their traditional class time.

There was a winter storm warning in effect until 6:00 Monday night. Freezing rain and three to five inches of snow and ice accumulations up to one half inch was expected with visibility reduced to a quarter mile during the heavier periods of snow. Lovely. We had almost been lulled into thinking an early spring would soon be ours—Jimmy the Groundhog of Sun Prairie, Wisconsin, had told us so. [12]

DAY 8: MONDAY, FEBRUARY 21, 2011

ON MONDAY MORNING, WE HAD 196 STAFF ASSIGNED TO THE INTERIOR Branch. Given that it was a furlough day with only two formally permitted rallies planned for noon and 5:00, both to include music, we were over-staffed. I silently reflected about my eighteen days 'til "freedom date."

Overnight, Undersheriff Kurt Pickerel from Walworth County had been the Interior Branch Incident Commander. Approximately

---

[11] A teach-out is when the instructor teaches a class off-site in reaction to some political issue. In this case, classes would be relocated from the classroom to the Capitol.

[12] Jimmy the Groundhog is Sun Prairie, Wisconsin's version of the famous Punxsutawney Phil, a prognosticating rodent from Punxsutawney, Pennsylvania. According to folklore, if it is cloudy when a groundhog emerges from its burrow on this day, then spring will come early; if it is sunny, the groundhog will supposedly see its shadow and retreat back into its burrow, and the winter weather will continue for six more weeks.

417 people slept overnight in the Rotunda, plus an unknown number in offices and meeting rooms. There had been no issues. The winter snow warning had been downgraded to a winter storm advisory, and only another inch of snow accumulation was expected.

City street crews and UW ground crews had been out clearing the streets so the roads looked pretty good. Metro buses were running without any issues. All campus events were still on, as we were not on furlough. The K-12 school closings or opening delays were too long to list, but suffice it to say, the closings were due more to the weather than any other reason.

AFSCME had published their bus schedule for all the rallies on Monday and Tuesday. Once again, the list covered every corner of the state. The Madison school district announced it was closed for the fourth straight school day.

It was the land of continuous improvement in the Interior Branch. We added a dispatcher from University Police to the Operations Room. It helped knowing that the CP was now officially out of the dispatch business for the Interior Branch. We were able to get the doors open by 8:00 am for the first time since February 17. This was a significant improvement milestone. We were briefing faster, and thanks to Randy, the entire process was becoming more streamlined each day.

Kevin Wernet had arranged a ride to take us to the Public Safety Building for the 8:30 meeting called by the general. The agency heads were all supposed to attend, including the Director of Wisconsin Emergency Management. We all talked through the challenges of the increasing crowds and the lack of logistical support. The city and county were taking care of most of their own needs themselves. The University had supplied most of the computer equipment, printers, office supplies, metal detection equipment, and all the support staff for the Interior Branch.

Still unresolved was the reimbursement for law enforcement agencies that were coming to assist inside the Capitol. We talked about how the rancor caused by the political situation was becoming increasingly heightened. Emotions and simple exhaustion was taking a toll. While the discussion went on, my mind was on all the work that needed to be done before tomorrow's budget address.

The Incident Command Structure was discussed and it was reiterated that everyone needed to report to the Incident Commander. We reaffirmed that we were going to continue to handle the Capitol activities as one event. At the time, that seemed logical but as things progressed and became ever more political, the idea of having us stay together as if managing one event would become awkward.

While everyone around the table was in agreement about Incident Command and following the directives of the Incident Commander, I was feeling it was more lip service than real commitment. Nonetheless, I decided not to push the issue or start an argument. As noted earlier, Madison city police had made it clear they would not cross the street to be on state property, which meant they would not enter the Capitol. The County Sheriff's deputies had decided that they would not enter the Capitol to assist with the crowd, but that they would take lead responsibility for the Square's lawn and ground level sidewalks.

My impression was that if the city or county disagreed with a directive from the Incident Commander, they would not follow it. I knew the players well enough to know that no "Incident Commander" was going to be able to tell the city police how to run their operation in their own jurisdiction.

I wasn't getting cynical, just reflecting on what occurred on Friday night when the directive to close the Capitol was given by Chief Charles Tubbs. Chief Tubbs was ordering the Incident Commander to close, yet the Chief Warden and I had agreed not to follow that directive. Further, I had decided that if ordered on Sunday to close the Capitol in a similar manner, I would not follow that order. It was clear from their Friday night actions, the sheriff and city police chief agreed with my decision. Although I didn't know how the superintendent of the Wisconsin State Patrol felt about all of this, I wasn't sure it mattered at this stage. Bottom line, not one of these agency heads were compelled to follow the Incident Commander's directions. Although we were all making attempts to collaborate through the auspices of the Incident Command System structure, we were struggling to make it work.

Clearly this was not one operation. There were several simultaneous operations commanders making decisions. There was a host of area commands, each with its own tensions wrapped up in a shared political drama. We were attempting to co-exist and collaborate when there was agreement, and lines drawn when there was disagreement. Our failure to recognize this and deal with it frankly would lead to many more tensions as the days progressed. Decisions were being made by going around certain people, avoiding communications, and often made without disclosing motivations.

At the close of General Dunbar's meeting, there was a lengthy discussion about how others among us needed contact with the state political "bosses" who were likely to attempt to dictate enforcement resources and tactics. Chief Tubbs and DCI Administrator Wall had access now, but not the rest of us. The city chief had access to the mayor; the sheriff had access to the county executive. The Incident Commander and the Interior Branch had no access to the political leadership at any level, yet we were the ones being ordered about.

We all agreed that sitting down with the political staff would be helpful. It was decided to hold that meeting at 12:45 p.m. in the Senate Clerk's basement office.

By the time Kevin and I returned to the Capitol at 10:00, 1,187 people had entered the Capitol. AC Brian Bridges was meeting with representatives from the city and county about civil disturbance plans.

Thanks to University Police Captain Karen Soley, I found the explosive ordnance detection plan completed. When Karen signs off on a plan, I have every confidence that it is correct. This one was no different. Captain Soley had increased the staffing and bomb sweeps and had diversified the pool of canines so that no dog was scheduled too frequently.

Kevin, my extraordinary aide, pulled me aside to inform me that County Executive Kathleen Falk wanted all county dispatchers removed from the CP. She also wanted any county resources being used to be returned to the county. She did not direct any specific comments toward the sheriff or his staffing. Kevin's computer was owned by Dane County, and if he had to return it, he would be without one.

I asked Kevin to find me a quiet room where I could make a call to County Executive Kathleen Falk (Democrat). Within minutes, we were talking. She greeted me with "What can I do for you, Chief?" I took a deep breath, realizing that although we had been on a first-name basis for close to 15 years, this was going to be all business. She was firm and made it clear she wanted Dane County to have nothing to do with assisting this operation. I explained to her that this operation and my mission were about protecting First Amendment rights. She was skeptical, but respected the job I was doing under trying circumstances. She assured me that she would not make any attempt to influence the sheriff in his responsibilities. However, she shared that county dispatchers were no longer dispatching now that the Interior Branch had taken over. She was correct. We ended our conversation amicably and I ordered a University computer for Kevin.

University Police Captain Steve Rogers called to inform me of a development at the University he felt I should know about right away. The University of Wisconsin System Board of Regents was calling a special meeting for Friday, February 25, to discuss the New Badger Partnership, which had been proposed by Chancellor Biddy Martin for the University of Wisconsin-Madison. The new Badger Partnership proposed flexibility be granted to the Madison campus to allow UW–Madison to continue to compete within the world economy. The twist that was emerging—and why I received a call from Captain Rogers—was that Governor Scott Walker was proposing in his full budget that the University of Wisconsin–Madison become a Public Authority and be separated from the UW System. To say that the UW Board of Regents was upset by this turn of events was indeed a gross understatement.

> The University of Wisconsin System was formed forty years ago as part of a budget bill. The system consists of thirteen four-year campuses throughout the state. In addition, there are thirteen two-year colleges. The third component of the System is UW-Extension, which has several buildings on the UW–Madison campus. With over 174,000 students and close to 39,000 employees, the University of Wisconsin System is the largest component of state government.
>
> The system is headed by a President and system administration offices are located on the UW–Madison campus. The system (as a whole) reports to a Board of Regents, which meets regularly in Van Hise Hall on the UW–Madison campus. Van Hise is a 19-story structure that towers over the campus. The top five floors house system administration, offices, and conference rooms for the Board of Regents. From a policing standpoint, it is a challenging location if a demonstration or meeting

turned ugly. So it was important for me to connect with the President and share my concerns about the logistical issues at hand.

President Kevin Reilly came to the leadership position in 2004, following a 12-year term of President Katharine Lyall. When I first arrived on campus in 1991, Katharine Lyall was a senior vice President for the UW System. She was named President of the system a year later. She quickly became a mentor of mine.

Despite her busy schedule, she has always made time for me. It was Katharine who started the tradition of having the UW–Madison police chief take responsibility for advising the President on system security and policing matters. I have always enjoyed the ability to speak directly to the President as needed. President Reilly has continued the practice of conferring with me about matters of security.

President Reilly took my call and we talked about the political climate and the inaccessibility of Van Hise meeting rooms for large crowds to move about easily. We discussed five alternate meeting sites and both favored one of the UW-Extension buildings, located on the edge of the UW–Madison campus. With a location tentatively agreed upon, I began to work with campus officials to ensure the availability of the Pyle Center and to anticipate any and all logistical needs.

I talked to Incident Commander DC Blackdeer and asked him to consider opening another branch in the ICS system to handle the special regents meeting. The day of the regents meeting was supposed to be my "tap out" date, my first day off in twelve. He agreed to open a branch and to have EPS locate staffing beyond what the 13 UW System campus police departments could muster.

Looking ahead to Friday, University Police AC Brian Bridges and I selected University Police Captain Karen Soley to head up the branch. Captain Soley was ready for her own command. The chancellors from each of the campuses would be present, along with all members of the Board of Regents. In addition to the normal Board of Regents attendees, we were expecting significant media attention. This would be the regents' first public airing of the New Badger Partnership (NBP) with the Public Authority component. I referred to it as NBP on steroids.

Although I was going to be off-duty from my assignment at the Capitol, I would be attending the Regents' meeting as a member of the campus community supporting Chancellor Biddy Martin.

Chancellor Martin had arrived at UW–Madison after a lengthy UW–Madison search process in July of 2008. She sized up UW–Madison quickly and proposed the Madison Initiative for Undergraduates (MIU). Essentially she argued that students who could afford to pay more for college should do so. The families in the state who earned less than $80,000 annually would be held harmless from the tuition increases. This initiative, coupled with the "Great People, Great Place" campaign to increase need-based aid, was the Chancellor's strategy to move UW–Madison forward, while maintaining access for students who couldn't afford a college education. The MIU also offered ways for the University to hire new faculty and support student services, particularly advising.

As soon as the Regents approved the MIU, Chancellor Martin created a new vision of attracting more international students. Watching the international scene and the strong emergence of China, she visited that country twice and forged new agreements between several Chinese universities and the UW–Madison.

She continued to focus on strengthening the UW–Madison for future challenges. Recognizing that layers and layers of bureaucracy cost money, time, and resources, Chancellor Martin proposed that UW–Madison be granted some flexibilities that would allow for increased efficiency and reduced costs. She dubbed the idea the New Badger Partnership (NBP) and outlined the basic concept at a Chancellor's Cabinet meeting in September of 2009. We were all intrigued and knew that if anyone could get flexibility from the state, Chancellor Martin was the person to do so.

Early in 2010, the state's political season began in earnest. The chancellor met with all three gubernatorial candidates from each of the two major parties. After the primary, she continued to meet with the lead candidates Tom Barrett (Democrat) and Scott Walker (Republican). Because she had spent significant time with each of the candidates, she knew when Scott Walker won, he would be open to giving UW–Madison more flexibility. As time went on, the UW System too began talking about greater flexibilities. In fact, the concept of the public authority model for the entire UW System was introduced into discussions. The Governor, however, modified the idea and decided to only suggest public authority for UW–Madison.

For the UW System to have its flagship campus "break away" was in the regents' view, catastrophic. UW–Madison brings in $1 billion of research dollars to the state each year. By comparison, the next closest University in terms of research funding is

UW-Milwaukee, which brings in $60 million. The system President and many of the regents were adamant about keeping UW–Madison in the fold. Conversely there were others at UW–Madison who believed that the University must break free in order to survive in the competitive world of higher education. A public showdown, so to speak, was scheduled for February 25, 2011.

In taking a bit of a break from the discussion about the regents meeting, I returned to planning for my first meeting with the Chief of Staff to the Governor, Keith Gilkes. Then, a little while later, with Kevin in tow, I headed off to the meeting. The State Patrol Superintendent, the Sheriff, the Administrator of DCI, Chief Tubbs, DC Blackdeer, and I represented law enforcement in this meeting. Also attending were General Dunbar, the Sergeants-at-Arms for the Senate, Ted Blazel, and Assembly Anne Tonnan Byers; Senate Chief Clerk Rob Marchant; Assembly Clerk Patrick Fuller; John Hogan, Chief of Staff to Senate Majority Leader Scott Fitzgerald, along with a handful of others. Keith Gilkes arrived a few minutes late and took a place at the head of the table. He was pleasant in his opening remarks, but didn't bother with introductions. We had hoped a representative from DOA would be present; however, that didn't occur.

I handed out the agenda I had prepared earlier. We reviewed the scope of operation for the Interior Branch. We went over life safety issues first and then discussed property issues, along with the coordination of all activities in the two houses of the Legislature, the Executive Branch, and the Supreme Court.

I discussed the Incident Action Plans and the tactical plans we had been working on since Friday, Day 5. At that time, the CP Planning Section appeared to be in disarray so in just two days, the Interior Branch created or improved upon escort plans, capacity management, evacuation, tunnel security, mass arrest, civil disturbance, fire response, EOD bomb and canine response. Catastrophic planning for the interior and exterior of the Capitol was underway. We reported that the Interior Branch had created a mission statement that Randy, Brian, and I felt was vital to forming a team from the disparate agencies that were sending staff to assist us.

WELCOME TO THE INTERIOR BRANCH

This Branch was established on February 17, 2011 at 3 p.m. Since that time we have attempted to operate by the Mission, Values and Strategies outlined below:

Our Mission:
Working as a team, using the principles of community policing, the mission of the Interior Branch is to maintain a safe environment for everyone entering the Capitol, allowing citizens to exercise their Constitutional rights and our government to continue to operate, through our law enforcement and community policing presence. We will utilize commonly accepted strategies and tactics of crowd management, demonstrate a respect for everyone, demonstrate fidelity to the U.S. and Wisconsin Constitutions and employ safe and sound law enforcement practices.

Our Values:
In order to achieve our mission we believe we must model the following core values:

- *Professionalism at all times*
- *Respect for everyone*
- *Integrity; leadership by example*

- *Dedication to duty*
- *Enthusiasm for the mission*

Our Strategies:
To the extent possible, we will work collaboratively with others to achieve our mission. We will be firm and fair, giving people clear and fair warning so they understand the choices they are making and the consequences of their decisions.

Command Post Logistics had yet to find us an offsite briefing location for the next morning. I made it clear that this was an unacceptable level of performance. I reviewed the crowd monitoring and management efforts and discussed the overcrowding of the previous week and the fact that it could not continue. Everyone agreed. I also described how I had established a capacity number based on measurements and what I believed to be reasonable safety levels. Again there was agreement. I did not share any of my numbers. Keith said he preferred I manage to the number I had established, but asked that I not share the number with this group or anyone else as he preferred that the numbers not become political. I agreed with his request.

I then turned to my remaining concerns. We needed to continue to meet the staffing levels each day. This meant that EPS must begin a reimbursement process so the chiefs and sheriffs would know their budgets would not be depleted. Sheriff Mahoney spoke up and talked everyone through the process.

Chief of Staff Keith Gilkes agreed to discuss some sort of Memorandum of Understanding that towns, villages, cities, and counties could sign with the state to recover costs. I wondered why the mutual aide statutes were not being invoked. We needed hotel support because some officers were traveling considerable dis-tances and could not be expected to "commute." Essentially we laid everything out for the Governor's Chief of Staff as I had for Senator Fitzgerald on Friday. I was concerned about the support of our staff. We had to ensure that the staff working in all these different roles knew they were supported in what they were doing, and the level of second guessing going on by the political appointees and politicians was taking its toll.

Our people were growing tired. Chief Tubbs, for example, had not had a day off since early February, so we needed to have a master "tap-out" schedule. Charles admitted he was tired, but kept saying he was fine. Having lived through long stretches of disaster or demonstration work several times in my career, I had noted that sometimes the only one who thinks the leader is fine is the leader. Almost everyone else can see through the façade.

Chief Tubbs might have had the authority to carry out directives from his political bosses, but unless he could do it all with his small staff of Capitol Police officers, he really didn't have the ability to carry out the assignment. He had a lot of adjustments to make under mounting pressure. This made for an interesting dynamic to work around. Charles was trying so hard to be a strong leader. Yet what he didn't realize was how many people were working around him instead of with him. In the structure of Incident Command, there is supposed to be civilian oversight at the policy level. However, it was unclear to me if the Governor and his Cabinet had ever been exposed to Incident Command, the National Incident Management Systems, or the National Response Plan. The Administration was so new it was unlikely they had been trained.

I also wondered why the Secretary of the Department of Administration (DOA) wasn't meeting with us. It was the Secretary of DOA who was responsible for the Capitol and all state buildings. While I liked and respected COS Keith Gilkes and his style, I was mindful he was a political operative who had worked in politics since his graduation from UW–Madison. His being in charge of the group made things feel more political.

Speaking of politics, my final concern that needed to be addressed with COS Gilkes bordered on the politically dangerous. I decided to go ahead. I asked him who was calling the shots. I wanted to know who was behind the directives to close and evacuate the Capitol. I wanted to understand the overall goal from the Chief of Staff's perspective and the Secretary of DOA's perspective. My questions hung in the air.

Keith Gilkes took a long breath and said that he thought that Incident Commander Dan Blackdeer was in charge of the police and the response. He noted that the overall policy had to be an executive function. I pushed back, asking how he saw that working. I wanted to know exactly what he meant. How often did he and Dan coordinate? When had Dan last spoken to the Secretary of DOA?

Across the table, I sensed that General Dunbar understood what I was trying to get at. Keith, on the other hand, seemed to think there were a number of larger issues that wouldn't be resolved today. Keith was a political animal and even though his COS role was just six weeks old, running campaigns was not new to him. Everything had a political angle.

Chief Tubbs had not been attending the two daily CP briefings, so it was at the Policy Group meeting that we first learned that Charles had been meeting every day with union leaders, talking over their plans for demonstrations, rallies, and marches. Charles, it appeared, had built a solid relationship with all the groups who were in opposition to the Governor's position. This kind of relationship building and overall information was pivotal in the success of all law enforcement agencies. However, it was unclear, and would remain so, what the police, via Charles, were receiving from the talks with the union in terms of re-establishing order.

We all turned our attention to the Governor's Budget Address scheduled for the next day. The Supreme Court would be in session, as would the Assembly and the Senate (although there was doubt as to whether the Democratic senators would return.) The unions were making another big push to generate large crowds. The Interior Branch was expecting around 500 police officers. This was the largest number of officers to date. Keith shared that the Governor's address might be postponed a week given the current situation. We had heard the Governor may even hold it off site, but that plan had been quickly abandoned.

Keith proposed we all meet every day at 1:00 p.m. at this location to go over policy questions. He agreed there should be no more surprises. Finally, I thought I had gotten what I had come for: access to the policy-level decisions that were being made. Of course, I was mistaken in that assumption but I wouldn't know that until a week later.

At the CP briefing later that day, the MFD leadership suggested the Interior Branch conduct a quick health screening for the Interior Branch commanders. I had never seen a police operation do this before, but then again, I had never been in a prolonged situation like this one. I supported the idea, knowing of the stress everyone was under. Paramedics began to come to the Operations Room to check our vital signs—pulses and blood pressures—and ask some general screening questions. Because they felt they could not share specifics about their "patients" with me, they agreed to give me colors: Green = good to go; Yellow = caution, needs to make adjustments; or Red = time to stop work and de-stress. The color was based on the individual's medical history shared with the paramedics and on the person's screening numbers.

We made this check mandatory for anyone who had worked four or more days straight, and available for any others who might want to be checked.

In our initial check, my health checked out as a solid green, while one of the folks in the Interior Branch Operations Room was "red" and two coded at "yellow." It was now my job to sit with each of them and talk through sending the "red" home and changing something so that the "yellows" would drop to green. Of course, no one wanted to go home. The individual in the "red" category hadn't had a day off in more than two weeks. He reluctantly left and scheduled the next day off.

My assistant Kevin suggested that as a result of the health checks, we should change up the kind of food we were all eating. Day after day of eating pizza and subs was obviously taking its toll. Kevin also noted that we needed to reduce our soda intake and increase our water consumption. More fresh fruit and a nutritious hot meal would be better for everyone.

After the 4:00 p.m. Command Post Briefing, we were still unclear where the offsite briefing would occur the next morning. DNR Chief Warden Randy Stark had a team of folks waiting all day to set up the briefing location the minute it was established. Moving 500 police into an area from all over the state and getting them organized and mission-focused were critical if we were going to be successful.

The DNR staff had important and relevant experience with logistics and support of wild land fires. In bringing those fires under control, they brought in staff from all over the state and in some cases, the entire country. The DNR had to account for them, ensure they understood the mission, had the proper equipment, proper supervision and leadership. All of this was not only important—it saved lives. The DNR staff had systems in place they could use in this Capitol setting that had been tried and worked well in locations and situations that were far more dangerous and chaotic.

Just after 5:00 p.m., we were told by the CP that we would use the Marriott Hotel in Middleton (about 7 miles west of the Capitol Square) for staging and briefing. It was a great site with parking and a lot of room; however, it was a 20-minute drive by bus to the Capitol. We would have to factor in an additional ten minutes for loading and unloading. We were going to need several buses and police escort vehicles. The DNR team excelled at this type of work. We set staging (check in) for 5:45 a.m., briefing at 6:00 a.m., with transports to begin at 6:30.

At 7:00 p.m. that evening, University Police Lieutenant Mark Silbernagel reported for the evening shift. Mark was a recently appointed lieutenant and was wise beyond his direct experience. His temperament is perfect for a leader—unflappable. He is also kind and a fantastic listener. For Mark to come in that evening and take over the reins from the CPD sergeants who had been bearing most of the overnight load was appreciated by all, especially me. With Mark there, I knew the Capitol Police would be supported, the protesters would be well served, and I would sleep easier and also stay "green."

With the operations turned over to Mark, we could concentrate on ensuring all of the needs of the next day would be met. We were still working late in to the night when word came that the Governor's budget address would be postponed until March 1, 2011, giving us another week to prepare. It also brought with it the realization that we were going to be here even longer. I had hoped to return to the University by February 23. That clearly wasn't going to happen.

Protesters marching up State Street to the Capitol. (Photo by Joe Lynde)

Crowds in the snow (Photo by Joe Lynde)

Officers from various agencies observe the crowd in the Rotunda. on the With the snow outside, the crowds were smaller on Sunday. (February 20, 2011) (Photo by Mark Golbach)

CHAPTER FOUR

THIS IS WHAT DEMOCRACY
LOOKS LIKE

THE CHIEFS MAY HAVE BEEN BUILDING ON 20 YEARS OF SHARED history, but the officers they oversaw began their day with barely twenty minutes together. During the height of the protests, the Interior Branch took responsibility for daily briefings for up to 500 visiting officers who would be providing security for the next 12-hour shift. The makeup of any particular group of officers varied from day to day. Some folks were able to serve multiple shifts, while others were with us for just one day. With their common bond being law enforcement, this group of strangers came together as a team. Within a half hour, each team learned its purpose, its protocols, and where the bathrooms were located! While these teams worked their "beat" inside the Capitol, the Interior Branch, the Command Post, and the Policy Group were working toward a shared understanding of the overall goal of this mission.

An effort to facilitate participation in democracy and allow people to exercise their Constitutional rights was competing with a more practical desire to "get the building back under control" and return some sense of normal government operations. The hands-off approach made returning to normal difficult to achieve. Try as we might to plan for the days ahead, a series of unexpected developments, including a prank phone call, and a strange ploy by the Senate to lure back the "missing" senators, kept us busy in the midst of Week 2.

DAY 9: TUESDAY, FEBRUARY 22, 2011

FEBRUARY 22 WAS SCHEDULED TO BE A BIG DAY. WHILE I WAS EXCITED TO be a part of it, I didn't exactly leap out of bed at 4:00 a.m. Running on about three hours sleep does not place me in my best form. We slogged through the snow to get to the morning meeting at the Marriott. The team from the Department of Natural Resources (DNR) had done a fantastic job getting the space ready. They had sign-in tables set up for officers, deputies, and troopers as they entered and had organized the ballroom into several seating sections. Each section corresponded to an assignment within the Capitol, and each area was properly labeled so people knew where to report. The sections each had the exact number of chairs to correspond to the number needed in the assignment. All of the supervisors, regardless of jurisdiction, were seated closest to the stage.

The Interior Branch Operations staff had compiled a Power-Point presentation to standardize the briefing information. All post assignment cards were divided into the various working groups and given to the correct supervisors. Gear was organized and stowed.

The first hiccup of the day came when Randy let me know that we only had half the buses we needed. Fortunately, he was already whipping up a two-staged transportation plan. I briefed the police escort officers about the need to make the seven-mile trip to the Capitol with full buses, then make a quick and efficient return trip to do it all over again.

Chief Tubbs appeared with his usual infectious spirit and warmth. While he was bearing much of the weight of the operation on his shoulders, you wouldn't know it from his affect, nor would any of the officers in the briefing suspect that Charles was also dealing with a family emergency. He and I shared a quick moment talking about his family concerns and then turned our attention to the work at hand.

The briefing began as I introduced Charles. His brief remarks were heartfelt; he encouraged the officers to recognize the historic nature of what was happening and made sure everyone knew about the unparalleled cooperation of the crowds. The attention of the nation had been drawn to Wisconsin, and everyone present had a role in ensuring that this protest continued to be peaceful. With the officers inspired about the significance of this work, I ran through the briefing PowerPoint.

There were 500 police officers, troopers, and deputies in the room. There was activity but very little noise. It was early in the day and the officers had many unanswered questions about what they would be doing. I had 30 minutes to take them from disparate strangers to a unified team. We needed to form different units that would act cohesively and not overreact or under-react to whatever might come their way.

As I looked out over the crowd of cops, I realized some were alone, just a single individual from a small agency, while others had come in groups from their county or municipality. The officers had come with whatever equipment they had thought to bring. Most had radios; some had clothing appropriate for outdoor duty; a few had tactical gear. They had brought an array of guns, Tasers, pepper spray, batons, and a multiplicity of protocols for using these items. Some had driven half the night to arrive in Madison for their shift at the Capitol, often after working a full day in their home jurisdictions. A surprising number had never visited Madison or the Capitol before, and only a few were familiar with the mazelike hallways of the building. Many of the out-of-town officers came from jurisdictions with lesser populations than the number of people they would see in the Capitol's Rotunda. I gave them what direction I could, and left the rest to their good judgment and the oversight of the supervisors. Typical of one of my talks, it ran a few minutes long. Randy was getting nervous about the time and the transport issues.

I turned the podium over to Randy to begin the complicated process of transporting the officers to their posts in the Capitol, which went very well. In less than five minutes after the end of the briefing, the first group was out the door of the hotel and on their way to the Capitol. The next group was organized and lined up for buses.

Arriving at the Capitol a little before 7 a.m., I saw more evidence of the DNR's thoroughness. Randy's staff had been busy getting signage up from the drop-off point through a series of tunnels into the Capitol and through the maze that was the Capitol basement. Without the signs, the chance of a police officer, deputy, or trooper getting lost en route was high. There was so much about this event that we couldn't predict; it felt good to have some basics like signage under control.

University Police AC Brian Bridges was busy at work by the time I reached 400 NE. He hadn't attended the massive briefing at the Marriott, but instead, had gone straight to the Capitol to run the Interior Branch. I received an update from him on the developments overnight.

Over the past week, the number of people sleeping overnight had averaged around 510; last night's tally was 762. There was one person who needed to go to the detoxification center due to incapacitation from alcohol. We had seen an increase in homeless people with no permanent address, or "NPAs, " taking part in the sleepover. In some cases, the homeless were mixing well with the protesters, in other cases they were not. There were no immediate threats, but it was a tonal shift we wanted to keep a close watch on. Some individuals about whom we had concerns or had previously made threats had now returned to the Capitol overnight. They had not acted out.

Around 8:00 that morning, Charles called to let me know he needed to leave for a while to deal with his family emergency. The extended nature of these work hours was taking a toll on everyone. We were on Day 9 with no end in sight. Life was happening beyond the Capitol and our families and departments needed us. In Charles' case, the need was acute and urgent. We told him to take whatever time he needed.

We began our now-routine morning Interior Branch meeting with the division commanders and turned from the overnight update to what we needed to watch during the day. The number and size of the mattresses (king and queen), along with an even larger supply of inflatable mattresses being brought into the Capitol was, in my view, getting unreasonable and unsafe. I certainly could not blame folks for wanting to sleep on a mattress; the marble was cold and hard, yet I worried about the fire and evacuation hazard the mattresses presented. We decided to place "mattresses" on our agenda for the CP briefing at 10:00.

The challenges kept coming. Restroom signage was not a class taught at the Police Academy! The mazelike quality of the Capitol made finding restrooms difficult even on a normal day and with all the enhanced security, it made finding a restroom near impossible. So we had requested men's and women's restroom signs that we could post around the building for folks to find proper and sanitary relief.

All we wanted were 8½ x 11 pieces of paper printed with "MEN'S RESTROOM" and "WOMEN'S RESTROOM"—directional signs with arrows, nothing fancy. When the signs arrived five days after they were ordered, they were quickly posted with blue painter's tape.

The division commanders and I added another capability to our response protocol in the form of the Police Extraction Response Unit (PERU) of the University Police. PERU is the only unit of its kind in the state. Comprised of sworn and non-sworn members of University Police, the unit is trained to extract protesters without harming them from secured devices such as bike locks, quick-set cement, and sleeping dragons.[13] While we had no intelligence or information that the protesters would engage in such activities, it was good to have PERU on scene with their equipment if we needed them.

The Interior Branch group ran through our list of known activities and events for the day. At 9:00 a.m., the Governor would be holding a cabinet meeting in his conference room. The press conferences were yet another opportunity for the crowd to disrupt things by jamming the entrance hallway to the Governor's office suites. Simultaneously, Assembly Republicans were scheduled to caucus in the Grand Army of the Republic (GAR) room on the 4th floor. At 10:30, state corrections officers, along with a band, would march around the Capitol Square. Also at 10:30, the teaching assistants and others would start their all-day "teach out" by walking to the Capitol via State Street.

The Republicans needed an escort from the GAR room at 11:00 to the Assembly floor where they would go into session. At the same time, the Senate would go into session, still without the fourteen Democratic senators.

---

[13] A "sleeping dragon" is a set of handcuffs strung through the middle of a PVC pipe and then used to connect multiple protesters; the pipe prevents the handcuffs from simply being sheared off with bolt cutters, making the extraction of pro-testers more difficult and time-consuming.

The teachers' union, WEAC, was going to rally at the State Street side of the building at noon and 5:00 p.m. There was a hearing scheduled at 1:00 p.m. on a bill requiring citizens to present photographic identification to be allowed to vote. It was contentious and the first meeting where we provided metal screening services.

Staff and Republican legislators had become increasingly concerned with their security. There had been several instances in which protesters had encroached on personal space. In some situations, physical contact had been made. No one had been injured, yet there was an uneasiness that was palpable. There were ever-increasing requests for legislative escorts throughout the building. The amount of "in your face" antics increased and I was concerned we should do more for the average staffer, but with the crowd size, that wasn't always possible.

As part of the University Response Plan, campus leaders use an Action List, or "AL" for short, to keep us organized during complicated incidents. ALs allow us to track assignments, establish deadlines, and schedule check-in times for progress reports. We felt that it was time to put an AL in place for the Interior Branch. Carol Gosenheimer, a key member of our planning team, had joined the Interior Branch the day before and had taken yesterday to size things up. She completed an AL and updated everyone on where we were to date and on next steps. Carol's first AL listed 67 items needing action. With Carol organizing things, nothing would fall through the cracks. The AL made a nice organized agenda for me to use for the 10:00 CP briefing.

The Interior Branch conferred with the CP via speaker phone. An attempt was made to connect us via video conferencing but the closest hook up was six floors down in the Capitol Police headquarters. We praised the Logistic section's work on the choice of the Marriott West as our briefing location, although we knew it was only available for a few days. We asked that the CP find a new briefing location soon and not wait until our time was up at the Marriott. Once again, CP Logistics explained how difficult it was to get contracts via the state process. They were hoping to expedite things via the DOA Secretary's office.

The Interior Branch directors and command staffs were concerned about the need to conduct metal screening in various locations simultaneously because of the difficulty in sustaining that capability for a long period of time, given that just UW Police were trained in screening. The division commanders recommended training more law enforcement officers in the screening process.

We had word the Assembly would begin at 11:00 and probably go through the night, which potentially meant more screening as the building had to remain "open." Everyone, including the Assembly sergeant-at-arms assumed was that the Assembly would eventually go on for one night and into the first half of the next day.

We asked about the plan for finding local hotels for police coming from out of town. We learned that Incident Commander DC Dan Blackdeer's state credit card, along with his assistant's credit card, were "maxed out" and weren't being accepted at area hotels or at the office supply stores. After the briefing, I checked with University Police Captain Michael Newton to see if our University emergency credit card was available through the University Response Plan. If push came to shove, we could use that card with its $1 million limit, but I hoped the CP would straighten out the purchasing issue soon with DOA. With that, we ended the call with the CP.

In the Interior Branch, we had created plans for seemingly every contingency, yet there hadn't been time to share our plans with the division commanders. We knew it was time to have a "what would we do if … ?" discussion. We walked through a handful of God-awful scenarios such as a bomb detonation, finding a

Day 9: February 22, 2011. The Interior Branch reviewing the Action List. (Photo by David LaWall)

Interior Branch Deputy Director Brian Bridges talks with Capitol Facility Manager, Ron Blair. (February 22, 2011) (Photo by David LaWall)

suspicious device, a shooting or a mass casualty shooter, a hostage situation, and an orderly and non-orderly evacuation.

We also considered the impact of significant property damage, fire, an anarchist action, and a wholesale blocking of entrance ways or evacuation routes. We talked all the scenarios through until we felt confident that with this many police inside the Capitol, we knew how each would be handled. Because officers had come in from all over the state, it was critical to have the supervisors on the same page. We genuinely believed that the high number of law enforcement officers would deter people from acting out in any one of these ways.

Reports came in that said workers from all the unions on campus were having open discussions about how "rolling" strikes might be implemented in an effort to highlight the importance of workers without crippling the institution. Fortunately, folks back on campus seemed to have things under control, and I turned my attention back to the Capitol.

It was usual to receive reports of missing children and parents. (We figured if we had the child, it was the parents who were missing.) Periodically, I would leave the Interior Branch Operations Room and walk throughout the building to stay in touch with crowd size and demeanor. The noise of the drumming and public mic was constant and reverberated off the marble. I moved through the building, talking to people and officers on every floor. I was usually recognized in my traditional navy-blue police uniform.

Something in the mood of the crowd had shifted. The drumming had stopped and quiet haunted the staircases. I couldn't remember the Capitol during the day without the drumming and chanting. Someone had seemingly pulled the plug on this First Amendment stereo system. The silence was deafening—and then the entire crowd of thousands began singing the national anthem. (This incredible event can be viewed on YouTube, February 16 and 17, 2011.)

I looked over the railing near where I was standing. No one was moving. Hats had been removed, many had their hands placed over their hearts. It was incredibly moving. This is what democracy looks like. My emotions swelled and I felt that tell-tale lump in my throat. There is always something very stirring in seeing and hearing a group of Americans singing our national anthem. I had been so caught up in thousands of swirling details, yet for just the few moments of song, I was reminded how precious our form of government continues to be. The First Amendment was on complete display all around me. I was experiencing what it means to have the freedom to speak, to peaceably assemble, and to petition the government for a redress of grievances.

From the land of the free and the home of the brave transitioning to policy and procedures was a little easier now. It was time to head to the Policy Group meeting in the basement. There were some new additions to the group: Jodi Jensen from DOA Secretary's office and taking the place of Superintendent Fitzgerald was WSP Major Darren Price. Once again, past relationships helped. Darren and I had known each other for at least a decade and we often saw eye to eye on things. All other members of the Policy Group, except for the Assembly Clerk, were present.

We talked at length about people sleeping in the Capitol and the fact that the numbers were increasing. I expressed wanting to use a soft-sell approach to limit the size of mattresses to smaller than king size, beginning that night. That received a chuckle and in a "you had to be there" moment, we shared a quiet laugh about the Capitol not being designed as a hotel.

In addition to the 762 some sleepers from the previous night, we knew there was another group over whom we had less control; the people who had been allowed to stay in representatives' and senators' offices overnight. We had made no effort to count those folks because they had permission to stay, but they were nonetheless contributing to the overnight population of the building. Chief Senate Clerk Rob Marchant asked how to make the situation better for us.

Quickly I explained that while we understood that late-night sessions and proceedings occasionally require a representative, senator, or members of their staff to stay and sleep overnight, having non-staff staying in those offices was problematic in getting the building back under control. Representatives and senators were currently giving people permission to stay overnight in their offices, regardless of whether either house was in session. Rob said he would work with Assembly Clerk Patrick Fuller and talk to the majority leaders of both houses to see what could be done about the office sleepovers.

John Hogan from Senator Fitzgerald's office was present and seemed in agreement. We suggested that if they could change the rule, we would like it to go into effect Saturday night, February 26. Chief Tubbs stated he would talk to the union leaders about this potential change so it wouldn't come as a surprise.

Next we discussed the alcohol intoxication issues. I wanted to ban alcohol coming into the building, as it served no democratic purpose and had the potential to create additional problems when we already had our hands full. Everyone agreed to the ban and if we saw any alcohol with those already in the building, we should ask for it to be removed.

The officers would be instructed to use a soft-sell approach tonight. I felt strongly that an abrupt change to any of our enforcement protocols would likely work against our goal of compliance. Chief Tubbs added the alcohol ban to his list of what he needed to talk with union leaders about. He thought that the leaders were likely to welcome this change, as many of their members were concerned about intoxicated people coming into the building to sleep who weren't members of the protest group.

We turned to issues still needing resolution such as wage reimbursement and hotel stays. Sheriff Mahoney led the discussion and Jodi Jensen from DOA stated the matter was being worked on in the Secretary's office. We all welcomed that development and moved on to the final topic of the meeting.

News was that the Wisconsin Law Enforcement Association (WLEA), which represented the State Patrol, UW Police, and the Capitol Police, was going to participate in two rallies on Thursday at the Capitol. They would be partnering with members of municipal police associations. The WLEA officers were asking their members not to wear any specific agency attire (unlike Corrections or those in the fire service, who regularly wore their uniforms or attire designating their department when they participated in the protest).

These rallies were interesting from a few different angles. Would the off-duty police officers be armed? By law, they had the right to carry their weapons concealed.

We were not concerned with an officer acting out; rather, our concern was with protesters who were not law enforcement who might be alarmed by the sight of a weapon. What would happen if the protesting police had to face off against fellow police officers, deputies, and troopers who would be working at the Capitol?

Since some officers were not keeping their benefits, the tension between the Capitol Police and University Police toward the parent union of WLEA was significant. After a thorough discussion, we thought it best to reach out informally to the police unions and talk this through with them.

Meanwhile, the situation in Wisconsin had spread throughout the country. In Indiana, Democratic legislators refused to show up at their statehouse, temporarily blocking a Republican-backed labor bill. In Ohio, protesters descended on the State Capitol in opposition to a bill put forward by Republican lawmakers that would restrict collective bargaining rights for public employees. In New Jersey, the Republican governor was deciding to link property tax relief to sharp increases in government workers' payments for health insurance. Throngs of union supporters shut down the Massachu-setts Statehouse on Tuesday to show their solidarity with public employees in Wisconsin.

The rest of the afternoon held more of what was now considered our normal updates, trouble-shooting, and reviewing plans. Health checks were now expanded to all the officers and were working well. When health issues were discovered, staffing changes were made. We closed out the day with a quick CP check-in at 4:00 and then one last check-in with the Interior Branch at 5:30.

We were set for the demobilization of 500 officers; it would be our largest one to date and we were about to limit alcohol and king-sized mattresses. Now that we had capacity management in place, we had a better sense of our resource needs. We were in good shape and had decided to reduce the number of police we would need for the coming days because the school districts would be open starting tomorrow and the budget address had been postponed until March 1.

It had been a busy operational day in the Interior Branch, with approximately 40,740 visitors to the Capitol. We even managed to facilitate "Superior Days," in which the residents of the City of Superior, Wisconsin, visited the Capitol to inform and lobby for things their city needed from the state government. Tomorrow we would start to plan for returning to our normal jobs and for normal operating hours at the Capitol.

DAY 10: WEDNESDAY, FEBRUARY 23, 2011

EVIDENTLY AT ABOUT 3:00 A.M., WHILE I WAS HOME SLEEPING, REPORTER Judith Davidoff of the *Capital Times* newspaper, posted a story about the Koch brothers opening a lobbying office at 10 East Doty Street in downtown Madison, just a block off the Capitol Square.

When I had gone to bed, I didn't know who the Koch brothers were, but I would soon learn. These wealthy brothers were linked to Americans for Prosperity, which had organized the Tea Party rally the previous Saturday, and had made sizable campaign contributions to gubernatorial candidate, and now Governor, Scott Walker. If I didn't yet understand the significance of those contributions, the implications became clearer as I read on. Davidoff noted that: "The expanded lobbying effort by the Koch brothers in Wisconsin raises red flags in particular because of the little discussed provision in Walker's Budget Repair Bill that would allow Koch Industries and other private companies to purchase state-owned power plants in no-bid contracts." At least one of those power plants was located on the UW–Madison campus.

Chief Warden Randy Stark and his staff began their day at the Marriott with the full officer briefing at 6:00. Brian and I headed to the Capitol at 6:15. We arrived to be briefed by UW Lieutenant Mark Silbernagel. Overnight there had been 421 sleepers, down significantly from the night before. The Assembly had continued throughout the night and as we spoke, was still in session. There had been one event in the gallery and the person had been removed without incident.

In the relative quiet of the overnight shift, Lieutenant Silbernagel had time to reassess our resource deployment. Mark felt that we could consider letting some of the troopers and police demobilize by 3:00 a.m. because issues, calls, and service needs grew fewer and fewer as people settled down to sleep. We agreed that if we could get by with fewer officers working fewer hours, by all means, we should do so. I let the CP and WSP Lieutenant Brad Altman know.

In spite of the new alcohol policy, overnight there had been another person, an NPA, who had to go to detox. Mark noted an increase in the number of NPAs compared to the number of protesters staying overnight. Several folks had commented to the police throughout the night that the NPAs were getting more aggressive and had been "eyeing" people's belongings. Unfortunately, many NPAs also had a noticeable and very pungent body odor.

While the protesters respected the NPAs' right to be in the Capitol, some were leery of the behavior, stench, and the volatility some of them demonstrated on a regular basis. A few of the homeless periodically lost control of their bodily functions and left human waste in a few hallways. The building custodians attempted to stay on top of this, but occasionally the waste cleanup was delayed. Some in the media and some politicians linked the "lifestyle" of the homeless to the protesters, but the police respected the differences and did what they could to distinguish the two groups and their respective needs.

In sharp contrast, the protesters who remained overnight had regular cleanup activities—they collected trash, washed floors, and organized the various tables of food, literature, and medical supplies. The protesters never relieved themselves outside of a bathroom. They paid attention to requests from us or the marshals. They made agreements with the custodial staff on how best to stay on top of their new living conditions. They took their chant seriously: this was their house.

In the often bewildering days that month, it became all too easy for some in the media or in politics to oversimplify the situation in an attempt to divide people into camps or groups. They were trying to make sense of what was happening and why. Law enforcement needed to avoid the trap of "us versus them," lest we misunderstand the very circumstances we were trying to manage.

We set our Interior Branch division commander check-in for 8:30 a.m. We welcomed Sarah Pfatteicher to the Interior Branch today. Sarah was another leader of the planning group within the University Response Plan. As an expert in emergency management and disaster recovery, she teamed up with Carol Gossenheimer and Kevin Wernet to keep us on task and provided necessary back-up to Carol and Kevin.

Chief Warden Randy Stark's ability to adapt to things on the fly was proving invaluable. It seemed he had a few staff shortages but would shift resources as soon as the check-in briefing was over.

The protests were unprecedented, newsworthy, and historic. Nevertheless, the next 12 hours of my life would be filled with the minutiae of parking arrangements, coffee shortages, and organizational charts. As Day 10 got underway, the activities of everyone working in 400 NE had begun to shift from fast-paced planning and reacting to an occasional thought toward the future.

With a week and a half of experience under our belts, we had naturally begun to establish routines enabling us to do more planning. Major briefings for incoming officers and deputies were held at 6:00 in the morning and at 6:00 at night. The officers were on 13.5-hour shifts. Command officers' shifts were 6:00 a.m. to 10:00 p.m. The commanders had begun each day by sketching a draft agenda for our 16-hour shift, so by Day 10 it was clear that the outline of that agenda was settling into a pattern: Command briefings and meetings at 6:30, 7:00, 8:30, 10:00, 1:00, 4:00, and 5:30, interspersed with establishing staffing plans for the following night and day.

With this growing knowledge, the personnel in 400 NE could plan for the day's briefings even before seeing the agenda posted on the wall. We knew we would be in place until at least March 3.

What had been manageable in the short term now had to become sustainable for a much longer haul. We needed a more varied and healthful meal plan. My aide Kevin had brought this up to the CP several times before. Personnel who had been working since this all began would need time off and within the Interior Branch itself, we needed tap-out schedules for everyone from clerical staff to the commanders.

DNR Assistant Chief Karl Brooks began this scheduling process. We also knew that it was important to document everything in case any one of us had to be replaced: plans, org charts, meeting schedules and agendas. Karl would lead this effort with support from University Police ESC Dave LaWall and Bill Curtis. Kevin Wernet had compiled a handbook of templates of the various job tasks and responsibilities. It was personally very rewarding to see everyone pitch in to get these jobs done.

Our purpose in the Capitol had begun to gel. When we first arrived, it was with a vague mission around providing for safety and security. By Day 10, we knew that the ultimate goal was to return the Capitol to a state of relative normalcy. Even as we settled into our routines, we were preparing to make ourselves irrelevant. Emergency workers and first responders always work to secure the immediate situation and to support a return to normal (even if it's a new normal)—in short, we work ourselves out of a job and prepare ourselves for whatever is next.

In the midst of the ever-changing situation at the Capitol, it was hard to grasp that we were here to facilitate getting this all back to normal. Knowing the goal is not the same as knowing *how* to get there. Obviously, if the Capitol was to return to normal, sleeping in the building overnight would need to come to an end. Between the mundane details of my day, I would work to establish some consensus on how and when to clear the building and how to manage the building's capacity. We would take today to plan a return to normal operations on or about Sunday February 27, just four days away. In much the same way that we had begun the soft sell of no alcohol or king size mattresses, I requested we develop a step-by-step, gradual re-establishment of order.

In emergency operations, the Command Post is intended to be exactly that—the place where commands (as well as plans, logistics, and press releases) originate. But in this experience, the CP was becoming less and less relevant to our daily work. We had our own planning section and our own logistics section within 400 NE. I received my guidance and authority directly from the policy meetings every afternoon. The CP was becoming an unnecessary middleman. The challenge, of course, is that the CP didn't view the situation in the same fashion as the Interior Branch.

Regardless of whether the Assembly was still in session or not, we decided early that 77 cops would be sufficient to handle the night shift. There was no way for us to know if we would be short staffed, yet we were trying desperately to establish some regularity in our staffing numbers. We all speculated the Assembly would be finished by evening; after all, how could they continue for 36 continuous hours?

We settled on 235 police as our default daytime number for the Interior Branch, which we would draw from three sources: troopers, DNR, and EPS. We would not count the UW and the Capitol Police in the general numbers because they brought specialized training and skills, such as metal screening and knowledge of the building, that could not be readily provided through the other sources.

We knew that our staffing numbers were exceptionally high. Unfortunately, in order to be prepared for the unexpected, we had to have sufficient staff available. Since the next political move was rarely ever shared in advance and the political rancor had been high, both sides were unwilling to share their thinking and plans with us. In the end, the state taxpayer paid the price for the government's dysfunction—a dysfunction that caused us to have to constantly scramble in reaction to political arguments.

Our staffing levels reflected a policy choice. After his last order to close the Capitol on Day 7, Chief Tubbs had changed his stance considerably. He kept stressing no arrests and no hands-on action by the officers. While good in theory, it meant a single trooper using only verbal commands when trying to keep people from passing through a 6-foot-wide opening could easily be ignored. Protesters quickly learned there would be no consequences for ignoring a verbal command of a police officer, deputy, or trooper. Officers often stopped the verbal commands altogether. Instead they decided to have two or three cops at each entrance. Protesters would have to force their way through, which didn't make for the ideal situation, but few protesters were willing to attempt such use of force. The no-arrest, no hands-on method merely resulted in the division commanders arguing that they needed double and triple the staff to successfully hold an area.

> *In law enforcement, it is best not to start what you cannot finish. Officers are trained and taught to start with their presence, and then give verbal commands. If necessary, they place a hand or two on someone to gain compliance, continuing to escalate only as necessary and as reasonable. Officers are likely to grow frustrated if all they have in their toolbox short of a felony arrest are verbal commands. They become increasing frustrated when those commands are ignored. This is not to say that everyone who fails to comply with a verbal command should be arrested, rather allowing an officer to reach out to take a hold of an arm and stop or redirect someone is likely to be sufficient. With the "no hands on" policy of Chief Charles Tubbs, even this mild form of*

enforcement, far short of arrest, was not available to the officers.

Flexibility is a key component of successful crowd management. There is a fine line between an early "surgical" arrest that nips bad behavior before it gains momentum, and an arrest that ignites a spark that turns a crowd against the police. This is more of an art than police science and it is necessary to think about it as a delicate matter.

An early surgical, well-communicated arrest, coupled with a clear directive and explanation will usually be successful. If on Day 1, the Command Post would have allowed troopers, deputies, and officers to stop certain behaviors early by stopping bedding, sound systems, large quantities of food from entering, we could have reduced unexpected chaos. Maintaining some structure and a sense of boundary is critical in managing crowds.

In the spectrum of enforcement from heavy-handed to hands-off, I felt we needed to be sensible where we maintained a high tolerance for crowd behaviors, but with surgical arrests as needed. By the time the Interior Branch was established on Day 4, all boundaries were gone. Now Charles wanted only voluntary compliance, which became an inflexible strategy.

Many staff in the Interior Branch Command had independently accomplished what needed to be done, yet as a group, we needed to know and understand what had been completed. Carol spent time going over the Action List (AL) and as of today, the majority of the 67 items were completed and of course, we added more items to the list. Our focus was on sustainability. In a big leap forward, Kevin reported fewer pizzas and subs and more box lunches with fruit!

I had my scheduled briefing with the CP on another threat to the Governor that Capitol PD and DCI would investigate. Although I appreciated the intelligence, I was only looking for general information that could be made open to everyone. A few days earlier, I had assigned one member of the Branch to scan websites, Twitter, Facebook, and the like, to learn what people were saying about the size and the mood of the crowd. I wanted to hear the most recent chatter about the rallies. I wasn't looking for anything illegal or nefarious; I just wanted information to keep up with the crowd. DCI said they could not collect information on non-criminal matters.

That was a key moment for me. There is a very large difference between intelligence and information. They are not the same.

All Americans have the right to engage in Constitutionally protected activities. How people go about exercising their Constitutional rights is certainly not something law enforcement should actively monitor and document. DCI used fusion centers and the center's activity was outlined in law (US Code of Federal Regulation 28, Part 23). The role of fusion centers during these protests was to keep us informed of threats and to assist in the investigation of those threats.

The type of information I was seeking from these other sources would help the Interior Branch maintain crowd management, prevent criminal activity, protect state dignitaries, protect the crowds themselves, aid in assessing the staffing needs for paramedics, firefighters and police and of course, protect the state Capitol building. I clarified my intentions with the CP and was freed to build the information apparatus within the Interior Branch.

We discussed at length what might happen if the Assembly passed the Budget Repair Bill. They were still in session with no end in sight. Yesterday, we had been told that they would probably finish by noon today. That didn't seem too realistic, given that they had to work their way through dozens of amendments introduced by the Democrats.

The Republicans had the majority in the Assembly, so it was believed by those "in the know" that the Bill would pass with few, if any, amendments. The Democrats were trying their best to stall the outcome. The Assembly galleries remained open without too much disruption or fuss.

The CP had arranged to have a bus on standby for Republican assembly members to get to their remote parking site after the final vote. It would take a phone call and a few minutes to put it in place. This, too, was an added expense. Although we stayed in close contact with Sergeant-at-Arms Anne Tonnon Byers, we couldn't imagine that the bus would be on standby for three and a half days.

Information was filtering in about a large sleepover tonight for corrections officers. The information seemed credible, and we thought we should get that information to Chief Tubbs to see if he knew anything more or could gather more from his contacts. Finding Chief Tubbs had not gotten a whole lot easier over the last ten days—and so the hunt was on.

It was time again for me to switch hats for an 11:30 a.m. teleconference call with my fellow University of Wisconsin Police chiefs. We normally have a monthly conference call, but because of the special circumstances, today was a special meeting. These twelve individuals ran full-service police departments at their respective campuses. UW–Madison is far larger than the other schools. For instance, UW-Milwaukee is the second largest campus, and is about half our size. In addition to my UW–Madison responsibilities, I have overall police policy responsibility for the UW System Administration, the Board of Regents, UW-Extension, and the thirteen UW colleges located around the state.

It is rare that we all are present on the conference calls, but all were present today. Not surprisingly, the first order of business were the ramifications of the Budget Repair Bill. Most of the chiefs thought the components of the Bill that didn't exempt our officers was unfair, though not all opposed ending collective bargaining. In the "fraternity" that is law enforcement, loyalty and mutual support are highly prized—on the job, our lives depend on it. Having someone outside of law enforcement trying to drive a wedge between two groups of police just riled our defenses.

The UW Regents meeting was scheduled to occur this Friday and given the importance of this meeting and the size of the crowds in Madison, we needed law enforcement staff from our system colleagues. All UW Police departments routinely provide mutual aid to one another, much as EPS does across the state. It was agreed that we would start the Regent detail at 8:00 Friday morning. Depending on distance, some campuses would send staff the night before. I had them coordinate all the staffing details with University Police Captain Karen Soley, Director of the University Branch.

After the conference call, I met with Captain Soley and heard her initial plan for Friday. Karen is so sharp and on top of things that her initial plan is often more detailed and complete than most other people's final plan. Today was no different. Karen laid out the floor plans, post assignments, resource needs, communication plan, meal plan, post rotation plan, transportation plan, and briefing schedule. The only thing left was to call the CP and make her resource requests.

I was going to be off work on Friday—my first day off in twelve—so more than anything, I was looking forward to sleeping past 5:00 in the morning! I would also be attending the Regents meeting to support Chancellor Martin and her shared vision of the New Badger Partnership (NBP). Although a number of people on campus had been privy to the Chancellor's NBP plans to propose a more independent operational footing for UW–Madison, the new twist of the Public Authority came as a surprise to many in the University.

For me to not work a day when the Board of Regents was meeting meant I had complete faith in my staff. It was so satisfying for me to see Karen take charge, develop all the plans, shoulder the responsibility, and just plain lead. I was very proud.

Following my meeting with Karen, I returned to the Interior Branch. Dave LaWall was working on logistics issues. For instance, we needed more earplugs to survive the incessant drumming. We needed things like sticky notes and tissues. The police break rooms had run out of coffee. Dave and I shared a laugh that on Day 10, Logistics at the CP appeared to be still struggling with acquiring simple supplies. Our momentary laugh ended abruptly when Kevin asked me to step outside with Captain Mike Newton. We went to "our" corner of the hallway and they told me the morning wellness checks had discovered a potentially serious health issue with AC Jerry Jansen. It seemed Jerry had gone from "green" status yesterday to "red" today. In fact, he was so "red" it was recommended by the paramedics that he be transported by ambulance to the hospital, but he had opted for a UW Police car instead and was already at the University Hospital Emergency Room.

I immediately tried to connect with Jerry via cell. He answered and it was good to hear his voice. The doctors were running some tests. They believed it was dehydration so they would be starting IVs and pushing fluids. There were some other serious concerns they were checking out as well. He had not yet talked to his wife, who was still in Arizona because he didn't want to worry her. He said he would call her from home once it was all sorted out.

Jerry's wife, Diana, is a friend of mine and the more I thought about it, the more I realized we were all very busy here, and no one could really watch out for Jerry or his needs appropriately. I asked an officer to stand watch and deny access to the 4th floor women's bathroom. I entered the bathroom for some privacy and called Diana. Very calmly, I told her what I knew. Diana is a practicing nurse and has spent most of her career in emergency medicine. I knew that she could handle the call without becoming overly emotional. She thanked me profusely and said she would check with her former medical colleagues at University Hospital, and then she would speak to Jerry. As the days passed, we learned that the simple wellness checks we were conducting had helped find a serious medical issue and saved Jerry's life.

The 1:00 policy meeting started in its usual fashion, covering events since the last time we met. There was a great deal to cover. The DOA Secretary's office had made substantial progress on the memorandum of understanding (MOU) for the EPS agencies to use. The MOU covered hotels, salaries, overtime, and mileage. There was discussion of how much all this was costing each day, as we had averaged over 200 police inside the Capitol for the 7:00 a.m. to 7:00 p.m. shift.

Incident Commander DC Dan Blackdeer raised the issue of two possible claims of workers' compensation that had already developed. Two officers had been injured: one had slipped on the marble steps and slightly injured an ankle, and another had cut his hand. Keith Gilkes and Jodi Jensen said they would check on workers' comp and report back to the CP. Again it struck me as odd that we simply weren't using the statutory language for mutual aid that was already available. The statute clarifies who pays for what and when, precisely so that conversations like these wouldn't be necessary in a time of emergency.

The DOA Secretary's Office shared a memorandum from Cari Anne Renlund, DOA Chief Legal Counsel, addressed to the Governor's Chief of Staff Keith Gilkes and DOA Secretary Mike Huebsch, and dated the day before, February 22, 2011. The memorandum was focused on restricting access to the State Capitol. It outlined clearly that DOA and the CPD had the authority to manage the building. In part, it stated:

> *DOA may prohibit any use of the building or grounds that:*
> 1. *Interferes with the prime use of the building or facility;*
> 2. *Unduly burdens the managing authority;*
> 3. *Is a hazard to the safety of the public or state employees,*
> 4. *Is detrimental to the building or facility; or*
> 5. *Exposes the state to the likelihood of expenses or damages that cannot be recovered.*
>
> *Based on this authority, DOA and the Capitol Police can evacuate the building and continue to limit its use while any problematic conditions, such as risks to public health and safety are remedied.*
>
> *In addition, DOA had the authority to require groups to obtain permits.*

At the bottom of her memo, she cited all the relevant statutes.

This was an important document for me to have. I was glad it was being shared at this meeting so we all would know exactly what we legally could and could not do. As noted earlier, I had taken measurements of floor space and exit capacity and established a capacity for the Capitol. It was reaffirming to know that our work on capacity was supported by statute. The Interior Branch would continue to manage using that number.

This document was helpful in another way. Within the memo, Ms. Renlund had mentioned that Deputy Secretary Cynthia Archer was concerned about the public health conditions inside the Capitol. In spite of the valiant efforts of the protesters and the Capitol cleaning crew, the building really needed a thorough cleaning. Many of the same folks had slept in the building since February 15.

A week after the protests had begun, we learned that DOA had legal authority to expel the protesters and close the building at the end of each day (as long as the Legislature wasn't in session). The issues were in how to exert that authority and how to achieve the agreed-upon goal of "normal operations."

The Governor's Chief of Staff, Keith Gilkes, was interested in returning the Capitol to "normal" by March 1, the new date of the Governor's budget address. He defined normal as safe, clean, and reasonably orderly. He explained the legislators were feeling intimidated and that the stench in certain parts of the building was unbearable. No one disagreed that normalcy would ultimately need to return. The debate was how and when to get there.

The Interior Branch had been targeting February 27 as a closing and clearing date. We would create a tactical plan to accomplish the goal. I explained to the Policy Group that I favored a scale-down, step-by-step approach. We would announce a day in advance what would be restricted the next day. Even though we didn't know what the complete plan would entail, we had already warned people about a ban on alcohol and king-sized mattresses.

I had decided we would not remove any of the items already in the building. Removing things might lead to an unnecessary escalation, so for now we would just stop certain items from coming in. Moving toward closure and clearing would require broad effective communication dissemination to the general public, in addition to the people within the Capitol.

While Charles would be the best person to share this informa-tion with the union leaders, he was not acting as a Public Informa-tion Officer for the entire event. I therefore renewed my request for a Public Information Officer (PIO) in the Interior Branch. The communications to date with the general public and with the protesters in particular were inadequate to the task of effectively communicating any scale-down, step-by-step plan. In compliance with our strategy of giving notice of any changes, we would have the police give friendly notice that tomorrow we would restrict queen-sized mattresses, cooking items, and additional tables.

Jodi, from DOA, was pleased to talk through having a Public Information Officer assigned full-time to the CP. In my mind, the Interior Branch was the better place for the PIO, but getting one to the CP was a good first step. We hoped that a PIO would also reduce the time and length of approvals before something could be released by the CP.

DCI Administrator Ed Wall announced to the Policy Group that the U.S. Capitol did not allow demonstrations inside of the building. Most of our group felt things were a bit too far along to adopt that policy right now. He mentioned that Ohio had closed its state capitol after seeing what happened here. He pointed out that Wisconsin's Capitol was seen as being occupied and was beginning to become the laughing stock of the nation. Things got a bit tense in the group.

It could have been semantics, it could have been fatigue, but I had heard enough. It is so easy for those who have little to no skin in the game to make such unhelpful pronouncements. DCI didn't have any uniformed cops on any line or on any post. They were working the crowd in plainclothes, but not as part of the Interior Branch. They were there to feed the CP intelligence. Wall and his staff weren't dealing with the countless logistical details that my team faced each day.

The desire to close the building seemed more political than practical. True, the daily crowds and the overnight sleepers posed a significant disruption. Also true, the Capitol could use a good scrubbing. Yet the law stated that the Capitol would be open whenever the Legislature was in session or conducting business. This building had a proud history of keeping its doors open, and the state had long placed a high value on transparency in government operations.

Even in the days and weeks following the September 11, 2001 attacks on our nation, the Capitol building remained open to all. There were no queues, no backpack searches, and no metal screening. Normal building hours had remained in place. Additional security measures had been taken, but they were largely invisible to visitors. If that deadly attack on our nation had not been sufficient to seal up the state Capitol and keep the public out, how on earth did the presence of some inconvenient and noisy, non-violent protesters warrant such a response? The reality was that the Assembly was meeting through the night, and by law, the building could not close.

Charles Tubbs had spent countless hours over the past two weeks building up a tremendous amount of trust and goodwill with the Unions and all the protesters. This good faith, with open dialogue and communication every day, had kept things peaceful and as orderly as one could have hoped under the circumstances. The thought of abruptly switching gears and having uniformed police clear people out for no particular reason except "today is the day" struck me as fundamentally wrong. It is a lesson I learned a long time ago and try continually to teach to new police officers: "Can I?" and if yes, "Should I?"

Can I muster enough police officers to empty this building by 6:00 tonight? You bet. The mass arrest plans were in place, the civil disobedience plans were in place, the hard (riot) gear for police was on-site and ready for use, and the University Police force's Police Extraction Response Unit (PERU) was here, along with the EOD canines. Unlike last Friday or Sunday, today I had everything I needed to make this happen.

Should I? No. It would be a ridiculous tactic, bad philosophy, and constitute an egregious use of power. The Assembly was still meeting and the building had to remain open. There was nothing to be gained from the spark that would ignite or the firestorm that would follow if we forced people out of the Capitol today. If we thought the crowds were big now, imagine how large they would be if we proceeded to shatter the trust and evict protesters without warning. Just to achieve the goal of clearing the building because we can made no sense.

The protests had begun in response to the Governor's Bill, but they were fueled by a sense that the democratic process was being ignored. The Governor was on record as not intending to negotiate the terms of his proposal. The Republican members of the Joint Finance Committee had closed their hearing because they were tired. Assembly Republicans were systematically rejecting Democratic amendments one after another, while the Democrats tried every tactic to stall. Senate Democrats had left the state in a desperate attempt to get opposing views heard and to slow down the legislation. Closing the Capitol abruptly would simply be taken as one more sign that the Governor and his administration wanted their opponents to go away. It would be a sure way to make them stay.

My goals to facilitate the First Amendment, provide for a functioning government, and keep everyone safe led me to believe that it was not my job to agree or disagree with either side. Rather, it was my job to understand crowd psychology and behavior and to put that knowledge to use in order to maintain the peace. The administration's goal, by contrast, was to get its Bill passed and proceed with business. As I understood the Administration's position, they did not feel it was their job to understand or engage the crowd. They simply wanted us to make the unpleasantness go away. The Democrats wanted to stall and for the dysfunction and chaos to continue, which was equally difficult.

The protesters wanted to be heard even though they knew it was unlikely that they could sway the eventual outcome. There was hope that some Republicans might reconsider their hard stance about the Bill if enough protesters from across the state demanded to be heard. The Administration seemed convinced that quick passage of the Bill would quell the crowds. But the Administration and the Republican speed and impatience were precisely what drove so many people to turn up at the Capitol day after day.

Charles Tubbs did not want law enforcement to be a flashpoint. He had been talking to the unions and protest groups about the idea of returning things to normal. He felt they were also interested in discussing returning to "normal." Though I am certain Charles never would have said so, the relationship he had developed with the protesters was everything the Administration's relationship with them was not.

In an attempt to find some consensus, I mentioned that at some point, arrests may be necessary. However, if the scale-down, step-by-step approach was successful, we would reduce the number of possible arrests to only those individuals who thought being arrested was a necessary symbol of their protest.

As part of the overall tactical plan, we aimed to have educational and information components about what we were doing and why. To be successful at re-establishing normal, we needed guidance on how many people were usually in the building on an average day prior to the protests. The number that I had established and continued to keep somewhat secret was a maximum capacity for the building at one time, not a typical day's occupancy.

What number to choose for daily occupancy was a difficult task. Any number short of capacity would seem manufactured and political. Someone proposed that we use the capacity of the Senate and Assembly galleries as our target occupancy number for the public. Arguably, these were the spaces of most importance to the protesters, and we had a definitive number of seats for each gallery. The full occupancy number of the building also needed to include legislators, administrators, and their staffs, as well as Capitol tours, constituents' visits, hearing room capacity, and the Supreme Court hearing room.

As the meeting ended, my shorter-than-usual fuse was becoming more evident to others and just another indication that we all were under a significant amount of stress. Three of my commanders had serious health issues. So I knew we all had to look out for one another and I was responsible for seeing that we did.

Each day, I tried to touch base with Chancellor Biddy Martin. I wanted to ensure that the University was getting everything it needed from the police and emergency management. Chancellor Martin's energy and drive were remarkable. She was facing a tremendous amount of pressure over the New Badger Partnership, the Public Authority proposal, and the collective bargaining provisions that would potentially impact all state employees benefit packages.

We spoke by phone just before 3:00 p.m. She inquired how I was doing, and I told her about the wellness checks we were conducting and how people who looked and felt fine when checked, were not actually healthy nor fine. I asked if she would be open to having a paramedic in plainclothes come to her office and take her blood pressure and other vital signs. Unobtrusive, no one needed to know the result beyond her. She agreed. A little while later, she texted me that she had the blood pressure of a 25-year-old. It was some of the best news I had gotten that day.

Returning to the Interior Branch, I was told we would be short 60 officers for the day shift Thursday and 30 short for Wednesday night. So far there had been 9,343 people in the building today, not including staff and the elected officials as they came and went through staff entrances. The division commanders made their adjustments.

CPD Lieutenant Marc Schmidt reported that we were now expecting up to 30,000 correctional officers to protest tomorrow, and Jimmy Hoffa's brother might even appear. We wondered if Marc meant Jimmy Hoffa's son, rather than his brother. Then we mused about how long does someone have to be dead before you are not always introduced as their brother or son? We all had a laugh.

We had known for several days that we had to switch out of the Middleton Marriott briefing site starting tomorrow morning. Unfortunately, the CP logistics section had yet to find us a suitable location. So once again, the DNR folks were itching to begin setting up, but had no place to go. Chief Warden Randy Stark reported that the transition of cops getting on and off the bus had become a media fascination at the Marriott. We all quipped that it must be a slow news day. With the number of police fluctuating, Randy had developed a transition plan to move certain groups of officers in the order of their post's sensitivity, making shift changes even smoother.

Then things got a bit bizarre. Sarah Pfatteicher (when we took roll call during our meetings, we always said "Sarah Pfatteicher, common spelling"—that always got a laugh in policing circles) reported on three things we needed to know from the news headlines of the day:

1. A prank phone call involving the Governor. Some prankster had gotten through to the Governor on the phone and had a 20-minute conversation posing as one of the Koch brothers.
   The prankster had recorded the call and posted it on his blog. It appeared the Governor genuinely believed he was speaking to David Koch, a significant supporter of his campaign. The two had supposedly discussed the protests and the strategy for reducing the unions' political strength

and actual numbers. Sarah would get a printed transcript of the call so I could read what had actually been said.

2. The Koch brothers supposedly opened offices just off the Capitol Square. This move probably would have garnered less notice but for the prank phone call. This gave the protesters another location beyond the Capitol building to show their frustration.

3. An Indiana government official's ill-conceived suggestion that we should use weapons with live ammunition to scatter the Madison protesters. Someone in the Interior Branch quipped, "When did we become a Middle-Eastern country that shot our citizens for exercising their Constitutional Rights?" We dubbed the official the "Indiana Idiot."

No doubt the crowd would have some reaction to all of this and no one knew what that could be. Our challenge was to figure out if any of these developments would impact our activities, or simply be bizarre distractions.

The wellness checks were progressing and more staff were having issues. We needed to push water and less soda to the officers. The food was improving daily; in that regard, Logistics was coming through for us.

At the daily 4:00 p.m. CP briefing, we learned the Senate would be going into session at 7:00 the next morning, but this information was not for public consumption. Like so many things these days, I found it odd that the Senate could convene, but the time wasn't public. Only staff and senators would be allowed in the chamber, no media or public. It was reported that the Senate would convene at 7:00 and then would quickly recess and then resume again at 11:00. What was that about, I wondered?

We were still awaiting the vote in the Assembly. The bus was on stand-by, and at this point, no one was willing to guess when the Assembly would be finished.

As we met, word arrived that a new briefing area for the incoming officers had been established on Packers Ave, midway between the Capitol and the airport on the city's northeast side. The Secretary of DOA just had to sign the lease. Randy's staff headed out to prepare the space for the next morning. The word was passed to EPS so they would tell the arriving officers, deputies, and troopers where to report.

We again talked about the scale-down plan, which the Interior Branch nicknamed "Operation Squeegee." Anyone sleeping near an egress area would be asked to relocate. With this part of the plan executed tonight, tomorrow we would take the next step, with all of the protesters and their belongings out by 4:00 Sunday afternoon. DCI Tina Virgil had started planning for a spot where protesters could retrieve any confiscated items. The custodial staff could thoroughly clean on Monday and have the building ready for Tuesday's Joint Address on the budget.

I reported to CP that the UW Branch would open Friday to cover the Regents meeting. We were attempting to muster as many staff as we could from the 13 UW Police departments and would only use EPS if needed. The extra radios the UW Police had on loan to the Interior Branch were recalled for use by the UW Branch. The communications folks would have to figure out how to make sure everyone in and around the Capitol was covered with radios. A person in the CP Planning Section had been assigned to gather information, not just intelligence. This was a small, but overdue, victory.

Madison Chief Noble Wray called me to talk about the Walker-Koch prank call. Noble wondered what I thought of the call. I told him the truth—that I hadn't heard it nor had I read a transcript. He summarized the components of the call he found troubling. In particular, he was concerned about a reference being made about placing people in the crowd who might be troublemakers or agitators. He thought certain references to planting troublemakers in the crowd could rile the public further.

So far we had noticed some signboards referencing the call appearing in the Capitol, but most of the people seem focused on the marathon Assembly session that was still underway. We agreed to keep each other posted if we heard more and I committed to reading the whole transcript of the call.

I sat down to read the transcript when I received a text from my sister. My mother was worried about me because Fox News was reporting that the Wisconsin Capitol was under siege, that the police were fighting the crowd, and that people were relieving themselves throughout the building instead of using the bathrooms. I assured my sister that depending on the news station—CNN, FOX, MSNBC—you were likely to see three very different versions of the event—none of which were completely accurate, and some of which were downright false.

Later in the day, I called my 83-year-old mother in Pennsylvania to reassure her I was just fine. I told her to alternate TV stations to get a fuller picture of what may be going on at any one time.

In reading the David Koch-Scott Walker prank phone call transcript, I marveled at how anyone could actually pull this off. While this was "only" a phone call, could someone dupe his staff and get physically close to the Governor? As there were a number of threats made to the Governor in the past 10 days, I made a note to talk to WSP Lieutenant Brad Altman in the morning about the Governor's physical security. The transcript indicated that the Governor had thought about planting troublemakers (in the crowd), and then went on to argue against the idea. It seemed a non-issue at this point; however, once an idea is out, there could be someone willing to act without "authorization." The remainder of the transcript to me was all about political strategy and had nothing to do with my role as a law enforcement leader.

Just as I finished reading the transcript, in the door came Ted Blazel. The Senate sergeant-at-arms needed me to arrange support for his staff charged with going to the home of four of the Democratic senators. He requested that state troopers be sent to the homes along with his staff. I brought WSP Lieutenant Brad Altman into the conversation. The troopers' role, Ted explained, was simply to be present and to provide assistance if requested by the staff. The visits would be early in the morning in residential neighborhoods, and Ted wanted to make sure his staff wouldn't be mistaken for individuals attempting trouble. I wasn't going to assign troopers from the Interior Branch, so I told Brad he needed to use his chain of command to work out the details. It was up to the superintendent to decide whether or not to use troopers in this manner. Brad made a quick call and arrangements were worked out.

Ted relayed that conversations were occurring between various leaders and a few of the missing senators. Some of the senators had intimated that if they were found in the state, they would return to the Capitol. This was more political theatre. Now it made sense to me why the Senate would begin at 7:00 in the morning and then recess until 11:00. For the sergeant-at-arms to have authority to take formal action and retrieve the senators, the Senate must be in session.

As was my usual practice before I left for the day, I checked the University's Emergency Operations Center (EOC) log to see what had happened or what might be brewing for the campus tomorrow.

Anyone who has had to work in an EOC or CP knows
there are times when you are so busy you can easily use
ten more people to help you. There are also times when
things are so slow that all you want to do is read a book

or play cards. Under the University Response Plan, we were able to run a virtual Emergency Operations Center (EOC). The University has the technology to link members of the EOC without having to co-locate them.

Each workday during the Capitol event, an EOC manager held a face-to-face coordinating meeting and then ran the rest of the twenty-three hours of the day virtually. The EOC manager always has the choice to bring people face to face with an hour's notice. This method of operation dramatically reduces staff fatigue and slashes costs. Staff can stay at their regular jobs, yet be in quick contact with the EOC if their services are needed.

My daily commute into and out of the building provided me with, in the language of emergency management, "situational awareness." Today had been a busy day for me. I checked on the Teaching Assistants' sponsored dinner that started at 7:00 p.m. in the Capitol. It was going just fine. The talk of the evening was the Koch-Walker call. Walking through the Capitol, I once again stopped to hear what some of the protesters had to say about life "under the dome." It was a reminder for me of why we were here—because thousands of Wisconsin residents and visitors from as far away as the two coasts of the United States felt strongly about the issues of the day and wanted their voices heard, while the government continued to function.

I noticed two women lying on a queen-sized mattress, both wearing matching red T-shirts. I knelt down and started to chat with them. They were both nurses from New Jersey. They were in town for the week and would be heading back home on Friday.

As a kid, I had spent several summer vacations in New Jersey in Wildwood. I had visited Atlantic City, Townsend Inlet, and Sea Isle along with Cape May. My father had been stationed in Cape May during part of World War II and I had cousins who lived in Sparta, New Jersey.

It was like we were old friends after just a few minutes. They shared some stories about their time in Wisconsin, how friendly and genuinely kind folks are here. They asked if my police department sold T-shirts to benefit our foundation efforts. Since I came from the East Coast, I was familiar with this practice, even though we didn't engage in it here. They really wanted one of my department's shirts. I gave them my card and told them if they sent me two of their T-shirts, I would send them two University Police T-shirts. We struck a deal.

I spoke to some other folks I had seen day after day and asked them how things were going. They wanted to talk about the Koch-Walker phone call and asked what I thought. I would always pause and offer a gentle reminder that I wasn't here to talk politics; I just want to ensure they were physically doing all right. Most people switched quickly to the topic of the building and what I thought would happen next. Would the Assembly finish tonight? I told them it was anyone's guess. All I hoped for—and that was all it was, a hope—was that someone would give us a 30-minute heads-up before the vote would occur. Of course, I didn't share that the only reason the Interior Branch would get a heads-up at all, was so we could ready the transport bus and get the cops in place to escort the Republicans out of the building safely.

As I left, the visitor count for the day was 15,284 people, not counting staff or elected officials. The reopening of schools throughout the state had decreased the numbers of protesters significantly.

Day 11: Thursday, February 24, 2011

THE DAY STARTED LIKE THE OTHERS AND ON MY WAY THROUGH THE Rotunda and up to the Interior Branch, I noticed only a few people had stirred awake. I greeted a few who acknowledged me, trying to keep my voice soft so as not to disturb the others. I met a man and a woman from Los Angeles, who had arrived on a bus the day before and were proud to have spent their first night in Madison in the Capitol. They remarked about how friendly everyone was—even the police. They posed for a quick picture with one of the signs they had brought with them. "LA Supports You."

As we got started inside the Branch, I was anxious to know how the new briefing/staging location was working. Chief Warden Randy Stark and his DNR crew had once again taken the lead. The Capitol basement area was ready for the arrival of the incoming officers and the night crew was definitely ready to leave.

We had 476 sleepers overnight and I was told the Governor was already in the building. There continued to be issues with the NPAs ("No Permanent Address," or homeless). Unfortunately, many had become aggressive toward the protesters and several had "helped themselves" to items or belongings that were not theirs. Theft throughout the building was becoming more common. A few had been in shouting matches with each other, causing some of the families staying overnight to express concern to the police.

Someone had placed a supply of feminine hygiene products and condoms in the various restrooms throughout the building for people to use. Unfortunately, it seemed a number of people not necessarily associated with the protest decided to fill the condoms with water and have water "balloon" fights. The "fights," along with the messy result, were dealt with by the night shift, who put a stop to the use of condom balloons.

In the Land of No Dull Moments, the police had also made an arrest of an NPA for lewd behavior and masturbation. We were mindful that there were children in the building, some staying overnight. People were also trying to find a quiet spot away from others. We had to be cognizant that kind of isolation could facilitate a sexual assault. Officers reported that there was a fair amount of consensual sexual intercourse occurring among people staying overnight.

As the organized sleepovers continued, the number of smaller air mattresses increased. My guess was that the average age of the people staying overnight was somewhere around 35 years of age. After the intensity of the last eleven days, I felt really old—and I wasn't sleeping on the floor. Many said they had jobs that they were juggling. Some worked an afternoon shift so they could spend the night, leave for their shift, and return the next evening. Some had called in sick and others had taken leave. I was struck by the fact that these were everyday working people just trying to make a point.

The NPAs certainly added some interesting dimensions to the scene. Most of the homeless would enter the building at night to gain some relief from the cold. They would socialize mainly with other homeless people, but occasionally they would attempt to engage with the demonstrators. They wanted to be fed. None of them smelled very good. In the morning, the homeless crowd would wake and leave the building. Some of the homeless told me that they wanted out of the Capitol during the day because there were too many people and too much noise.

The Senate start at 7:00 a.m. was perfunctory. There were 100 people in the Assembly gallery as the Assembly continued to debate the Democrats' 120-plus amendments. We were able to listen in to the Assembly proceedings via *Wisconsin Eye*, a live online video broadcast. The cable connection we requested from the CP came accompanied by two new flat-screen televisions. This helped us tremendously with situational awareness, information we needed, although we missed relying on the quaint rabbit-ears antenna outside on the window ledge.

Preliminary word on the four home visits of Democratic senators was that none of the senators were found. We would wait official word from Sergeant-at-Arms Ted Blazel. If the four senators had returned, the Senate would have enough members present to take up the Bill. It was expected to pass the Senate with a Republican majority. If all of this drama came together, it could make for another interesting day.

I needed to avoid the politics and move forward with executing the plan to clear the Capitol for cleaning by Sunday at 4:00 p.m. If we made the announcement today, we would have given more than 72-hour notice. Chief Tubbs joined the 10:00a.m. CP briefing for the first time. I mentioned to him how much the crowd marshals were doing and wanted him to know their value to us.

It was important for UW Police Captain Soley to join us for the CP briefing because she would be in charge of the UW Branch. I had dragged AC Brian Bridges and Chief Warden Randy Starks with me to a few meetings so they could run the Interior Branch for my day off. We went to room 415 NW, where a video connection had been set up for me to reach the CP. While it had taken eleven days to obtain, the equipment used to make the connection was top shelf and worked flawlessly.

Captain Karen Soley talked about the UW Branch and that EPS would be tapped for a few officers. The officers involved would stage in Parking Lot 60 on campus, be transported to the Pyle Center, and briefed there by Captain Soley. According to the CP Logistics team, the necessary buses would be available. Karen was estimating a crowd of around 1,000 people to show up at the Pyle Center on campus.

The Student Labor Action Committee (SLAC) was planning an 11:00 a.m. rally in front of Bascom Hall, where the chancellor's office was located. It was believed they would then march to the Pyle Center on Langdon Street, where the Regents were meeting, and then on to the Capitol. The planned speaker for the SLAC rally was to be Ben Mansky. We at University Police were very familiar with Ben; he most recently ran for State Assembly but hadn't been successful.

I reminded everyone that I would be tapping out on Friday and that I would be attending the regents meeting as a citizen. We joked a bit about me being civilly disobedient and needing to be dragged from the room. If I wasn't so tired, that might be possible.

We talked about the large rallies on Saturday at the Capitol with crowds expected to be over 50,000. Live music and various political speakers were being planned. The event time was looking like it might be 2:00 in the afternoon instead of the usual 12 noon. Charles said he would talk to the organizers today to learn more about their plans. Charles then talked about closing at 4:00 on Sunday afternoon. He wanted as much voluntary compliance as he could get. He had been speaking with union leaders, telling them that he really had to get the facility back to normal. The leaders seemed to understand.

I made sure all of our officers were getting their wellness checks twice a day. As a result of the wellness screenings, the Wisconsin State Patrol (WSP) was moving toward a two-day rotation for troopers and inspectors. It may be difficult to understand why all of this was so stressful. Imagine listening to the banging of drumsticks on 5-gallon buckets or drums while standing for twelve hours on unforgiving marble in a building that smelled of unwashed bodies just waiting for something to go wrong day after day.

While someone in the CP was reporting, I turned to Charles, who was seated next to me and quietly asked him if he was getting his wellness check twice a day. He replied he was not, but that I should be assured he was good.

After the meeting, it was time for my own morning health check. I sat in the chair in the hallway outside the Interior Branch and the paramedics asked their questions and followed their procedures. I was still "green" and good to continue. There were a couple of "yellows" but no "reds" for the morning round.

We needed to implement "Operation Squeegee." I gathered my division commanders together in a room down the hall, thinking a change of venue would do everyone some good. Carol Gosenheimer, a professionally trained facilitator, led the discussion and planning. We made a master list of things that needed to be restricted.

After brainstorming, we divided the list into categories: Fire Safety, Health, Public Safety, Disruption, and Miscellaneous. We had a good discussion about returning the Capitol to "normal." The previous night, we had successfully moved sleepers down from the 4th floor, limited mattress size, and prohibited alcohol.

We would turn the focus to fire safety issues starting tonight and continuing Friday. This was the largest category of items needing restriction. Fire safety was something everyone could readily understand. Next, we would ask sleepers to relocate to floors 2 or lower.

Starting on Friday and continuing into Saturday, we would focus on health-related items. By Friday night, we would have all sleepers relocate to only the first or ground floors and begin to remove all restricted items on Saturday. Also on Saturday, we would not allow sleeping above the Rotunda ground floor. Thanks to new restrictions announced in both houses, Senate and Assembly members could no longer allow non-staff to sleep in their offices overnight.

On Sunday at 4:00 p.m., we would plan to close the building and escort everyone out. If there was a group that wouldn't leave, we would walk through a step-by-step relocation plan one person at a time, and if necessary, pick them up and physically move them outside. We would have plenty of police on hand with at least three hours to relocate people and their belongings before shift change.

We designed a communication strategy with Chief Tubbs playing a considerable role. Our plan included Charles sharing the closing plan with the union leaders. We would ask that he fully brief the marshals and gain their cooperation. We would ask the marshals to talk things over with people who had been staying overnight in addition to other crowd members. The marshals had been so terrific to work with and were wonderful at relaying information, and it was concluded that we should definitely team up with them.

We were informed that the Milwaukee police would be gathering information and intelligence and sending us information that was relevant. Now the CP and the Milwaukee police had someone searching open sources while the Interior Branch focused more on Twitter and Facebook, both major sources of communication among the protest groups. Milwaukee Police Chief Ed Flynn and I had spoken earlier in the week about what was going on in the Capitol and the role his folks and mine were fulfilling.

I had known Ed for close to sixteen years, since his time in Massachusetts. He and I had served in the International Association of Chiefs of Police, the National Association of Women Law Enforcement Executives, and the Police Executive Research Forum. Ed had been the Police Chief in Arlington, Virginia on September 11, 2001 and his organization was involved in the response to the attack on the Pentagon. I consider Ed a friend and a very knowledgeable police chief.

We talked a bit about tactics and use of staff. We discussed how best to educate and inform folks of our plans and how things would be carried out under the circumstances. There is an art to drawing lines and setting boundaries with crowds. We agreed on virtually every point. Ed committed to sending me staff until my departure date, which I believed was March 3.

The division commanders wanted to create signs and handouts, listing items of what was permitted and what was restricted each day. We figured this information would get to the press quickly, which was another good way to get the word out that it was time to return the Capitol to normal. Pending DOA approval, we would also issue a press release. Tina Virgil had also learned that DOA had a policy regarding abandoned property and lost and found; this would allow us to retain items for five days and then dispose of them.

Heading back to 400 NE, I was told sarcastically by one of the officers standing post on the 4th floor that the Senate had just concluded some "critically important" business. They had just voted to declare January 26th *Bob Uecker Day*. The officer went on to tell me that Senator Lassa had made Senator Kapanke imitate Bob Uecker's home run call before the vote. We chuckled that it was good to add a bit of levity to a tense week. [14]

By the time I headed for the Policy Group meeting with my scale-down plan in hand, 6,734 members of the public had entered the building that day, so far. The capacity management plan was working well, and the officers and troopers were at the doors, ensuring that recently prohibited items were not getting in. The room was beginning to get crowded. Some of the players had changed.[15]

---

[14] Bob Uecker was the long time announcer for the Milwaukee Brewers professional baseball team. He was a man with an amazing recollection of baseball facts coupled that with an endless sense of humor. His telltale "Get up, get up, get out of here" call whenever the Brewers hit a homerun is legendary.

[15] In attendance were Keith Gilkes, the Governor's Chief of Staff; Ed Wall from DCI; Rob Marchant, the Senate Chief Clerk; Jodi Jensen, DOA; John Hogan, Senator Fitzgerald's office; Ted Blazel, Senate Sergeant-at-Arms; Anne Tonnon Byers, Assembly Sergeant-at-Arms; Sheriff Dave Mahoney; AC Brian Bridges; Chief Charles Tubbs; DC Dan Blackdeer; General Dunbar; plus AC Randy Gaber and Captain Tom Snyder of the Madison Police.

DC Dan Blackdeer began talking about a rally on Saturday with possibly 50,000 to 100,000 participants, although there was no permit request yet. The WLEA police union was rallying today and so far there had been no issues. There would be a rally at the Koch offices at 4:00 p.m. in response to the prank phone call. Protests were now being held around the state in various cities, instead of busing everyone to Madison. The Assembly was still meeting. The CP had a report of a bus arriving from Los Angeles. I was able to confirm that from my morning meeting and photo op with the couple from LA.

Word had spread, incorrectly, that we were going to close the Capitol on Friday night. We received word from DOA that they were thinking of saying something publicly that the Capitol was not closing on Friday. We supported that idea.

Because there had been greater public interest in the various proceedings than there were seats in the various galleries, the Assembly sergeant-at-arms had put several large screen televisions with sufficient sound in the Rotunda several weeks ago. Crowds of people had gathered around the TVs each day the Assembly was in session to watch the proceedings. Sergeant-at-Arms Anne Tonnon Byers had received a request from the protesters to turn the volume down on the TVs at night so that they could sleep better. The whole point of the TVs was to give access to people to watch the government at work. The group agreed that if the TVs were there, they should remain on, including the sound.

We returned to the business at hand for Tuesday, March 1, and the Governor's Joint Session Budget Address. It was believed that the Supreme Court justices would be in chambers, and the Assembly and Senate would be in session prior to the address. There are traditions of escorts when moving members from one house to the other for a joint session. In my mind, all of that would be relatively straightforward to carry out if the operations were at a normal level. For this Joint Address, tickets were issued in advance for the seats in the Assembly gallery. Those attending would be known in advance with one exception; there were twenty tickets that would be available for the general public the day of the speech.

The discussion shifted to the scale-down plan to bring us to closing on Sunday. I presented the plan and the group agreed the fire safety items should be done right away. Some still argued for even quicker action. A few wondered aloud if there was sufficient time for staff to clean the building by March 1.

Incident Commander DC Blackdeer spoke up and said he was still worried about law enforcement becoming the flashpoint. He wanted a balance between the functioning of the building and officer safety. Others countered quickly with concerns that the homeless have taken up residence and would never leave. Ed Wall mentioned that whenever large crowds gather, there is a chance that someone will see it as an opportunity for a terrorist strike. He noted that the terrorism may not have anything to do with the cause or the protest, but a large crowd is a good place to hide before one attempts some horrific act. He went on to say that because these events were on a national stage, they were therefore a large target and the building was wide open with no screening in place.

The Capitol Police, WEM, and DCI were working on having a vulnerability assessment completed. One of the keys in any assessment is whether regular building hours are maintained and whether the building is secured after hours.

This was an interesting and serious point. However, this was Day 11, and while someone attempting to injure the crowd or cause extensive damage had been discussed, it was never framed as possible terrorism. I felt this was a bit dramatic, but I would reflect on it before the Joint Address.

We discussed needing a screening system for people entering the building so we could eventually reduce the footprint of law enforcement. Screening would reduce the prohibited items from being brought in and would help keep the Capitol from becoming messy. It was suggested that we should screen out backpacks as well.

Getting back to the plan in front of them, I pointed out that the division commanders in the Interior Branch had brainstormed a list of the items that we had been seeing. Between now and Sunday at 4:00 pm, I thought it unwise to deal with anything beside fire safety and health. Given all of the "stuff" that was currently in the building, we had already lost a lot of public safety ground. It seemed ridiculous to prohibit backpacks until we cleared the building. A point was raised that as we tighten up, we should at least begin looking through backpacks. Once we get past Sunday's closing, then the group could consider searching or prohibiting backpacks altogether.

The representative from the DOA Secretary's office, Jodi Jensen, said that when we closed the building on Sunday, it should be completely cleared. I agreed with Jodi. DC Blackdeer said he didn't want law enforcement to be seen clearing the people out of the building. He didn't want to rush them. He wanted to maintain the good will that the police had nurtured, keeping the posture so the cops were still seen as friendly people. Dan also felt we should allow a reasonable number of people to remain if they wanted to do so.

WSP Major Darren Price spoke up. He thought Sunday had to be the day when everyone left to allow the building to be cleaned for health reasons. Basic sanitation was suffering. Having people sleeping in the Capitol indefinitely was not normal. He was convinced people were getting ill, as were some of the troopers. He might even favor an earlier closing on Saturday instead of Sunday. Ed Wall of DCI agreed with an earlier closing.

I added that a Saturday closing was a bad idea and clearing people out after 4:00 pm on Sunday was a sound idea. We had three more nights to gradually reduce the sleeping space. We had three more days to deal with reducing the items in the building. Our plan was predicated on scaling down to Sunday in a gradual manner, reducing the chance of the spark with which Dan seemed concerned. This Saturday we were looking at potentially the largest crowds to date with an organized sleepover planned for Saturday night. We should stick to Sunday closing at 4:00 p.m., continuing with cleanup on Monday.

Charles Tubbs spoke up and said he felt the scale-down plan of closing on Sunday was still moving too fast. The unions were saying 100,000 people would show up on the weekend. He said he was speaking to the unions about voluntary compliance—they were listening and in favor of making the Sunday deadline voluntary. He felt strongly that law enforcement shouldn't be heavy-handed.

Ed Wall quickly followed with, "Wisconsin is becoming a national example of how not to manage an event like this." I absolutely disagreed with that assessment. At this point, it seemed we had three options under discussion. Close and clear Saturday night, close and clear Sunday, or close but don't clear on Sunday.

It was interesting to have watched and participated in the morphing of people's stances over the past week. Less than a week ago, Charles had entered the Interior Branch demanding we close and clear the building within 20 minutes of 6 o'clock and on another occasion within four hours. Now a proposed closing with 4½ days' notice was too quick. My view had been that once we determined the goal of normal operations, the building should be closed and people cleared out. We needed to give reasonable notice, and we needed to make that change in an organized, step-by-step fashion as I explained.

General Dunbar spoke up and said, "None of us know for sure how anyone will respond, but we need to establish reasonableness, set a policy, and in the future, think about inside and outside being permit based. Right now, we have legislators who are afraid because of the threats received." He added that there are significant health issues with the food preparation and serving occurring in a building that hasn't been cleaned in two weeks. The General finished by noting that there has to be a reasonable approach going forward and no plan should place us in a position to be heavy-handed.

Most felt the unions had to be reasonable in their expectations as well. Our plan called for the unions to have two more weekend days for their large gatherings, and could continue to make their points. Then we would close the facility on time at 4:00 on Sunday and have it cleared and cleaned. Charles thought we should regroup tomorrow and discuss this further, but Keith Gilkes pressed on in an effort to have the decision made. I agreed with Keith and said so.

I was growing weary of the indecisiveness of some of my colleagues. The group was not aligned and was not getting any closer to alignment from my perspective. Leadership—who was actually in charge and who was really making decisions—remained unclear. We were now discussing issues like no inside protests and the need for further permits and screening outside the galleries. Some of the dialog struck me as sounding potentially threatening to the public. I returned to the health issues as the main reason why I favored a Sunday night close and clearing with the scale-down approach to get us there.

Keith agreed with my points and instructed Chief Tubbs to get on message. He was to tell the unions that the Capitol would close at 4:00 p.m. Sunday; that we need to get this place cleaned up. The sheriff said that this group will need to discuss future access with restrictions at some point, but for now, we needed to have the union leadership understand the health and cleaning issues, and we needed to tend to the fire safety issues immediately. The group recognized we needed to prepare for a flashpoint, should one occur despite our best efforts. We should have ended the meeting then.

However, the discussion switched to Monday and beyond. Keith and Jodi raised the need to clear the building nightly at the posted building hours. They floated the idea that maybe the building, once cleared, should just stay closed Monday to the public so that cleaning could continue. The sergeants-at-arms reminded folks that there were hearings and meetings scheduled for Monday.

We talked at length about limiting movement in the Capitol on Monday to only those meetings and hearings, but not having the entire place open for anyone to wander through. Charles reminded us that the public tours of the building had, for the most part, stopped. He would like to get them restarted as soon as possible. He was especially sensitive to the school children from around the state who were looking forward to their field trips.

We once again returned to limiting the public to the capacity of the hearing rooms and the galleries. What would the numbers be if we limited people to those spaces for Monday and in the future—a number less than one thousand? The past week we had been screening for weapons in the galleries and for major meetings and hearings. Would our screening protocols need to change?

These questions hung in the air unanswered. To get them answered, the Interior Branch would once again return to planning. Since I was going to be off tomorrow, I wanted to use Saturday as an ambitious planning day in the Branch to ensure that we success-fully closed and cleared on Sunday. Everyone seemed okay with that.

As we prepared to wrap up the discussion, the question was raised if we were willing to draw the line in the sand for Sunday. I certainly was ready and thought the scale-down plan that was already underway with the mattress size reduction and alcohol prohibition was going well—and it was logical.

Anyone walking the Capitol halls could see that the extension cords running everywhere were tripping and fire hazards. Food was being left out unrefrigerated for hours on end. There were people staying in the building with serious medical conditions. The police were getting sore throats, colds, and flu-like symptoms. The wellness checks on staff revealed the toll this situation was taking on everyone. Three of my commanders had been red-lined and WSP had modified its rotation because of health concerns. In addition, the whole Capitol smelled like unwashed bodies and human waste.

Keith summed up that we wanted to get the number of people on Sunday as low as possible through voluntary compliance with union leadership on board. At 4:00 p.m. Sunday, there would be no more food deliveries and no overnight sleeping. Jodi would post the media release on Friday. Anne Tonnon Byers wanted to be sure constituents would be able to visit their Assembly representatives on Monday. It seemed to me to be decided. Sunday closing and clearing at 4:00 pm.

I had asked if I could meet with General Dunbar and the Chief of Staff for a few minutes after the meeting. Chief Tubbs asked if he could join us. I said I preferred he not join us as I had to discuss some University business. This wasn't entirely true, but I was concerned about how things were going, and I didn't want to get my signals crossed since I would be away tomorrow. Charles was very gracious and left the room.

I explained to Keith and the general a bit of the dynamics regarding the regents meeting. I then returned to the discussion of the Sunday closing and clearing. I totally agreed with voluntary compliance and had no desire to have law enforcement carry people out of the Capitol. However, if I was to return the Capitol to normal operations by March 1, then allowing only voluntary compliance was problematic. If people realized there was no consequence to staying after closing on Sunday, then why would they leave? The scale-down plan would continue to reduce the footprint of the group gradually each day until Saturday night when the last area for sleeping was the ground floor of the Rotunda (reminding them that even offices and meeting rooms would be prohibited.) All of that would lead to the next logical step: no sleeping anywhere in the Capitol Sunday night.

Over the years, I have found most people to be reasonable and rational. The overwhelming majority of the people we had encountered over the past eleven days were law-abiding, hard-working people who believed in their position and had done everything to avoid violence or any sort of physical aggression. It seemed to me that with Charles' efforts, they were likely to leave in large numbers.

It was also important to consider that several people or groups would resist. In my experience, for whatever reason, certain people would not want to comply with our plan. Some may feel it was "the principle of the thing" and that, to make a point they would need to be physically carried out and/or arrested. I felt it was important to accommodate and facilitate their needs as well, and to carry them out and/or arrest them. It would be done with minimal force and as safely as possible for both the officers and the protesters.

Strange as it might seem, forcing compliance would meet the goals of some of the protesters—fulfilling a desire to be arrested—and the goals of the administration—a functioning building. Keith and the general agreed with me and said they felt some people simply wouldn't leave just because they wanted some confrontation they had yet to achieve.

While I thought Charles had done an amazing job communicating with the main union leadership, I was concerned that Charles may have spent too much time with union leaders and as a result, was unwilling to use any tactic beyond voluntary compliance. The plans of the Interior Branch for the remaining few days contained a variety of tactics to meet the goals and the final day would involve removal and, if necessary, arrests. Both men wished me a good day off to attend the regents meeting.

Returning to the Interior Branch Operations Room to ensure everything was in place for tomorrow, I found Randy and Brian confident and on task. The attempt earlier in the day to compel some of the senators to return had not worked. I decided to call Kathleen Vinehout, one of the missing senators, to see if she would talk to me about what was happening. I called her cell phone and left a message. It wasn't a surprise that she never called back.

The Assembly debate would continue for many more hours. The shuttle bus plan remained at the ready for whenever they finished. It was time for me to tap out.

Protesters waiting for results of the Assembly hearing. (Photo by Mark Golbach)

Chapter Five
Voluntary Compliance

There are 5.5 million residents of Wisconsin; all deserve a functioning government. Over the past 12 days, just over a million of them had come to Madison to make their voices heard, and they had been heard. They had met with their representatives and senators, testified, marched, observed, sang, wept, slept, laughed, talked, chanted, posted signs, prayed, sang the national anthem, and in doing so affirmed their Constitutional rights. In that time, remarkably few had been arrested, of which three had little or nothing to do with the protests.

Day 12: Friday, February 25, 2011

Shortly after midnight, some Assembly staff members woke the sleeping crowd inside the building. After a session that lasted over 61 hours straight, the Assembly was preparing to vote on the Budget Repair Bill. The crowd, realizing what was happening, gathered itself together quickly. They had been waiting for this moment for three days. The protesters had listened, watched and tweeted all about this vote since the Governor had introduced the Repair Bill on February 11.

After what was believed to be the longest continuous session in state Assembly history (there being no records to the contrary), the vote lasted all of 17 seconds. The Assembly adjourned about 1:00 a.m. The crowd that remained inside the Capitol was agitated about the 17-second vote. The police were understaffed at this point (neither the Interior Branch nor the Command Post was given a warning as to what time the vote was to come), and the situation was tense. Holding the upper floors was not easy, but the officers were able to maintain the scale-down plan.

Some Democratic members of the Assembly mingled with the protesters and gave a few short speeches. The police were able to clear the second floor wing by about 5:00 a.m. After things settled down, 864 people had stayed through the night. There had been two arrests, one dealing with a drunk and the other an emotionally disturbed person.

Since I was tapped out that day, my Branch responsibilities were divided between AC Brian Bridges and Chief Warden Randy Stark. The focus of the protests would now be on the Senate, since the Assembly had adjourned and would not reconvene until Tuesday. The Senate would convene later in the morning.

Today was the "junk detail," as the Branch nicknamed the mission. This was the detail to separate people's belongings from the items that had been abandoned around the building and were now truly "junk." Overnight, the staffing had been only 47 officers. They had a hard time keeping up with the crowd using the soft-sell approach that was so vital to making the scale-down program successful. Fire prevention and health safety were to be the focus of light enforcement today under Assistant Chief Warden Karl Brooks' leadership.

Meanwhile, Randy had formed the contact teams to deal with anyone who might show resistance toward the scale-down plan. These contact teams were the principal negotiators and sales persons of the scale-down plan. He selected UW Police officers for the task because he felt their crowd experience and interpersonal skills matched the assignment best.

There was significant confusion surrounding the roll out of the scale-down plan. Although flyers had been printed and given to the officers, the public only had bits and pieces of information and was filling in the gaps with whatever they "heard" or what the rumor mill supplied. There is nothing quite like Facebook and Twitter to help spread rumors far and wide. Speaking of which, rumor had it that the building was closing Friday at 4:00 p.m. or Saturday at 6:00 p.m. The actual time was to be Sunday at 4:00 p.m.

At the 1:00 meeting, the Policy Group moved further away from getting people out and closing on Sunday night. The group decided the close was now to be a voluntary effort with no one being moved out. Something had shifted overnight in the DOA and the Chief of Staff's thinking. Chief Tubbs' belief that he could negotiate his way to complete voluntary compliance to clear the building was to be the strategy going forward. A few in the Policy Group recognized that some number of people remaining on Sunday wouldn't leave on their own and that number was anyone's guess.

The stated goal was to resume normal building hours on Monday (8:00 a.m. to 6:00 p.m.), with staff being able to work in the Capitol under the same conditions they had before all this activity began. The Administration wanted to establish a much smaller number of people who would be allowed to demonstrate in the Capitol, beginning on Monday. In my view, to differentiate the purpose of why an individual was entering the Capitol could be considered unconstitutional because it addresses the content of why someone was entering the building.

In the Constitutional rulings of the United States Supreme Court, the government may control time, place and manner of speech, but not the content. Law enforcement could, under the law, enforce building hours. We could enforce regulations on capacity. However, asking a person who is not an employee of the building, to state the reason he or she is entering the building and then screening that person based on the answer could be viewed as limiting content. Others would argue that limiting the people who are coming in to protest, regardless of what they are protesting, was restricting only the manner in which they were going to protest. If the manner was defined as entering the building to protest, the argument could be made the state could control "manner," i.e., restrict access.

The Policy Group then derived the capacity of those allowed in to be the number of seats in the galleries, which stood at 354. That number was exceedingly low given that we allowed up to 9,000 visitors in at one time, and the average number of total visitors each day since we put capacity management in place on February 19, was 19,772. It was too restrictive, but the Policy Group agreed to it anyway.

Another immediate complication in establishing a capacity number different from the actual building capacity was the fact that legislators invited an unlimited number of visitors to the Capitol. There would be no true visitor limit, unless something (or some- one) restrained the legislators' authority for unlimited visitation. It appeared the Administration was willing to pursue some limit on the number of people the Legislature could invite inside. The idea of limiting the number of visitors of each legislator would have to be pursued with the clerks and the sergeants-at-arms in the days to come.

Information reached the Policy Group from the protest groups that if the Capitol closed at 4:00 p.m. today, Friday, the protesters were going to try to "charge the doors." Because the doors would not actually be closing today, the "charge" might just lead to overcrowding in the building. Chief Tubbs and DOA's Jodi Jensen shared language that would go out to the media and the public trying to give accurate information about Sunday's closing.

More information was reaching the group about Saturday's activities as well. As of midday, the projection for Saturday's rally and crowd was the largest yet.

I wondered if the fact that I wasn't there played a role in the Chief of Staff changing his position about closing on Sunday. Months later, I would learn that Gilkes did not believe I would or could muster law enforcement to remove people against Tubbs' wishes.

He had viewed me as arrogant. Yet I knew Randy Stark and Steve Fitzgerald would agree to have me use their staff to clear the building.

Meanwhile, it was my day off and I was attending the Regents meeting in support of UW–Madison Chancellor Biddy Martin and the New Badger Partnership. While there, I received a call from a Jerry Matysik, the City of Eau Claire Police Chief. He was concerned about the use of law enforcement and in particular, state troopers, to help in the attempted "roundup" of the missing senators that had occurred the day before. He felt that it was inappropriate to use law enforcement in this way and called to get my take on things. I filled him in on my role in the Interior Branch and the role, as I knew it, of the State Patrol in assisting with the attempted retrieval of the missing senators. Jerry had no idea I was involved with the day-to-day operations at the Capitol.

I explained to Jerry that behind the scenes, some Democratic senators had been discussing the issues and their possible return to the Capitol. Some had signaled, or had been thought to have signaled, that if they were found in the state, they would return. We talked about the role of law enforcement in the current atmosphere and the fine line of trying to stay above the politics of the moment. It was kind of him to tell me he had faith in me and respect for my ability to lead and police these events going forward.

About a week later, Jerry authored an opinion piece in the Eau Claire (Wisconsin) *Leader-Telegram* newspaper about the use of the police and politics.

Searching for Legislators is a Misuse of Police Powers

(Source: Eau Claire Leader-Telegram, Eau Claire, WI, March 4, 2001, Opinion Page, used with permission)

I have closely followed news reports that during the past few weeks the State Senate has been out looking for absent legislators. Recently the Senate passed a resolution calling for the Sergeant of Arms to, with or without

*force and with or without the help of any law enforce-
ment officers, take the missing members into custody
and bring them to the Capitol—any time day or night.
Although the Senate can engage in seeking out its
members, I would certainly hope and expect that police
agencies will refrain from allowing their officers to be
used for partisan purposes. I am concerned that the
public may be left with the impression that police
participation in such a search is a legitimate use of
police powers.*

*Police powers, represented by the badge and uniform,
should not be used to intimidate politicians or to curtail
political freedom. To do so would undermine the public
trust and confidence that the law can be applied in a fair
and impartial manner. If police executives were to allow
their agencies to act as the enforcement arm of either
political party, the effectiveness of the police would be
severely damaged. Police can only be effective if the
citizens are assured that dissenting political views will
not leave them vulnerable to unwarranted enforcement
actions.*

*Police officers, like all citizens, are entitled to exercise
their own personal political views while off duty.
However, when on duty, they have a professional
responsibility to apply the law in a fair, impartial, and
even-handed manner. This is, admittedly, a challenge for
officers but it is nonetheless a goal we must insist upon.
To do otherwise would negatively impact the
relationship between the police and the communities
they serve.*

*Although most citizens see the main role of police as
law enforcers, law enforcement is, in fact, only part of*

the job. Perhaps the most important police role is to
protect and preserve the Constitutional rights and civil
liberties that all citizens enjoy, regardless of their
political views.

I agreed with Chief Matysik's argument on the need for police to be politically neutral. For some outside observers, the use of law enforcement to retrieve the senators was the most obvious example of mixing policing and politics. For those of us with duties at the Capitol, the interactions with politicians and staff of the Legislature were frequent and complicated.

After speaking with Jerry, I returned to listening to the Regent's proceedings. Captain Karen Soley's plan worked well and she had the situation well in hand. Chancellor Martin finished her remarks and other chancellors presented their views as well. I left the proceedings around 2:00 to take a nap. I was still tired.

In Ohio and Indiana, demonstrators held support rallies for the union cause as the scenes near those state houses became increasingly chaotic. Over 50 unions rallied in the wind and rain outside the New Jersey Statehouse in support of collective bargaining rights for public employees.

By the end of the day, approximately 22,367 visitors had come through the Wisconsin Capitol.

DAY 13: SATURDAY, FEBRUARY 26, 2011

THE ROUTINE OF THE DAY REMAINED ALMOST TOO FAMILIAR. THE SLEEPER report was 571 from overnight. There were some intoxicated people to deal with, but no one had to be transported to detox. Some protesters had been giving instructions for civil disobedience actions. We had a copy of the instructions and read them over. It seemed quite well written and illustrative of standard civil disobedience tactics. There was nothing in the instructions that concerned me.

Protesters had moved down from the upper floors. At 4:00 in the morning, things were so quiet, sixteen troopers were sent home. Overnight, the scale-down worked as designed. Items that were now prohibited from being brought into the building stayed out of the Capitol, and some items inside had been voluntarily removed. There would be no weapons screening going on today, as no one was in session. All floors would be open all day to the public, but the Assembly and Senate galleries would remain closed. This would free up a number of officers for other tasks. It was snowing outside and predicted to continue throughout most of the day. The day's program:

Today at the Capitol: Saturday, February 26, 2011

10:30—Correctional officers march
10:30—"U.S. Uncut" Rally in front of the Koch offices
11:00—UW Health Radiology march to the Capital
11:00—U.S. Representative Tammy Baldwin march from Library Mall
       up State Street to the Capitol
Noon—"Move on" and Madison Teachers Rally
1:00—Tom Morello concert
1:30—Service Employees International Union (SEIU) Rally
2:00—Students for a Democratic Society
3:00—Main Rally WEAC teachers, auto workers, AFSCME
       and entertainment celebrities

Several in the law enforcement community were concerned that the Tea Party folks or a "lone wolf" type might enter the crowd and attempt to cause trouble. The Koch prank call to the Governor was still a topic of conversation, during which "planting troublemakers" in the crowd was raised. Law enforcement dealing with the exterior was staffed up to deal with those issues, which I hoped would not spill into the building.

There was a rumor floating on the blogs and in other social media that the War Memorial inside the Capitol had been defaced because posters had been hung on the memorial. I made a note to go and see for myself. When I did, either the offending posters had never been there or had been taken down because the memorial appeared untouched.

There would be no meeting of the Policy Group today. If needed, a meeting could be called and the participants would respond. Within the Interior Branch, we grudgingly accepted the reality that the resources assigned to Planning Section in the Command Post continued to be inadequate. Once again, our day in the Interior Branch would be spent planning for what was to come and for things we hoped wouldn't come to pass. We would also spend time dealing with a series of imminent challenges set forth by the largest crowd to date. Having to do this level of planning in the Interior Branch caused us to have less time to supervise our staff and less time to adjust operations that would have led to greater effectiveness in setting staffing levels. Regardless, it was time to make the planning assignments for the day.

Because I had not attended the Policy Group meeting on Friday, I didn't know about the decision *not* to move people out who were reluctant to go after 4:00 p.m. Sunday. When Randy filled me in, I was frustrated and disappointed at this turn of events, because the scale-down plan was working.

I certainly did not relish having to order law enforcement to go "hands-on" with a group of people. Yet I knew from experience that some people really felt strongly that they must be "carried out" to prove that they had given their all to the cause. I felt strongly the vast majority of the 9,000 people who could be in the building at one time would leave voluntarily with their heads held high. To allow a few dozen to a few hundred to stay would place those few in a situation of having a greater influence on events than the rest.

If we cleared the building and had it cleaned, the public could return to protesting during the day (no sleepovers unless the Legislature went into session overnight), the school tours could begin again, and all three branches of government could function.

The Capitol Police Department (CPD) and Department of Administration (DOA) had made public statements on Friday reaffirming the building would close at 4:00 Sunday and protesters must leave. DOA and the CPD had been very careful about their public statements up to this point. To not follow through on what had been said publicly would bring into question all that government officials might say regarding these protests. Information management is always an issue when dealing with large numbers of people. In addition, getting the right information out reliably and at the right time is a challenge. Social media can help—or hurt.

Official word, once given, travels quickly, and so do rumors. In this environment of distrust we needed to be sure we weren't adding to the confusion. We needed to be sending consistent, accurate messages. Again, I wondered where that Public Information Officer (PIO) was that we'd been asking for. The big "we" were struggling to keep ourselves on one page. If I didn't understand the latest plan for Sunday's closing time, we certainly couldn't expect the crowds marching toward the Capitol to know it.

If people were left to stay overnight in the Rotunda after Sunday night, the presence of protesters could be an excuse for the Administration to severely restrict the public access to the building on Monday. In my view, that restriction would cause even more problems. With no true deadline to enforce on Sunday, I recognized we were again going to be way overstaffed for the day.

In the Interior Branch, we went on to discuss the plan I dreaded, but one I knew would be needed the minute we didn't clear the building Sunday night—some form of queuing up visitors to enter the building. The responsibility to develop the plan went to

Assistant Chief Dale Burke and Sergeant Ruth Ewing of the UW Police. The plan for Monday needed to limit the capacity of the building to that of galleries (354), coupled with providing exterior queues that would, in essence, sort people by the purpose of their visit.

I chose to interpret this new capacity number of 354 as the number of *additional* people who could be permitted to enter without showing an appropriate state employee ID or other proof of their official business in the Capitol.

To track all this, we decided to set up separate entrances for separate purposes: staff would enter through one door and press would enter through another door, where posted officers would check credentials. Those with appointments went to another line, where officers would contact the appropriate legislators and ask that an escort meet their visitors. Anyone else was directed to a separate queuing area where officers were tracking the number of people being admitted.

Once we reached the magic number of 354, we would allow admission on a 1-in, 1-out basis. Anyone without an appropriate state employee ID card was given an ID badge at the door. It was illogical and only happening because closing and clearing the building on Sunday was no longer an option. I just shook my head.

Given that the Command Post Logistics team had been overwhelmed by the red tape involved in obtaining simple restroom signs, we held little hope that they would be able to provide all the necessary badges and other equipment by 8:00 a.m. Monday. Contrast the CP Logistics with effective, efficient logistics of Chief Randy Stark's DNR staff processes at the morning briefing, I thought.

The plan for Tuesday, when the Governor would give his Budget Address to a joint session of the Legislature with the Supreme Court in attendance, fell to University Police Assistant

Chief Brian Bridges. Wednesday and beyond—what we termed the "new normal"—needed a lot of work. As of now, the "new normal" was supposed to involve queues, metal screening, visitor badges, and possibly escorts. Also to be considered in Wednesday's planning was the 100th anniversary celebration of the Joint Finance Committee with all former members invited to the event.

I instructed the Interior Branch commanders to format their plans into the Incident Command System (ICS) forms so that we could then send them to the CP electronically. The Command Post could then cut and paste the plans into the Incident Action Plan as needed. When I briefed the CP at 10:00 that morning on how we were proceeding, WSP Captain Teasdale said tersely that I was not authorized to complete the 202 incident objectives, 203/204 division assignments, 205 communications, or 215A (safety) forms. I thought, *Really? Are we now at the stage where we are going to squabble about who can fill out a form?*

I believe in the Incident Command System—the structure and uniformity it fosters is meant to help avert chaos in the midst of a disaster—but his response was bureaucratic and extremely unhelpful. However ridiculous, I followed his directive and placed the plans in both ICS and non-ICS formats so that the CP Planning Section would not have to reformat everything—all of which was truly a waste of people's efforts.

I had been told that Captain Teasdale was an ICS "purist." Everything had a box and every box had a place. I found this laughable, given the lack of logistical support, planning support, and operational decision making of the Command Post.

It then it dawned on me that the Command Post was staffed with people who had much more time on their hands than the Interior Branch division commanders. The Interior Branch was doing the planning, supervising 225 police officers, and carefully managing 20,000+ visitors. The Command Post still couldn't get the food delivered correctly. The resentment by the CP concerning my determination and leadership in the Branch was once again building toward confrontation. Everyone was trying hard to keep up, yet only a few of us had ever been a part of something this big and complex.

While ICS works well for emergency management and resource deployment, the twists of politics were adding to our challenge. When fighting a fire, the strategy established by leadership to extinguish or contain the fire can be understood and agreed upon. The winds may shift, it may or may not rain, and resources and staffing are quickly and efficiently adjusted to deal with the changes. Politicians don't usually weigh in on the tactical operations in firefighting practices. Nevertheless, we were faced with politicians proffering their opinions, pushing the envelope, deciding on the Sunday closing, and then changing their minds, seemingly without regard for our tactical response. Others were controlling the public information. Granted this wasn't your textbook ICS, but I felt the CP couldn't adjust to the varying dynamics of their alleged charge.

> *Months later, I learned that the Command Post had been very frustrated with me. In fact, they met about my actions from time to time and discussed my supposedly overstepping my role as Branch Director. One of my captains, Karen Soley, assigned to the CP, had suggested they elevate me to Incident Commander and have DC Blackdeer take the Interior Branch. That suggestion apparently went nowhere.*

By 11:00 that morning, my Interior Branch division commanders went through a status check of everyone's planning responsibilities to that point. We tried to resolve any issues or barriers. Plans were being developed at an amazing pace. People were working extremely hard and maintaining their focus. I was very proud of them. Periodically, I went down to the Rotunda or headed outside to take an estimate of the crowd on the entire Square.

Using the measurement of the square footage in each segment of the Capitol Square, including the streets, we calculated crowd density and capacity numbers for those moments or days' events. We were also curious about the Command Post's estimates versus our own. We thought their numbers were inflated. We estimated the outdoor crowd to be at 86,000 people using measurements and having two independent calculations completed. Other law enforcement agencies staffing the CP estimated the crowd at 115,000.

I received a call from a friend, Fran Breit, who was with a group of her friends visiting from out of state. They were outside the Capitol and very cold. She was wondering if I had time to get together for a few minutes. We met up at the North Hamilton entrance, where, once inside, Fran and her friends shared the reaction of so many I had seen.

At first glance, most people who hadn't been in the Capitol in a while were surprised, even stunned, at the amount of signage taped all over the walls and railings. Adjusting to the noise level while being bombarded by the visual overload took a moment or two before the desire to take pictures of signs, the crowd, the overall scene, and each other emerged. I had watched this process in hundreds of people over the course of the last twelve days. After posing for a few pictures, I wished them well and returned upstairs.

The preliminary plans developed by the division commanders and deputy branch directors had come through by the 3:00 p.m. deadline. The scale-down plan was looking very good through tonight and up to 4:00 p.m. Sunday. The plan still included all contingencies, including carrying people out of the building, arrested or not.

The queuing plan for Monday was the most complicated, and there were nine different options being contemplated within the plan. It took Assistant Chief Burke and Sergeant Ewing considerable time to explain the variations to us. While quite sophisticated and nuanced, it needed more work and logistical support for queuing lines and signage. The division commanders again voiced their concern about the Command Post's Logistics Section following through on obtaining the badges, signs, bike racks, or tensor barriers (the retractable material stanchions used for establish waiting lines) needed to make the queues operational.

From our point of view, to ensure the Governor's Joint Address on the Budget went successfully, all of the plans to date would be combined with the added pressure of having all elected state officials in one place. Since terrorism had been discussed at the Policy Group last Thursday, the Joint Address plan involved measures to counteract possible terrorist attempts. Few thought the protest crowd would attempt an act of terrorism, but with the Arab Spring underway and Wisconsin receiving national press daily, Madison was on a world stage and who knew what that might spawn. The plan necessarily contained increased explosive, ordnance, and detonation countermeasures.

As the Interior Branch planning review had gone a bit over the hour we had designated for reporting, I was late for the 4:00 Command Post video conference briefing.

Since people still seemed to be changing their thinking about Sunday's closing, there was still the possibility that we would have to carry out or arrest anyone who stayed past 4:00 p.m. The CP demanded that language in the plans about carrying protesters out at closing be struck. I countered to say that this issue should be weighed by the Policy Group again. If we were to reach the goal of having the building return to normal by Tuesday, we needed to have no one sleeping overnight in the Capitol.

I took a deep breath, and asked what would happen if we didn't clear the Capitol Sunday night. How would the protesters who stayed overnight figure into the new 354 capacity number? When would the sleeping in the Capitol end? I was met with silence from the Command Post.

My resistance to immediately yielding to CP authority made some people in the Command Post uncomfortable. Instead of talking it through and respecting my experience dealing with crowds and the like, the discussion was cut off abruptly. In addition, I began to suspect the Administration was making a political calculation. If people stayed overnight, there would be an excuse to keep larger crowds out of the building. Keith Gilkes had been behind the two previous attempts to close and clear the Capitol this past week. Now he had reversed his position by 180 degrees. It didn't add up. I didn't sense anyone within the Command Post was grasping the larger game that was being played.

* * * * *

To ensure communication and avoid surprises, Randy decided to make flyers to place upon the piles of blankets, sleeping bags, and various personal items that had been left unattended. The flyer was a reminder that the belongings would be moved to a "claim" room in the Capitol by Sunday at 4:00 p.m. The officers were given the flyers to distribute as they made contact with the protesters.

My latest health check showed I was still in the "green," but my blood pressure was the highest of my checks to date. I had let some of the artificial nature of life at the Command Post, especially the forms and the bureaucratic hoops, affect me earlier in the day. I also was troubled by the change from fully closing and clearing the building at 4:00 p.m. Sunday, to the voluntary closing. I believe when it comes to notifications from the police, the public should know that what is said and communicated in press releases is solid and accurate, or law enforcement loses credibility.

The DOA had now repeatedly said the building would be closed at 4:00 p.m. The Command Post was backing away from that and in doing so, were damaging their credibility. The challenge for me was that my credibility with the public was linked to that of the CP.

While ruminating over all this, I was asked by Kevin Wernet and Sarah Pfatteicher to speak with them in the hallway. They relayed to me that certain members of the Command Post were frustrated with my argumentative attitude and my "uppityness" in the CP sessions. In addition, Kevin relayed that they were upset that I had been late for the 4:00 p.m. CP briefing.

This was the match to my gasoline. I was furious. First, I felt the Command Post staff were cowards in that they sent subordinates to tell me of their displeasure. Second, the Command Post world is so artificial compared to the Branch that it was a rare pleasure when we could start on time. Hell, what else did they have to do? I had waited for a TV for five days, and a week for a video conferencing hook-up. Computer hook-ups and wired phones had taken four days. More than once we had come to 5:00 p.m. the night before major morning briefings without knowing the location of the briefing sites. The CP had taken close to ten days to get the food organized. I was on a rant while Kevin and Sarah stood wide-eyed.

I didn't have just one boss to please in the operations chief; I had the whole damned Policy Group. Branches don't normally have to plan as we had done. The Planning Section at the CP was supposed to plan. That section hadn't planned diddly-squat. I rattled on that if I weren't so busy fixing their lapses, I would be early for the Command Post briefings.

Poor Kevin and Sarah. I hadn't merely shot the messengers, I had drawn and quartered them. Sarah peeled off and found my two deputies, Brian and Randy. She got them to join us out in the hall. Kevin and Sarah stood nearby as I relayed to Randy and Brian what I had been told. As I explained, I also acknowledged my frustrations and my temper. I wondered out loud if I had outlived my usefulness and effectiveness and asked them if I should step down.

Brian spoke first. He knew me best and I knew he could and would deliver hard news to me, even if it hurt. He shook his head and said the frustrations with the Command Post were shared by everyone in our Branch. The division commanders felt I was tough, demanding, and hard charging, and all were proud and amazed by all we were accomplishing.

The division commanders knew that work had to get done, plans had to be made, and if the Branch wasn't doing this—no one would. Brian insisted that law enforcement working in the Branch would go wherever I told them, do whatever I said, and answer whatever I asked of them. He reminded me that we were bringing in other officers from around the state (some 198 different agencies) and within a short period, we gained their trust, loyalty, and effort. He said my sense of humor, combined with my ability to focus on the needs of Branch staff, proved day after day that my priorities were right-on.

He went on to say that I had to remember that few of the members of the upper management of the Command Post had ever worked with a person, let alone a woman, who was as strong, determined, and un-intimidated by positional authority as I was. He concluded with a laugh, telling me that he can only imagine how crazy I must make the CP.

Randy spoke next, saying he was surprised by my reaction because he hadn't thought of me as someone who would step down in light of criticism. That stung. Randy talked about leaders and leadership challenges, telling me that leaders make the best of what they have, just as we had done in the rest of the Interior Branch. When we didn't have computers, we found some. When no one planned for us, we planned. When no one knew how to organize all the police, we did. While he understood my anger, he knew I wouldn't step down. Not because of what the Command Post had failed to do, but because I wouldn't abandon the men and women of the Branch. Damn, Randy was good. He played to my sense of responsibility, duty, and commitment.

Randy asked me if I had noticed how University Police Sergeant Ruth Ewing acted whenever I was around. I hadn't. He noticed that Sergeant Ewing watched every move of mine whenever she was in the Operations Room of the Capitol. He reminded me that I am a role model and admitted he thought some of what was being relayed from the Command Post had sexist overtones. He asked how could I ever put up with that. How would Ruth and others be impacted?

I put my fuse on hold while we finished tweaking the plans and turned things over to the night crew. As we walked downstairs around 9 p.m., we stopped and greeted people along the way. I saw a protester mopping the floor and another picking up the trash. The medical table was in full operation and we asked if they had any concerns. They said things were going well. Through donations of supplies, they were well stocked and through volunteer medical practitioners from around the area, they were able to keep up with demands. Some folks were being monitored for some significant health issues, but because of privacy rights, nothing more was discussed. The MFD had assigned a paramedic team to handle the law enforcement health checks and these same paramedics were in touch with the protesters' first aid station on a regular basis. If there was an issue, MFD would be on top of it.

I stood at the edge of the Rotunda, looked up, and marveled at this magnificent building. I slowly turned north, east, south, and west. I tipped my head back to look straight up all the way to the painting at the very top of the dome. As my eyes traversed the fourteen stories of mosaics, arches, and plaster reliefs, I thought again about democracy, our Founding Fathers, and the principles we all hold dear (or in some cases, take for granted) as Americans.

Then I noticed something was wrong with the painting at the top of the dome. My heart leapt to my throat. Oh, my God, how did that get damaged? I was startled by this discovery. I went up to the nearest Capitol Police officer and pointed up in horror.

He chuckled, "Chief, it's only a red metallic balloon filled with helium. Someone must have let go and it drifted up there. It happens from time to time."

"Oh, thank God. I thought the painting had been damaged," I replied with a sense of relief.

"I'll get someone up there with a leaf blower and remove the balloon."

"A leaf blower?"

"Yeah, we keep a leaf blower up on that level. You just turn it on and blow the balloon off to the side where you can then retrieve it, pop it, and throw it away."

"Really?"

The uppermost part of the Wisconsin Capitol dome. Errant balloons can be retrieved with leaf blowers. (Photo by Tony Barnes)

"Really. Chief. You need to go home now and rest up."

"Thanks. Good night." I was truly relieved. That is just what I would have needed—a priceless painting damaged. Geez.

I peeled off to the side in one of the alcoves and texted UW Chancellor Biddy Martin to ask if I could talk to her about some events at the Capitol. She replied quickly and suggested I come to Olin House. On my way, I texted my partner, Joanne, and suggested she meet me at Olin. Upon my arrival, I realized I was interrupting the late stages of another dinner party to celebrate the chancellor's 60th birthday with longtime friends, who had arrived from out of town.

She left her guests and we went to the living room where we sat and I explained the Command Post's feedback. She listened intently and asked probing questions. When I was finished with the whole saga, she acknowledged the challenges, the difficulties, and the exhaustion. She shared my frustration and pledged her full support. She reminded me crises never go as designed on paper. Adapting, persevering and meeting priorities were the focus needed to meet the goals. The nonsense with the CP was a distraction, added no value, and wouldn't help me with keeping the event successful.

Joined now by Joanne, Biddy invited us to stay and mingle with her guests. While we were tempted, I was too tired and didn't wish to repeat falling asleep on the ottoman as I had the previous week.

The Capitol was more than overcrowded by the protesters.
(Photos by Jim Escalante)

CHAPTER SIX
TRUST BUILT AND TRUST BROKEN

TWO WEEKS IN NOW WITH A BUSY WEEK TO COME. IN THE NEXT two days most of the protesters would leave the building, the Governor would give his budget address, and a court case would begin. For days, we had been planning to close the Capitol at 4:00 on Sunday afternoon—a key step in returning the building to "normal operations." Our hope was to clear the building on Sunday and re-open it to the public on Monday morning. The intent was not to prevent public access to the Capitol, but rather, to facilitate that access according to long-established building hours.

In its normal operations, our government reflects a philosophical compromise: that we should be ruled by the will of the majority while protecting the rights of the minority. The inherent tension in that arrangement poses challenges, but also provides for the checks and balances so essential to democracy. In the days to come, we would spend much of our time navigating that tricky middle ground. Could we continue to provide daytime access to the public at large if a few refused to leave at night? Would our goal of normal operations be better served by leaving them in place or by forcibly removing them? How far would voluntary compliance take us? And what options did we have if and when that approach failed?

DAY 14: SUNDAY, FEBRUARY 27, 2011

AS I LOADED MY GEAR INTO THE CAR FOR THE MORNING DRIVE to the Capitol, I began thinking about what was ahead for the day and how much remained in flux. If the final decision was to move the remaining people out of the building at 4:00 p.m., I would need to have the proper number of staff on hand. If we were staying with voluntary compliance, I would be overstaffed.

When I arrived for the day, the people in the Rotunda Community had a different energy about them. I had a different energy, too. The events of yesterday were maddening and had served to disrupt my focus. I told myself that today I would not get distracted from my mission. Today was the first day that Kevin Wernet would not be at my side in the Interior Branch. It was his first day off, so Sarah Pfatteicher would be in his place.

Many members of the Rotunda Community were talking about "last night" as their truly "last" for staying in the Capitol. Most were starting to pack up belongings and roll up sleeping bags, making plans for moving the items out before 4:00 p.m. Many called out and thanked me for "everything." As we made our way up the stairs, we noticed there were no people sleeping above the first floor and their belongings were gone as well. This indicated to me the scale-down plan continued to be effective. The protest signs were still taped to the walls; removing them was not part of this phase of the scale-down plan.

The offsite morning briefing went well. Officers were on their posts and at the doors with instructions to keep prohibited items from coming into the building. We were going to keep circulating the flyers with information about lost or misplaced belongings, along with the building closing instructions.

Overnight staff reported there had been a dance until 9:00. There had been a suspicious package found that the canines had checked and cleared. We all chuckled that with all the stuff around, how anyone found just "one" suspicious package was a miracle. At 11:00 p.m., five people had been found in the galleries and when asked to leave, they complied promptly. The officers found that after they closed the doors for the night, some people attempted to gain entry and were turned away.

The general public didn't realize we actually were closing and locking the building late at night when government business was adjourned. The officers had noticed that some of the windows in the first floor bathrooms had the locks removed, and some of the protesters were loading food through the windows after hours. These windows were antiques and window parts were not easy to come by—we would need to keep an eye on that.

After the tensions of the night before, I decided to inject some levity into the 10 a.m. CP briefing. I turned to Charlie Brown's faithful dog, Snoopy, for help. After all, every CP needs a mascot, so I placed Snoopy on the table next to me where Command Post staff could see him while we conferred. Snoopy was dressed in a navy blue crew hat, along with a navy uniform tie, complete with a state seal tie tack! In place of a badge, he was wearing a University Police

The Command Post mascot, Snoopy next to a flower arrangement given to me by the Interior Branch staff. (Photo by Bill Curtis)

logo pin on his chest. Snoopy was now 50 years old and like me, needed reading glasses. I let everyone know that when Snoopy's glasses were on, it was time to get to work! Everyone enjoyed my effort at lightening the mood.

Over the past two weeks, trust and goodwill had broken down, and the numbers we faced each day were not manageable with just the usual Capitol Police resources. We had continued to attempt to operate under a policy and expectation of voluntary compliance. The general public, the politicians, and the police all wanted a return to some level of normalcy, but had yet to agree on how to achieve that. The protesters who had spent the night in the Capitol back on February 15 had done so out of concern that their government was ignoring their interests, and though their numbers and their tactics were out of the ordinary, their goal was to ensure that their representatives were indeed representing them. Most would gladly return to their normal lives as soon as that faith was restored.

The politicians who wanted the protesters gone (not all did) argued that they could not do the job of governing in the midst of the noise and disruption. The politicians (mainly Republican) whose tactics of changing the ground rules for the Joint Finance Committee hearing by cutting off public testimony on February 15, or threatening to withhold Senate paychecks, were also acting out of the ordinary, claiming their actions were because they could not engage in what they saw as "business as usual." The Republicans argued that the Budget Repair Bill, while unpopular with some, was necessary for the state as a whole. They were frustrated that the discontented were preventing them from representing the majority of their constituents.

Then there were the fourteen Senate Democrats who took the extraordinary step of leaving the state, and the Assembly Democrats who introduced over 100 amendments to the Repair Bill. The

Democrats looked for every opportunity to stir up the energy in the crowd so that securing the Capitol would be more difficult. Some Democrats claimed more people as "staff" so they could bypass some of the rules; others allowed people to literally enter through their offices windows.

All parties had some hand in making the return to normal anything but easy. Few were listening to anyone with whom they disagreed. As long as the administration continued its public stance of non-negotiation with the Democrats and the 14 senators stayed away, the protesters would continue to surround the Capitol in large numbers. The large police presence would be necessary to keep the peace. Having Chief Tubbs negotiating and discussing issues of access with the major unions helped us manage day-to-day issues, such as which floors were accessible to protesters and which entrances to the Capitol were open, but it did not appear likely that this approach would return us to normal operations.

Police, emergency responders, and other incident managers are trained to have a Plan B, but now we were continually being told to return to Plan A (voluntary compliance and negotiation). What if voluntary compliance and negotiation didn't work, we asked. Stick with voluntary compliance and more negotiation, we were told by Chief Tubbs.

This was another peculiarity to me. Chief Tubbs spent an overwhelming amount of his time with the protesters. He rarely made a Command Post briefing. He played the role of the "public face" of law enforcement with the protesters and press. Yet beyond saying he wanted voluntary compliance, he wasn't a part of operations. Charles became a negotiator. In some ways, he spent so much time with the demonstrators, there was a point when he seemed to become their advocate. He used "shuttle diplomacy"—moving from demonstrators to the Policy Group and back again.

In police operations, the person negotiating is usually not a decision-maker because, at some point, negotiators can begin to identify with whom they spend their time. This identification and involvement was emotionally draining, making it awkward and difficult for him to disengage and maintain a distance that would allow the tough decisions. On Sunday, I thought Charles had taken the protesters' side.

As we tried to prepare to close the building at 4:00 p.m., I read a text message from the Governor's Chief of Staff asking me to delete from our planning documents any reference to having police remove people as an option for today's closing. It would seem the civilian authority had spoken. I acknowledged his message and ordered the draft of the plan changed accordingly. It was clear to me that after 4:00, "we" would not be in charge of the building. The protesters—be it 50 or 500—would be in charge, whether they fully realized it or not. Those remaining protesters—not the police and not the Policy Group—would determine how many would stay and for how long, because we had no agreement as to how to remove them.

It was also clear that the plan I dreaded—the queuing system that limited access to the building—would be put in place for Monday. If we were able to clear the Capitol completely on Sunday evening, we could open on Monday morning with some semblance of normal operations. But if even a few protesters were allowed to stay, we would be forced to limit access on Monday for fear that we would be unable to re-close the building that night. Thus, access to the facility would be far more limited on Monday and in the following days than if we just removed any remaining folks at 4:00 p.m.

If a few protesters chose to stay, it would be because they felt they were ensuring a toehold of access for the public. What they didn't realize was that their presence would do just the opposite and would be used to justify restricting access and increasing security even further. It also seemed that Charles didn't get this nuance either.

The argument I had made to remove any remaining protesters at 4:00 p.m. and then open the building to the public on Monday at 8:00 a.m. for "normal operations" did not carry the day. It was time to do the best I could with what remnants of the scale-down plan were still intact.

After the briefing with the Command Post concluded, I spent more time observing the crowds in the building. The negotiation teams of UW Police officers Chief Warden Randy Stark had established on Friday continued talking to people and moving from group to group. The teams had been remarkably successful as they, along with the marshals, union leaders, and Chief Tubbs, had gained voluntary compliance with every aspect of the plan to date.

The Policy Group convened at 11:00 a.m. There were 17 of us in the room, one of our largest gatherings to date. In attendance were:

- Dan Blackdeer, Deputy Chief of the Capitol Police, Incident Commander
- Ted Blazel, Senate Sergeant-at-Arms
- Donald Dunbar, General, Wisconsin National Guard
- Keith Gilkes, the Governor's Chief of Staff
- Jodi Jensen, Assistant to the Secretary of the Department of Administration
- Dave Mahoney, Dane County Sheriff, member of the Policy Group (Capitol Grounds, City Streets)
- Rob Marchant, Clerk for the Senate
- Dave Mathews, Assistant Administrator, Wisconsin Department of Justice

- Sarah Pfatteicher, UW Associate Dean, Assistant and Aide-de-camp of the Interior Branch Director
- Darren Price, Wisconsin State Patrol
- Susan Riseling, Chief of Police, UW–Madison, Interior Branch Director, member of the Policy Group
- Randy Stark, Chief Warden, Wisconsin Dept. of Natural Resources, Deputy Interior Branch Director
- Anne Tonnon Byers, Assembly Sergeant-at-Arms
- Charles Tubbs, Chief of the Capitol Police
- Ed Wall, Administrator of the Wisconsin Department of Justice, Division of Criminal Investigation
- Noble Wray, Chief of the Madison Police

Dan summarized the briefing I had given him earlier. We then turned to the 4:00 p.m. plan the Interior Branch had developed. The plan had already been adjusted to reflect the directive that the police not touch the protesters in an effort to clear the building. I was still convinced that not moving the few remaining protesters out of the Capitol would actually lead to far greater restrictions on protesters and the overall public.

It wasn't a matter of my agreeing or disagreeing with the protesters or the government; it was that I felt a professional obligation to protect the public's right to express their thinking and to have access to the state Capitol when the government was conducting business. I believed the majority of people would comply and leave. A small group of people should not be allowed to stop that or be manipulated in such a way as to end access. Yet that was exactly where we were heading.

The group accepted the plan as drafted. The union working group had the idea to line up and march the crowd out of the State Street doors. Those doors had been closed since February 19. The group agreed with Charles that this would be a very fitting way to end this part of the protest. The Capacity Management division commander would make this happen. We all agreed Charles and the union leaders should lead the exit march.

Charles had more ideas and passed out a draft document agreed to by union leadership. At 4:00, there would be a public address announcement asking the protesters to leave via the State Street doors and thanking them for their cooperation. It further stated:

> For those who feel strongly that they should stay in the
> building, we ask that you please go to the first floor
> Rotunda area, one level up from the main floor by the
> railing, so as to allow others to leave the building.

In my view, this line in the draft, if adopted, was an invitation to the protesters to stay in the Capitol past closing and was the antithesis of the scale-down plan.

Charles' plan had the cooperation of the marshals and outlined the marshals' roles and responsibilities. The plan called for the marshals to take the lead in approaching people after 3:00 and ask them to move down to the lower floors. Union marshals would eventually be posted on the second floor, asking people's cooperation to not go up to the higher floors.

Every entrance would be staffed with a marshal to encourage people to line up and exit via the State Street doors as part of the main crowd. This meant the police would stay in their usual posts and refrain from moving the crowd. The marshals would reduce the chance of law enforcement actions creating any type of spark. This portion of the plan illustrated the strong and valuable relationship between Charles and the union leadership. In this way, Charles' efforts had been truly remarkable.

According to the draft, after the main group of marchers paraded out, Chief Tubbs and a couple of officers would be joined by a few union leaders. As a group, they were to open a dialogue with those who had not left voluntarily. Charles would attempt to convince the remaining protesters to leave. Successful or not, Charles wanted to allow twenty people into the building to pick up trash and preserve the signs and posters.

Having closely watched the crowd inside the building for two weeks now, we became aware this was no longer "one" group in solidarity. Instead, the protest had segmented the groups into various factions. I wanted Charles' assessment of whether the union felt they were in charge and in control of the whole group any longer. Charles said the unions felt strongly they could direct the operations of most of their members. However, there were other folks who had joined the protests who were not within the union ranks. These non-members were sympathetic to the unions and supportive of collective bargaining, but they did not necessarily feel the need to follow union instructions about behavior. Many of these individuals wanted to be arrested to show their dedication to the cause of preserving collective bargaining.

These were the folks Charles was anticipating would stay behind. The Interior Branch had gathered intelligence that over a hundred of these protesters were eager to be arrested. They had developed a well-written message to give to the media outlets upon their arrests. Arresting those who wished to be arrested was a technique I have used before. Technique or not, facilitation or not, Charles was totally against any arrests. So, unknown to the protesters, no arrests of this nature were going to occcur.

Once the teachers had returned to their classrooms a few days into the protests, the people who stayed overnight had kept the protest in the national news. Signs around the Capitol reminded viewers "The whole world is watching," "America is watching,"

"Egypt is with us," and "Arab Spring during a Wisconsin Winter." This core group believed that the occupation of the Capitol building had begun on February 15, even though the building was legally mandated to remain open that night because Joint Finance was in session. Nevertheless, these "occupiers" felt that in order to keep faith with the "Wisconsin 14" (the Democratic senators who had left the state), they needed to stay put until the senators returned.

Their strategy was two-fold. If the Capitol was actually closing, then they would not leave without being forced. After they were forced out, they would have garnered widespread media coverage and shown their resolve. The other prong of their strategy was to have so many people remain behind such that the police could not logistically arrest them all, resulting in the building remaining "occupied," which would also draw attention to their cause. When they discovered that they were allowed to stay beyond closing, they would most likely believe the second prong of their strategy had worked—that there had been too many to arrest and they had then "won."

Regardless of whether the protesters stayed or left, the action of DOA announcing the closure and the appearance of the police standing by ready to enforce this action would begin to drive a wedge between the protesters and the police. If that didn't create the wedge, the queues and limited access on Monday certainly would. For two weeks, the protesters had seen the police as neutral, if not supportive. Our collaborative relationship was about to change, whether anyone liked it or not.

At this point, the tough-talking "throw the protesters out" language that I had heard in the Policy Group earlier in the week was gone. The State Patrol and Division of Criminal Investigation were silent. Something had shifted. Positions don't shift like that without a reason.

I realized that the Policy Group's refusal to allow the police to go "hands on" came not from a desire to keep the peace, but from a political desire to limit overall access. If the number of the general public could be limited, the silencing of dissent would occur because the legal ability to be loud and boisterous in an office or in the galleries was restricted. The legal ability to be loud and boisterous in the Rotunda was almost unlimited—there was no clear capacity limit, and no specific rules against disruptive behavior in this central space. From a political position, allowing a few dozen determined, but isolated, protesters to remain in the Rotunda was preferable to allowing open access to thousands each business day.

The Policy Group continued to consider plans for Monday. The queue plan had nine variations to choose from. There was a discussion with the Senate and Assembly sergeants-at-arms about constituent visits and queues for such purposes. After some discussion, it was agreed any senator or representative could have up to eight constituent visitors at any one time. The Command Post would design a badging system and signage for the queues.

The Logistics Section at the CP would have to supply what was needed. Given the difficulties we had experienced with the Logistics Section to date, I was concerned and asked Dan if the CP could handle all of the items we needed for the queues. He assured me that they would. What else could he say? Part of me wished he had just said "no," for then the Interior Branch would have found alternatives, but without having any access to Capitol Police Department funding, I needed to rely on the Command Post.

The Policy Group confirmed that if there were people in the building overnight, there would be no general access allowed for the public on Monday. Metal screening at the exterior doors would also begin Monday. Unless a member of the public had specific business in the Capitol to see a legislator or attend a hearing or proceeding, he or she would not be granted access. Large-scale food deliveries would end and ground-level windows would be re-secured.

The strictest queuing plan meant the general capacity number of 9,000 visitors in the door at any one time would now drop to 354, less the number of protesters left in the Rotunda. Using this formula, if 354 protesters stayed, not another soul from the general public would be allowed in the building, no matter how legitimate their business. I knew that could not be considered true access and I doubted it was Constitutional.

A slightly less restrictive plan called for allowing constituents with an appointment to enter, eight at a time per legislative office. If this plan was maximized, it would allow 792 members of the public to enter. A third variation on the queuing plan would allow additional access to folks wanting to attend a hearing, increasing access to the general public by a few hundred more. The Interior Branch would need to research the capacity of each hearing room and inform the CP's Logistic section so the badges and signs could be made for each hearing, as well as for each legislative office and the galleries.

We would soon be faced with additional complications, as some representatives made "appointments" with constituents and escorted them to their offices, only to then allow them to wander the Capitol as they wished. No more visitors for that representative would be admitted until an ID badge was returned to the officers stationed at the exit doors, who could then issue the badge to a new visitor. This required a good-faith effort on the part of visitors. If they didn't turn in a badge or went out a different door, the badge would be gone. Given the political and partisan rancor, good faith was hard to count on and it wasn't long before Democratic legislators ran out of badges for their constituents.

Much was still undecided about Monday's access, and the new routine for entry into the Capitol after Tuesday was still up in the air. In addition, the Department of Administration wanted us to initiate a permitting process for protests inside the Capitol. Ideas were still being generated for what the "new normal" might look like. There was a lot left to do, and we had yet to get through the day.

After the Command Post meeting, I talked with Incident Commander DC Dan Blackdeer. I told him that I understood we were not going to remove people, but that I needed to share my concerns that not removing people would result in greater restriction to the public than if we actually removed those who didn't cooperate. I believed greater restrictions would be fundamentally biased. We had gathered information about the strategy we attributed to the non-union members. He appreciated my concerns, but he didn't want law enforcement to create the flashpoint, and stood firm on maintaining voluntary closing and exit.

Moving to my next issue, I asked when the Exterior Branch was meeting, as I wanted to know about its Policy Group. I asked why I hadn't been invited to those meetings, as members of the Exterior Branch seemed to always be present at Interior Branch meetings. I wanted to review the city and county's practices, as they had certainly weighed in on the Interior Branch procedures.

Dan relayed there was no "Policy Group" *per se* for the Exterior Branch. He then confided that, indeed, there actually was no Exterior Branch. The city was an operation unto its own. The county, while more cooperative, didn't function as a branch either. Although Dan was the Incident Commander, he had no illusions that anyone from the city or county was truly going to listen to him and follow his instructions if they disagreed with him.

I instantly felt for Dan. What an awful position for him. There is nothing worse than to have the title and the responsibility without the authority or ability to control resources, procedures and decisions. The Command Post was bringing in hundreds of police officers, troopers, wardens, and deputies from around the state, partially because the City of Madison police and the Dane County Sheriff had refused to assist inside the Capitol.

I suggested to Dan that we establish "Area Commands," a management structure defined within the Incident Command System that is used to manage events. Area Commands have the responsibility to set overall strategy and policy, allocate critical resources according to priorities, ensure that incidents are properly managed, and make sure that objectives are met and strategies followed. Area commands are part of the national Incident Command System (ICS) and defined by the Federal Emergency Management Administration. (www. training.fema.gov).

In short, area commands allow for parallel management of different pieces of an incident, without an overall Incident Commander needing to coordinate what are essentially separate activities. This structure would relieve Dan of being the paper leader of the entire event, when he clearly wasn't in charge. I made the case that this structure would reflect what was truly happening. The City of Madison and its streets and the County Sheriff outside on the terrace could be their own area commands.

We at the Interior Branch were churning out lots of plans, handling most of our own logistics, dispatching our own units, and gathering our own information. I wanted desperately to have a public information officer and a one-way blog. Technically, the Interior was currently a branch, but over the course of the past ten days, it had become, in many ways, its own command.

Dan would not or could not agree with my suggestion. We parted amicably.

There was a flash mob scheduled for 1:00 that afternoon in the Capitol Rotunda, which seemed a bit ironic. The flash mob idea was to have an extremely large crowd gather, seemingly impromptu, in the Capitol Rotunda and sing *Do You Hear the People Sing?* from the musical, *Les Miserables*. The crowd had been here for over a week—

it was hardly a "flash." I wanted to be in the Rotunda to see this event, so I scrambled up from the Capitol basement and stood on a second-floor bridge to watch and listen.

Deep in the crowd, I saw my stepson Nate. He loved *Les Miserables* and has a good singing voice. At age 18, he had voted for the first time last fall. It was important to me that he take an active part in governance, regardless of whether or not I agreed with him. Sure enough, right at 1:00, the entire crowd began singing with great gusto and passion. When they finished the song, a large cheer went up and people began to leave.

On my way back to the Interior Branch, I made contact with COS Keith Gilkes. I explained that I understood the city and county law enforcement agencies would not enter the Capitol for crowd management purposes. Given their position, I thought that the state law enforcement agencies in the Capitol, responsible for keeping the government in operation and the inside crowd managed, should begin to meet without the city and county. He quickly agreed and said he would coordinate and attend an early morning meeting with Dan, Charles, DCI Administrator Ed Wall, General Dunbar, and me, starting the next day.

Upon returning to the Interior Branch Operations Room in 400 NE, I gathered all the division commanders and support staff to brief them on what items were needed. We needed instructions for the public that the officers would give to the people in queue, so that as they waited, they would know what was going on. With Monday's schedule in hand, we had organized the information needed for the signs and easels by event, hearing, or meeting. We were going to develop physical queues with bike racks. However, bike racks were not available on short notice, so we suggested the CP Logistics contact the airport and borrow some tensor barriers.

It was getting close to 3:00 in the afternoon. The union marshals were ready in accordance with the closing plan. People were starting to gather outside the Capitol to watch. We lowered the capacity inside to keep the crowd to a manageable level, less than 1,500 for the exodus march at 4:00 p.m. People were very cooperative and friendly and most people easily complied with the marshals' requests. I headed down to the ground-floor Rotunda, where the largest crowd was gathered.

The "Citizen's Mic" had been operating for weeks now, and allowed many people to come to the microphone to speak. This amplified speaking had given all of us a break from the incessant drumming. Various folks would use the mic to give a speech, others would read correspondence addressed to the protesters, and sometimes there were just announcements. The mic facilitated people being heard over the often noisy Rotunda area.

Using the Citizen's Mic, people were asked to raise their hands if they were going to remain after 4:00. Others made announcements in an effort to organize the marchers. Some folks were talking about civil disobedience instructions. A few Democratic politicians were present, and clearly they were not going to shy away from a microphone or the moment, to address their supportive public.

After checking to make sure that State Street doors were staffed with officers to allow protesters to exit only, I moved to the other exterior doors for the same purpose. Once people were out, they needed to remain out. Back in the Rotunda, Chief Tubbs was readying the group. The protesters lined up and at 4:00 p.m., over a thousand protesters marched out, with Charles leading the pack. I got in the line about twenty people back from the front with Sarah Pfatteicher next to me, and when we got outside the door, the crowd was cheering on the exiting protesters.

The outside crowd was large and I didn't want to lose Sarah. We stood together, to the left of the door, and I shook as many hands as I could. I thanked the folks streaming out and they thanked me. Many wished me good luck with the protesters who wouldn't leave. Several said they would see us tomorrow. I had my doubts.

People kept flowing out of the building smiling, cheering, and pumping their fists in the air. Only one person attempted to swim upstream and get back in. I was able to grab hold of him and turn him around. He seemed surprised that I had no intent to arrest him. I simply wanted him to move in the same direction as everyone else. The crowd quickly swarmed around him and helped move him away from the doors. When the last of the folks in the first wave left the building, Charles, some union leaders, Sarah, and I slipped back in the building and the doors were closed behind us. The crowd outside stayed on the grounds for a while.

About 500 people had chosen to remain in the Capitol. We had been told by some of the marchers on their way out that a small group of protesters was going to stay behind, attempt to open a door, and let people back in the building. The main march was over, so all the doors were closed and locked. We had suspected that those who remained behind would be less unified than the larger group had been, and we soon saw signs of that fragmentation. Two dozen protesters, all young adults equipped with a couple of drums, moved slowly from the Rotunda toward the State Street door.

I nicknamed the group the "Devilish Dozens," and ordered a team of twenty officers to stand on the inside of the State Street doors to prevent them from opening the door to allow others inside. The 24 protesters moved straight to the doors yelling and drumming, coming within feet of the officers.

Approaching the one appearing to be the leader—a title he would not accept—I asked him if he and his colleagues wanted to leave.

He replied. "Hell no, open the fucking door and let them back in."

I responded, "Not going to happen."

In fourteen days, this was the first time any protester had been less than courteous to me. The officers knew to stand their ground and keep the doors closed. I left them to do their job.

Returning to the Rotunda, I was stopped by a group of about 100 people who had wanted to watch the march, but had not been comfortable being in the large crowd, so they stayed back out of the way. Now, they wanted to leave the Capitol, but the Devilish Dozens were opposed to any more people leaving and blocked the way.

Several people in the group of 100 asked if they could exit out of a different door. Another team of officers led them outside without incident and without anyone else getting back in.

Meanwhile, Chief Tubbs was talking to one of the groups of protesters who had remained inside the Rotunda not wanting to leave. When the Devilish Dozens, near the State Street entrance, realized they were not going to be able to maneuver past the police to reopen the doors and couldn't stop others from leaving, they returned to the Rotunda, drumming all the way.

There were a considerable number of media inside the building from local, regional, and national outlets. They were all there to report on the arrests they thought were going to occur. Pat Simms, a longtime local journalist, asked me what was going to happen next.

I smiled and said, "Lots of talking." She asked when the arrests would begin and I just chuckled and said I had no idea. It was true.

She probed a little more, saying "Tonight?"

I replied that Chief Tubbs was going to talk them out of the building.

At about 4:45, I moved up to the second floor to view the whole Rotunda. About 350 people remained inside the Capitol at that point. I returned downstairs and mingled with several individuals. There were some people with children and they asked what would happen to their kids if they were arrested. I told them that I doubted they would be arrested, barring any violence. We had a good laugh. The kids looked afraid. I knelt down and talked with the kids for a few minutes in an effort to reassure them. I gave several of the kids little Bucky Badger police pins I carry in my uniform pocket. The kids love Bucky, even in a police uniform.

Others approached me and asked when the arrests would start. They wanted to get arrested, get processed, and then get home. Several talked about having to go to work in the morning. I explained I didn't foresee any arrests occurring that night. They weren't sure if they could believe me.

Representative Mark Pocan approached me and asked me when the arrests would begin. I told him what I had told everyone else: that unless the crowd turned violent, which I didn't anticipate, there would be no arrests. Charles was going to talk them all out. Pocan couldn't believe it.

I had known Representative Pocan for a number of years, having testified before committees on which he served. He asked if Chief Tubbs knew there would be no arrests; I acknowledged Charles did, and that Charles was attempting to convince people to leave voluntarily. Pocan said there were people who wouldn't leave, short of being arrested. He claimed, as I had stated before, some felt it was a matter of principle. Some wanted to be arrested for staying to express their views, and to stand against the Capitol being "closed." I agreed with his assessment. Of course, Representative Pocan had no way of knowing what was planned for tomorrow in terms of differentiated queues and identification cards. Rep. Pocan went to find Chief Tubbs, so we parted ways.

Charles was still committed to voluntary compliance and not forcibly removing people, so the 200 members of law enforcement were unnecessary. The commanders in the Interior Branch began the demobilization of law enforcement early.

Charles was continuing his attempts to talk to the protesters who remained on the first floor. At this point, it seemed he had given up trying to get them to leave the building. He was now focused on getting them to move down to the ground floor to consolidate all the protesters into one place.

An exception to the consolidation was the "Family Center" on the first floor, which Charles had negotiated to leave in place. The Family Center was no more than a hallway where children's handmade art had hung for the past two weeks, decorating the walls. There were toys, books, and blankets for children to use, and it was an important area for kids to find some stability with fewer stimuli than the rest of the building offered. However, to move all adult protesters down a level was important to us, as it would help us to reduce the number of law enforcement we needed to have on hand in the days ahead.

Meanwhile, those designated as sign collectors were inside the Capitol but reluctant to take down any of the signs, because not all of the protesters had left. The union-organized trash crew was making its way around, cleaning up the litter. The Capitol cleaning crew was working on the upper floors, but for now, the signs would stay.

Chief Warden Randy Stark and I joined up and talked about the lack of connection between what Charles might be negotiating and what we as the Interior Branch could logistically support and provide. We decided that Randy would stay with Charles as he continued his negotiations. We knew no one could out-talk Charles, but we also recognized Charles must have been dead on his feet from working non-stop since February 13. Somehow through it all, Charles kept his temperament very even with the protesters.

Today was the first time the protesters had been asked to leave. Those who were left now constituted an occupation. My professional view was that the remaining protesters held a minority opinion. The thousands of others who had taken part in the marches, rallies, sleepovers, testimony singing, drumming, sign-carrying, and flag-waving over the past two weeks had left the building, quietly acknowledging that it was time to return the Capitol to normal operations.

Those remaining within the Rotunda Community were now making a statement against the building operation hours of the Capitol. In some ways, it was evident that a few believed that if they gave up staying overnight, it would mean they had given in or allowed the Governor and Republicans to "win." It was important to this group of protesters to show they were still in control of "the people's house." Unwittingly, their presence would deny the access to the general public starting the next day.

Sarah and I went back upstairs so we could bring the Interior Branch and the CP up to speed on how things went for closing. We reported there were still 350 people in the building with fifty being members of the media. Another hundred wanted to be arrested quickly and would probably leave once they realized we were not going to be making arrests. The Interior Branch needed to turn our attention to the queuing plan for Monday.

The Command Post was concerned that it could not support the logistics of the queuing plan. While I wasn't surprised, I was disappointed. They had waited until 6:00 p.m. to tell us. They wanted to cut back on the number of badges they were required to make. We needed approximately 1,880 to properly make the queue work. The CP Logistics Section could supply 120. The tensor barrier borrowed from the airport was not to be used outside. This was problematic since the queues were supposed to be outside. As of now, without the logistical support, tomorrow was going to be a disaster. It was a recipe for failure.

In addition to little logistical support, the CP wanted us to make a corral for the protesters to limit them from moving throughout the building and to reduce the number of law enforcement needed. I asked if they had communicated this objective to Charles, since he was the one doing the negotiating, but they had not been in touch with Charles.

The Interior Branch started working on a plan that would give the protesters an area on the ground floor, complete with bathrooms and an alcove to store their belongings. If we did corral the protesters, we might be able to open the building to the general public without a queuing system. Some of our DNR division commanders went to work on that plan. If what they came up with would avoid the queuing, I was all for it.

After the briefing, Randy rejoined Charles, who was hard at work with the remaining protesters. By the agreement Charles had reached earlier, the protest group had a couple of marshals who

While the number of protesters inside the Capitol was significantly reduced, the buckets and drums remained. (March 2, 2011) (Photo by Kevin Wernet)

remained with them. The marshals negotiated food delivery. A few people wanted to stay on the first floor outside the family area. They were a small group of 20 to 24 protesters and at this point, Charles and Randy didn't think it was worth arguing over. This required us to relocate some law enforcement posts.

Another marshal requested to use a third-floor hearing room overnight. This request was denied. The food delivery occurred on schedule without incident. While the group was resistant to leaving, members were generally cooperative; it was not the police they were protesting.

As the evening wore on, most of the exterior crowds dispersed. An individual had erected a tent outside on the grounds, but once officers made contact, the tent came down. A group of people was getting ready to sleep outside the King Street entrance. We were impressed with people who believed so strongly in their cause that they would stay outside overnight without so much as a tent in February in Wisconsin, in temperatures far below freezing. They must be young, we quipped.

At 10:00 p.m., the troopers made another request to the marshals—to have all the sleepers move down to the ground floor. No one had moved. A short time later, Capitol Police again found the windows in a men's bathroom had been tampered with so the window couldn't lock. The window could open far enough for a person to climb in or out. Maintenance was summoned to fix the window. Tampering with window locks reoccurred over the next several days.

As the evening wore on, Charles tried his absolute best to convince people to leave voluntarily. The number of people remaining inside dropped from approximately 350 to 198. It looked like we would have to use the queue and the corral.

DAY 15: MONDAY, FEBRUARY 28, 2011

ARRIVING AT THE CAPITOL I MET UP WITH CPD OFFICER GINA RAY, WHO gave me a plan regarding a change to the security set up outside the hallway entrance to the "Rock"—the Governor's complex of offices. While troopers and wardens had been assigned with her since this all began two weeks ago, she still felt there were physical changes that were needed. Officer Ray handed me a schematic of her plan. She needed some equipment to carry it out and I authorized it right away.

In 400 NE, the signs over the door that changed daily read: *February 28, Day 15, T+ 11* (my retirement sign). There was a new posting that looked like a rural township's population sign found on a county highway in Wisconsin. It read: *Rotunda Community pop. 198*. We all joked with Randy that as "mayor" of the community, his job was to work on getting that population to zero.

The first queue was being established outside at the King Street entrance. Three trashcans were located nearby for disposal of prohibited items and portable toilets were added in case people had to stay in line for long periods of time.

By then, I should have learned that everything had a rule that governed it, and portable toilets were no exception. The plan called for portable toilets to be placed in a location near the queue so that people would use them and not just relieve themselves in place. However, according to CPD Lieutenant Marc Schmidt, some operational rule stated that portable toilets should never be placed on the Capitol grounds. The placement would have to be across the street on the city side of the Square, which meant the toilets would not be used, as people were not likely to get out of line to venture that far away.

We took another sleeper count and were able to lower the Rotunda Community population sign to 153. Kevin Wernet and I headed off to our first meeting with just the Interior Branch and Incident Commander. The meeting was to be held in COS Keith Gilkes' office on the first floor.

Keith welcomed Charles Tubbs, Dan Blackdeer, Ed Wall, Kevin Wernet, and me to his office. General Dunbar attended via phone. We brought everyone up to speed on the overnight. It was clear that Charles had slept in his office and looked a bit rough around the edges, yet he was his usual upbeat self.

The remaining 153 occupants included a group of about 35 who were interested in being disruptive and confrontational. There were 20 to 24 on the first floor outside of the "corral." Despite Charles' and Randy's best efforts, the group would not move to the ground floor last night or this morning. It was decided that unless the group would go to the ground floor, we would not open the doors to the general public.

I voiced my concern that we were keeping out the public because of the non-cooperation of a few, namely 20 to 24 people. I was adamant that we should not be giving that level of control to so few. Charles continued his insistence of voluntary compliance. While I supported voluntary compliance, there comes a point at which too few can keep too many from being able to access the Capitol. The decision not to move the group to the ground corral would cause the building not to open to the general public, and would turn the tide of public support away from us.

Charles felt that we should allow an exchange of people. If someone outside wanted to come in and someone inside wanted to go out, we could let that one-to-one exchange happen while he and Randy were attempting to negotiate with the group to move to the corral. Relying on voluntary compliance to clear the building was troubling enough, but now we were actively planning to support those who refused to comply by allowing the exchange of one-in and one-out. Would staying overnight when the government was not in session ever come to an end?

I wondered aloud if we still had the same goal, namely, of restoring the Capitol to regular business hours without people sleeping over. If that was our goal, then we wanted the 153 number to be reduced. The one-to-one exchange Charles was suggesting seemed counter to that. Despite my questions, no one seemed to want to clarify what our goals were at this point.

For now, the one-to-one plan and the general public queue plan to reach 354 were on hold until the negotiation ended with the 24 occupiers on the first floor. Charles predicted that it would take about an hour or two to get them to move. Every hour of delay in opening the doors added to the frustration of those lined up outside.

While Charles tried to work his magic, we needed to keep floors 2, 3, and 4 clear. We placed officers and troopers at the base and top of the stairs to keep the 153 protesters from accessing those floors. If the protesters failed to listen, law enforcement posted at the top of the stairs would escort the protesters back down. Offenders would not be arrested or ejected. If the person attempted a second run-by, he or she would be removed from the building. Hooray! This was the first change in the voluntary compliance plan. I was heartened to be able to place a new tool in the officer's toolbox that would allow them to maintain order. Something this simple would allow me to reduce the number of officers deployed.

We needed to get moving on this plan while the building was still closed. We decided to forgo the 10:00 a.m. CP briefing because we had just met. Charles and Randy were headed off to negotiate, and I was headed back to the Branch. I would check in with Randy in an hour to see if the doors could be opened.

As we were leaving, the Governor's Cabinet was meeting in the room next door to Keith's office, and we heard quite a commotion outside Keith's windows, which overlooked the King Street entrance where the queues were located. A protester had climbed the façade of the building and was attempting to gain access to the Governor's conference room.

CPD officer Gina Ray and two other uniformed officers had responded and were outside on the balcony. Officer Ray was attempting to talk the person in from the ledge. Before I knew it, Charles climbed through the window and out onto the balcony. I headed into the Cabinet room and stood near the window, watching the officers.

The Cabinet meeting went on uninterrupted.

After a few minutes of watching this new drama unfold, I was convinced the officers would be able to keep the Governor and Cabinet secure, so I left and returned to the Branch. Eventually CPD Officer Ray, along with the other officers, reached out and grabbed the individual, pulling him in and over the railing safely.

On my way back to the Branch, I decided to talk to some of the 153 protesters still in the building. It was there I met Janie.[16]

When I said, "Hello," she looked a bit dazed.

"I'm cold," she replied. "I need some hot water."

I looked around and spied a large coffee pot that was labeled "hot water." I said to Janie, "Let's go over to the food station."

"No, I don't want to get up."

"OK, I'll get you a cup. Tea, coffee, or hot chocolate?" I asked.

"No, just hot water," she replied. I retrieved a cup of hot water, returned, and as I handed it to her, she said "Thank you."

There were blankets lying about and so I picked one up and while it was far from clean, I asked, "Would you like this blanket around your shoulders?"

"That would be nice," so I helped her up, draped the blanket around her shoulders; we sat on a nearby bench.

---

[16] Janie is not the woman's real name. After leaving the Capitol, I never was able to reconnect with Janie to ask permission to use her real name.

Although a trained observer, I found it hard to estimate Janie's age. Maybe she was in her 50s or 60s? She had been in the Capitol along with her husband for a long time now. Sleeping on the marble floor had been unforgiving. She had showered since she arrived, because a system had been developed in which the protesters would take turns going to nearby apartments to take showers and get a change of clothes. However, such arrangements were now cut off.

She told me that she had cancer and was receiving chemotherapy. She had to monitor her blood pressure several times a day, but the first aid station was now gone and she had no one to turn to. She had more chemotherapy to receive, but that was a few weeks away.

She talked to me about why staying was so important to her. She felt she had to stay for all those who couldn't be here from throughout the state. She had worked all her life, often holding two jobs, but since she had been diagnosed with cancer, she had to cut back on working. I just listened, keeping to my professional position of not discussing politics or the merits of the legislation. She said she would not leave voluntarily.

In a short period of time, simply because I listened, we built a bit of trust between us. She realized I was not going to suddenly grab her and toss her out. Janie wondered if the government was going to starve the protesters out, and I told her as long as I was working here, no one would be starved out. She asked if the Governor would turn off the heat at night to freeze them. I said they might turn down the heat for conservation purposes—but I didn't think it would get below sixty. I made a mental note to check.

Using my radio, I called for University Police Captain Michael Newton to join me. He came down from the Operations Room immediately. Michael was an EMT and led our First Responders EMS group at UW-Police. I asked Michael if he would meet with

Janie several times a day to monitor her blood pressure. He readily agreed and he and Janie set a schedule.

I attempted to speak to some of the young people who had attempted to reopen the State Street door the night before. They were just waking up and were not as interested in talking to me as were some of the older, more seasoned protesters.

I met a nurse from University Hospital and her husband, a mason by trade. They had spent the weekend at the Capitol. He had a few days off this week and she didn't have to be to work until later tonight. They thought they would stay until this evening or until the arrests started, but weren't interested in being arrested.

Afterward, I headed upstairs to the Operations Room. The latest twist in my day was to learn of several Democratic representatives and their staff using their access control cards to allow hundreds of people to bypass the queues. I ordered the shutdown of the card access system.

CPD Lieutenant Marc Schmidt said he couldn't remember anything like this ever happening. He made the call to CPD dispatch and the system was shut off. Now we had not only blocked entry into the Capitol by members of the public, but were also blocking the automated access of elected officials. As before, we posted officers to check credentials of staff and elected officials. This was hardly a promising step in our attempt to return to normal operations.

Randy and Charles checked in, saying that there hadn't been enough progress yet in getting the protesters to relocate to the first floor to trigger the opening of the Capitol. This was very unwelcome news. In fact, keeping the doors to the building shut was becoming quite problematic.

The queue outside had all sorts of problems. The 120 constituent badges were utterly inadequate and the CP had not increased the supply. No wonder the representatives and their staffs attempted to bypass the queues. The people in the queues were tired of waiting for badges and were demanding to see their representatives.

University Police Assistant Chief (retired) Dale Burke had wanted to establish a police escort system for constituents because there were not enough badges. As we neared 11:00 that morning, Dale let me know that the queues were essentially shut down. This was unacceptable. We needed the 24 reluctant protesters moved, more badges made, and the doors opened.

Chief Tubbs had not been able to achieve a negotiated settlement. This situation was becoming indefensible. Charles needed the doors to remain closed to have leverage with the 24. If I just overrode everyone by opening the doors while maintaining voluntary compliance, which Charles insisted upon, we could have a real mess on our hands. Yet due to the inadequate logistics and negotiation stalemate, Charles had cut off legitimate access even more severely than our queue plan.

As I was trying to sort out the situation, I asked the Branch staff what else I needed to know at this point. Many of the division commanders said that because no one was being let into the building, we had about 100 un-needed cops. My initial thought was to turn them over to Dale to form an enormous escort system. That idea would take a bit of time to think through—and I didn't feel we had a lot of time.

Certainly no one had any patience with us. We still had no way to communicate with the public directly. The more time that elapsed with the doors closed and the queue malfunctioning, the more credibility we were losing. It was time to move the 24, whether they liked it or not. I tried to reach Charles to tell him but couldn't connect.

I suggested the hundred extra cops be sent to lunch and then we would replace those on post when they were done. That way, only half of the crew would be visible at one time. That was when we discovered there was no lunch. How could that be true? It was Day 15, for crying out loud. I called the CP and let my annoyance be heard.

WSP Captain Chuck Teasdale informed me the lunches had been delivered to Capitol Police headquarters in the basement of the building "an hour ago." CPD Lieutenant Marc Schmidt called his headquarters to find out what was going on. A moment later, he held his hand over the mouthpiece of the phone and asked, "Do you want more constituent badges or food?"

He explained that Sue Barica, the Capitol Police secretary extraordinaire, couldn't do both. I took the phone and talked with Sue. What she told me left me shaking my head. Again.

To my surprise, Sue was the entire Logistic Section—when we called the Command Post offsite, they called back to the Capitol to Sue to pass on our requests and needs. She was the one person who received all the instructions from the Logistic Section in the CP and was expected to carry it out all on her own.

The week before, I had assigned Sue a helper from my security staff, but I had no idea she was alone in her work attempting to fulfill all of our needs. Now it was clear why logistics were such a problem—no one person could possibly have met the needs of our entire branch, even if she had a helper. The fact that she had done as well as she had was simply amazing.

We sent a team of officers to the Capitol Police headquarters in the basement. Sure enough, when they arrived they found all the lunches. The officers knew what to do to get the food to the break locations and to the Operations Room.

I entered Sue's office. There she was, almost at her wits end, surrounded by pieces of plastic and photocopied pieces of paper with "*CONSTITUENT*" written on them. She filled me in on what her world had been like for the past 15 days. The state credit card Sue had been issued had a credit limit of $5,000 and was maxed out. She didn't know what to do about ordering anything else we needed. She had gone to a store to get supplies and at the register, she found out her state card was at its maximum and had to leave the store without any supplies.

Sue and the University Security Supervisor I had assigned to be her aide were working as hard and fast as they could and were stymied by the lack of resources. I told her to stop what she was doing and get something to eat. I gathered up the 150 or so completed badges and had an officer take them to AC Dale Burke at the queues to add to his current supply of 120.

Returning to Operations, I huddled up with University Police Captain Michael Newton. I told him that I wanted him to design a professional-looking color constituent badge by district, eight for each district, and to get proper holders. Next, I called Incident Commander DC Dan Blackdeer and told him what was going on with Sue and the badges. I requested he approve us going to an outside vendor to get the badges made. He explained his state credit card was also maxed out. I told him that I would place it on the University's tab via the University EOC Logistics Team. We had the 1,800 badges within two hours.

Word reached the Interior Branch that some representatives had again opened their windows on the ground floor to allow people in the building. Officers had been sent to talk to these legislators to dissuade them from continuing this practice. We understood their desire to provide access, but like the Rotunda Community's refusal to leave at closing time last night, this sort of behavior was actually hampering our efforts to re-open the building. Tension levels were rising. Charles' "negotiations" were not yielding results.

I headed off to the Policy Group meeting at 1:00. Incident Commander Blackdeer summarized the overnight report I had provided and I summarized the lack of logistic support for the queues and for the Interior Branch itself. Dan asked Keith Gilkes if Dan's and Sue's credit card limit could be raised above the $5,000 limit. Dan also indicated that he had told Logistics to send work to other places in the state government beyond Sue.

Randy reported that his goal was to have everyone downstairs on the ground floor by 6:15 tonight with one exception: a woman who would staff the Family Center. Members of the group wanted clarification that the Family Center was not in any way a daycare center. No one wanted the liability for what might happen to children in an unregulated daycare. Randy assured all of us the Family Center was just a gathering place for kids. At the moment, the only kids in the building were the children of the woman who ran the "center."

Randy reported that the 24 protesters were not going to move down to the first floor. The inside group of 153 felt under siege and were yet again dismantling locks on the windows of the bathrooms, this time allegedly to ensure food getting in, even though there was plenty to eat inside the Capitol. In an effort to stop the protesters from taking the locks apart, Randy agreed he would negotiate food drop-off times with them. It was part of a written agreement between the leadership and the Rotunda Community Randy had been working on. He wanted me to review a draft later. Randy and Charles were talking about keeping the Capitol closed for the whole day. This was very difficult for me to accept.

Information was not flowing to the people outside waiting. They had no understanding of why they were not being let inside. All they knew was that they had complied with our request to leave on Sunday and had been assured they would be able to re-enter today. They had rebelled against the queues by attempting to rush the doors around the building. Interior Branch officers were then placed outside the doors, as the Dane County Sheriff made it clear he wasn't going to have his deputies defend a "closed" building. The situation at the King Street entrance remained tense.

We needed better information and faster delivery of it. I again renewed my request to be able to use social media, as we do at the UW, directly out of the Interior Branch. The group agreed that starting tomorrow, a Public Information Officer (PIO) should be stationed in the Interior Branch. They were still reluctant to allow the use of social media. General Dunbar offered a retired colonel, Tim Donovan, who used to serve as Public Information Officer with the National Guard to act as the PIO for the Branch. I had known and worked with Tim on some projects since September 11, 2001 and would be glad to work with him again. More debate ensued and finally it was agreed the Interior Branch would have its own communications and a one-way blog with the public.

Senate Sergeant-at-Arms Ted Blazel and Assembly Sergeant-at-Arms Ann Tonnon Byers raised the issue that the queuing plan had not functioned as planned. Most senators' and representatives' staffs were very angry about the plan not being carried out. Both the public and staff members felt we had not kept our word about access. They were correct. We had allowed negotiation with 24 people to stop the rest from gaining access. Our lack of logistics support had helped bring the queue plan to a standstill. Both sergeants-at-arms asked that a message be sent to representatives and senators about what had happened this morning, and what was going to be done to fix it.

Several on the Policy Group, besides me, felt it was interesting that Charles would negotiate for so long and fully with protesters, but would deny legitimate access to other citizens wanting to conduct business in the Capitol. The pertinent question was why were we allowing the 24 protesters so much leeway and control? The answer from Charles continued to be his desire for voluntary compliance.

Ten days earlier, Charles had marched into the Interior Branch and demanded the building be closed in 20 minutes. No warning, no plan—just close it. Then eight days ago, he had again called the Command Post and told them to close and empty the Capitol within a few hours. That day there had been bad weather, little warning, and again no plan.

However, the Interior Branch had now gone through a very deliberate planning process and we had followed the scale-down plan over five days, and clearly gave plenty of notice for people to march out, be carried out, or be arrested for cause. The scale-down plan allowed for the building hours to be enforced, the building to be cleaned, and the overall Capitol operations to return to a more normal footing.

All that careful planning and execution had been ignored by Charles. Using voluntary compliance as the only strategy led us to cutting off the access control system for staff, cutting off access to the general public, resulting in poor public opinion of law enforcement and overall inefficiency—including a failed queuing system and the inability to control the number of police officers needed.

The Assembly had a listening session going on in an upstairs room, which led to another decision point. The building should close at 6:00 tonight, so what were the instructions to the Interior Branch if those in that meeting decided not to leave? Would they be allowed to stay? Would we be allowed to go "hands-on" then? If so, why "hands on" with them and not the 24 who were actually holding up access for everyone else? The Assembly sergeant-at-arms made it clear to the representatives that their listening session had to end at 6:00 and those in attendance must leave the building immediately. She was confident the representatives would comply. I wanted the group's direction for the possibility the people attending the listening session would not comply. No direction was given.

Since WSP Captain Chuck Teasdale was in attendance, I began a discussion about the evening shift and the need to change the rules. We agreed on the need to move to a point at which fewer police were required. However, going to smaller numbers was troublesome if we were not going to empower the police to take some level of enforcement action when their instructions were not followed. Because of voluntary compliance, the crowd's defiance was prevalent. Captain Teasdale was surprised. He couldn't fathom that we had been allowing people to disregard a directive from a police officer. This to me was another example of how out of touch the Command Post was with our life under the dome.

The group even seemed surprised at this, yet Chief Tubbs had repeatedly told the Policy Group: no arrests and no hands-on. As a result, the Policy Group had been under the wrong impression that folks were complying with the police when, in fact, they were not always following police officers' instructions.

The group agreed the officers' orders needed to be followed. However, these statements were then followed again with the advising that the officers use only voluntary compliance. It was unclear to me why some in the group couldn't understand that voluntary compliance was failing. We needed to use some level of enforcement to gain compliance. The discussion went in circles.

DC Dan Blackdeer noted that he and I would work out instructions for the officers after the meeting. This situation was bordering on ridiculous. Dan wasn't willing to override his boss, Chief Tubbs. I was getting very weary at the lack of strong leadership to clearly define and achieve goals using tactical methods that would work effectively.

I reminded folks that we had abandoned the scale-down plan at 4:00 yesterday before anything, including drums, had been removed. So the nonstop drumming continued. Chief of Staff Keith Gilkes insisted he wanted the drums gone, so the building could return to its normal operation. Charles said he would do what he could through negotiation. I tried hard not to openly roll my eyes.

The decision for now was that the building would not be opened to the general public. I groaned to myself. The new goal was to open at 8:00 tomorrow morning if we had a written agreement signed by the protesters who remained in the building, along with some of the union leaders. The group thought it would be better to have a volunteer marshal instead of a police person explain to the crowd what was happening at this point.

Randy and Charles would resume negotiations. Randy firmly believed in the scale-down plan and restoring the building to its normal hours and operations. He wasn't against arresting people. He was a skilled negotiator and believed in getting something when you give something.

Keith stated three goals to work toward by Wednesday:

1. To ensure tomorrow night's Joint Session Address occurred safely and on time.
2. To work our way to opening the building to a new normal (yet to be defined).
3. To dismantle the Interior Branch and not use the Branch or EPS beyond Wednesday, because we would be at the new normal.

Following up on several points in the meeting, Jodi Jensen from DOA and I talked through some of the issues we needed to communicate to staff, representatives, senators, and the public. I hadn't met Jodi until these events, and even during this time, we had only worked via these meetings. This was the first time we had direct contact and had to work through a problem together. Jodi was sharp and knew her business. She was easy to work with and it was helpful to think through complicated communication issues with her.

Now it was back again to the Interior Branch. We were having trouble getting enough law enforcement coverage overnight. I had thought it strange that not one municipal police department within Dane County had offered any overnight assistance in the Capitol. I called longtime friend and colleague, City of Fitchburg Chief Tom Blatter and explained what was needed. I requested he ask the chiefs within Dane County to send us some overnight help. Tom informed me no one had asked them to help and said he would be glad to reach out to the other chiefs. I gave him the particulars and he got to work.

* * * * *

If we ever stopped to think about the day-to-day experience it was all but surreal—yet we did our best to find irony and humor where we could. The Interior Branch was receiving correspondence from various representatives and senators, identifying individuals who were important to the office but who were not staff. Their goal in sending us the correspondence was to give greater access to a larger number of people. One of my staff showed me one such correspondence signed by Senator Lena C. Taylor (Democrat).

The joke we chuckled about was that if this missing senator had actually signed the memo, Senate Sergeant-At-Arms Ted Blazel should stop using the troopers to search the state for this senator and just go by and check her office. We joked about its authenticity, as we knew she was still out of state with the other Democratic senators. Clearly her staff had prepared it; however, we didn't doubt she authorized it.

I received a call from COS Keith Gilkes. He informed me that the AFSCME union had filed suit to get the building open and begin legal action against the DOA. He thought there would be a court order that would command us to reopen the Capitol without queues. He told me the state would file an appeal to that order and until that time, nothing involving access should change. I told him I would not violate a court order. He said the order was on appeal and while on appeal, Keith thought everything remained status quo. This was a reasonable point. For the time being, we would continue with our plans, but clearly changes were likely to come.

Keith then told me that when the state went to court to defend its action, he wanted me to testify on behalf of the state as the law enforcement official in charge. I balked. Why not the Incident Commander DC Dan Blackdeer or Capitol Police Department Chief Charles Tubbs? Keith explained that after discussion with DOA and the state Department of Justice, I had been selected to testify.

"Who exactly selected me?" I asked pointedly. Keith just kept referring to "they." "They" had discussed it and decided I was the best person to represent the law enforcement effort.

He went onto explain that the injunction was against DOA as the state agency charged with oversight and operations of the Capitol. The state Department of Justice Assistant Attorney General who would defend DOA was Steve Means, whom I had never met. Keith wanted to give Steve my number, to which I immediately agreed. He also wanted me to get an estimate of the costs to date that the University as a whole had spent staffing the protests.

"Oh, boy. Here we go," I thought. I immediately called UW–Madison Chancellor Biddy Martin and informed her of the latest events, as I understood them. She thought it was important that I inform Lisa Rutherford from the University's Office of Legal Services. Lisa would check with the Attorney General's Office and find out who would be representing me individually, not just DOA as an agency. She would also send University attorney John Dowling up to assist me. I thanked her. A short time later, Lisa informed me that she had spoken to Jack Sweeney of the Attorney General's office and that Assistant AG Corey Finkelmeyer would defend me. I knew Corey from previous cases and felt very comfortable with him.

I spoke briefly to Assistant Attorney General Steve Means by phone. He asked me some very general questions. I mentioned to him that I had a strong background in demonstrations, crowd, and capacity management, as well as homeland security issues. If he wished to explore the terrorism concerns some in state law enforcement had raised, he could do so, but not through me.

My reasoning, as I explained to AAG Means, was not a lack of knowledge of the topic or a lack of expertise. I have security clearance in the federal system; I had served on the US Attorney's Terrorism Task Force in Wisconsin, the FBI Joint Terrorism Task Force oversight committee for the Madison field office, and the International Association of Chiefs of Police (IACP) Homeland Security Committee for several years. In addition, I oversaw both the IACP Homeland Security and the IACP Terrorism committees.

The reason I didn't wish to testify about the subject was that all of my expertise led me to believe terrorism was not a viable factor or realistic threat in the Capitol protests. I told Mr. Means that Ed Wall of DCI was the one who thought the risk was present.

Mr. Means was concerned about the lack of time for preparation, as this case would probably be before a judge tomorrow. I told him that I had started on February 17 and knew all of this would end up in court someday, so I had been keeping records and notes. While it would be difficult to organize them in any helpful way overnight, the records did exist. He said he would have someone assist me in preparing for the case and asked if I would be all right with being prepped by a DOA attorney. I was fine with whatever he could arrange, given the short lead time.

I told the folks in the Interior Branch the latest information. Deputy Branch Director AC Brian Bridges was dealing with reports of problems at the King Street entrance. The crowd had rejected the queues and had come all the way up to the doors without any stand-off area. One of the doors had a panel kicked out of it.

University Police Lieutenant Kari Sasso immediately reacted and went to reinforce the entrance.

I went to the scene as Brian ordered Interior Branch officers to don coats, hats, and gloves, and move outside. When I arrived, one of the doors to the King Street entrance was off its hinges and a group of officers was attempting to repair it. Officers were holding fast knowing they could not allow a breach. The tension continued and the crowd was shouting and very angry.

With the officers beginning to establish a small standoff area outside the door, I inched my way outside to approach the crowd. I didn't get far as the crowd was very close to the doors. They were chanting and yelling to let them inside. My efforts to talk to them were for naught as their volume was far too loud. The crowd itself was sizeable, probably 5,000 to 7,000 people. Some of them close to me attempted a conversation. They told me the union had filed suit in Dane County court this afternoon to have the building reopened.

I said I understood and that DOA was appealing. Another recognized me from the day before and called me a liar. He said I had lied that they would be allowed back in today. He also shouted that I was mistreating those left inside. He claimed we were denying the Rotunda Community food and water. While I tried to explain, he just insisted I was a liar and not to be believed.

From where he stood, his beliefs made sense. Publicly, Charles had told the protesters they would be allowed to re-enter if they left peacefully on Sunday afternoon, and as of now, they couldn't. The irate protester had no reliable way to know all that I'd gone through to try to keep that option open, nor that I had insisted on food, water, and reasonable conditions for those remaining inside. For now, I was the one standing in his way and preventing the access promised just 24 hours earlier.

The officers were finally able to push out from the doors and establish a larger buffer. The door was back on its hinges, not too much worse for the wear. The panel had been reattached. Once again, a protester decided to climb the façade to gain access to the building. Officers were able to get him down. I came to find out, it was the same guy arrested for climbing the building this morning. On my order, he would go to jail. Charles' no hands-on policy did not extend that far.

Meanwhile, Randy informed us that it was "story time" at the Family Center. As part of the negotiations, the woman acting as the Family Center director had convinced Randy and Charles to participate. We all chuckled, envisioning Charles reading to a small tike perched on his lap. We learned later on that Charles had sat down on the floor to participate. Because there were no children or families in the building, Randy had to gather six troopers, wearing their trooper Smokey Bear hats, to be close to Charles and listen as the woman read a story. Later, when Randy told us this story, we laughed thinking about a man the size of Charles down on the floor near this very petite woman as she read the story to the group of cops. We wished Randy had taken some pictures.

The Assembly listening session finished at 6:00 as planned, and those in attendance left the Capitol without incident. The 7:00 p.m. shift change occurred and we were left with few officers in the building and a very large and agitated crowd out front. A candlelight vigil was planned outside on the Capitol lawn. We needed support from the Dane County Sheriff Department, which had been working the grassy areas of the Capitol Square and the sidewalks on the state portion of the Square since Day 1. As the night wore on, they discouraged people from climbing in windows or pitching tents and kept a watch so that no further damage to the doors would occur.

It was time to meet with Assembly Sergeant-at-Arms Anne Tonnon Byers and Joseph Fadness, Director of External Relations,

Office of the Governor, to complete a thorough review of all that was needed for the March 1 Joint Session.

The meeting covered hundreds of details, but Anne and Joe were highly organized and things went quickly. Our combined management plan for the day of the Address would begin at 9:45 in the morning and the timeline had every preparation item noted until approximately 7:00 in the evening. Everything looked like it was falling into place.

Back in the Interior Branch, my staff handed me what Randy had written as a draft agreement with the protesters remaining in the Capitol. The draft was the result of Charles' and Randy's discussions with the protest leadership. This was intriguing to me as I wasn't sure the leadership of the established unions were actually the leaders of the occupation group or the Rotunda Community. The agreement designated areas for sleeping, food storage, medical supplies, gathering spots, and the Family Center. Much to my disappointment, there was no end date for the occupation written within the draft.

I didn't see how the goals the Governor's Chief of Staff Keith Gilkes had established at the policy meeting earlier in the day would be reached if this agreement was signed by Charles. Although I wasn't enamored of the idea of a corral, I understood the desire to keep the Rotunda Community in one part of the building so that "normal" operations could resume. I was still concerned that Charles wasn't going to allow law enforcement to physically move people down from the first floor if they didn't want to go.

Thinking ahead a bit, I did not believe this queuing and badging plan was going to have a long useful life. So I asked Captain Michael Newton to draw up a plan for allowing entrance into the Capitol via one door with metal screening but no badging.

Randy Stark called me on my cell phone and asked if I could come to the Governor's conference room, where he and Chief Tubbs were meeting with Keith about the draft agreement. The Governor's conference room is a stunningly beautiful room, as elaborately decorated as any space in the Capitol, from the wood parquet floors to the marble fireplace and the 22-karat gold-leaf trim ringing the many murals. Kevin Wernet and I entered the Governor's conference room where Charles Tubbs, Randy Stark, and Jodi Jensen were sitting, along with a well-dressed gentleman, whom I had never seen before. Keith Gilkes was standing at one end of the imposing table.

There were no introductions as I sat next to Charles, who looked thoroughly dejected, and across from Randy and the gentleman in the suit. I had a copy of the draft agreement. It seemed everyone did. The tension in the room was noticeably thick. Whoever the gentleman in the suit was, he was very upset. He did not want to discuss the agreement Charles had reached with the protest leaders. He made it clear there would be no such agreement.

I had joined the meeting in progress, so I waited a few minutes to gauge the tenor of the meeting before I asked him what he did want. His reply was short and to the point; he wanted Administrative Code Chapter 2 enforced. I asked to see a copy. He had one rolled up in his hand and he tossed it toward me across the table.

In this rolled-up document were the legal rules and regulations for how the Capitol was supposed to operate. Several times over the past ten days, the Interior Branch had asked for these rules but a copy had never arrived. Four days ago, this code was referenced in a memo from a DOA attorney. I realized I was now face to face with the actual Secretary of the Department of Administration, Mike Huebsch. It was Day 15 and it had taken this long for us to meet. Evidently, with the Administration being just seven weeks old, he and others were just beginning to fully understand some of their job responsibilities. Secretary Huebsch had served for 16 years as a state representative from the LaCrosse area representing the 94th Assembly District.

He went on to describe that he wanted the protesters cleared out of the building. I thought of how the scale-down plan would have accomplished that by now had it not been altered. I couldn't help but think the situation would be so different now if he and I had met on Saturday.

Secretary Huebsch was frustrated and he did not mince words. No more food deliveries would be allowed. If the people occupying the Capitol wanted to eat, they could leave and go find food elsewhere. There would be no agreement with the protest leaders. Acknowledging his frustration, I confirmed his point that there was to be no agreement signed by Charles. However, I would not agree to deny people food.

While DOA had told the folks to leave on Sunday, we were all still operating under the voluntary compliance notion. I explained to Secretary Huebsch that moving people from one floor to another, or moving people to the outside, was far more reasonable than denying people food. He quickly acknowledged my points.

I continued by noting that at this time in the evening, we did not have adequate law enforcement to remove the remaining protesters if they chose to resist. My assessment of the protesters currently in the building was that 40 or so would resist, beyond just going limp. The crowd outside was angry and disappointed with the police. I had seen their frustration up close in my last encounter with them. To make any attempt to move these people tonight would be tactically unsustainable.

Given that the occupiers thought they were on the verge of an agreement that would allow them to stay indefinitely, I explained we didn't have a particularly strong hand to play with unilaterally deciding to remove these folks tonight. The building had been cleaned, which was one of the main reasons we wanted everyone out, so that argument had passed. The Secretary repeated that Administrative Code Chapter 2 (Use of State Buildings and Facilities) was all the reason he needed in order to remove the people. I reminded everyone that because the union had filed a lawsuit and the state was appealing, removing people now would appear to be politically based, and I wasn't going to use the police in that manner. I would await direction from the court from here on out.

I went on to say that if the entrance badges were ready, the tensor barrier in place, the proper signs made, and law enforcement scheduled in adequate numbers, the queues would be operational in the morning. Furthermore, the Rotunda Community should all be in Charles and Randy's corral, and the building would be open for the business of government.

Despite his obvious frustration with all of us, I instantly liked the Secretary and hoped I finally had a direct line to the policy decision-maker. If it turned out to be true, this command would get much easier. He asked if I would enforce Administration Code Chapter 2. I told him that I would go back and read it and I would enforce it as soon as I could reasonably and safely do so. My understanding is that in all likelihood, we were headed to court tomorrow.

This meeting was reminiscent of last week when Charles said to close the building. Instead, we had put together and executed a scale-down plan that gave plenty of notice. We were not allowed to remove people. Here I sat with someone who once again, without notice, wanted to have people removed. I felt like I was riding a yo-yo.

I knew I had further angered the Secretary by not agreeing to remove the Rotunda Community right then and there. It wasn't that we disagreed. I, too, had wanted these last protesters removed the day before. But the Secretary's entry to the scene without the context of the past two days, much less the past two weeks, and his expectation that abrupt action could simply be taken right then and there frustrated me. What might have been a reasonable action two days ago was now likely to stir more confrontation and trouble.

At that point, I envisioned another scale-down plan. This time, it would move more rapidly to the endgame, perhaps spanning one day, not five days as the last scale-down plan had done. If we did not give a reasonable warning, the plan would not have my support and the Secretary would lose the support of other law enforcement. I assured the Secretary that this scale-down plan would end with people being carried out or arrested if they did not leave on their own accord. It was clear to me now that voluntary compliance was no longer the only tactic to be employed.

We parted ways and as I left the stately conference room, I glanced up at the ornate ceiling. The quote above my head said, *"The will of the people is the law of the land."*

It seemed to me the "will" of the people was to be allowed back inside the Capitol, not to allow 24 people unwilling to move to a lower floor or the other 129 left inside allowed to dictate the continued closure. I was certain though that the crowd outside and the protesters inside would not frame the choice the way I had.

Randy, Kevin, and I headed out together. Randy and Charles were going to have to face the protest leaders and say "no deal." Charles looked dismayed. He had worked many, many long hours and if he slept at all, it had been in his office. His efforts today were slow and laborious, but well intentioned. He had tried hard and in good faith to reach an agreement. He was so averse to using physical interventions with the Rotunda Community. Today, we were all seeing our hard-won trust with the protesters broken by circumstances.

Later that night from home, I called Chancellor Biddy Martin and updated her on the meeting with Secretary Huebsch, I told her that I may be ordered to do things I ethically felt I couldn't do, like deny food. If that were the case, I would feel compelled to resign my command and return to the University. She stated she would support such a decision on my part.

As I turned in for the night, I knew sleep would not come easy. There were so many questions and so much pressure. I wrestled with the possibility of being a witness for the state, while living with my level of frustration about how the operation had gone to date. What direction would and should I go? Should I yield to the pressure of being a team player, or should I risk standing on my own? It could mean all alone. It wasn't a matter of truth. I would always tell the truth. However, how things are phrased, how I express myself, could have a considerable impact on the outcome of the court proceeding and this bizarre period in Wisconsin history.

If asked, how would I explain why I was testifying and not Chief Tubbs, Deputy Chief Blackdeer, or even the Operations Chief Teasdale? I felt like I was caught a between strong sense that I knew and understood the dynamics of crowds and police operations for crowds better than those with loftier titles who were currently attempting to control this incident. In the realm of authority, I lacked title and position, yet operated with the police as if I were in charge, while the protesters believed that I was simply taking orders. Both were true. And both were not.

Day 16: Tuesday, March 1, 2011

THE CALL TO FITCHBURG CHIEF TOM BLATTER HAD PAID OFF. HE AND THE other chiefs from municipalities in Dane County had come through. There had been 91 officers on the overnight shift. On the balustrade outside the entrance doors, there had been about fifty sleepers. While some attempted to erect tents or other cardboard shelters, they cooperated with law enforcement when told to stop. There were a lot of sleeping bags and blankets. No arrests had been made. Overnight, the officers continued to monitor the bathrooms to ensure the windows remained secure.

I walked around the balustrade and spoke to those who had stayed outside overnight. Originally, some thought they would be allowed inside the Capitol to sleep as the evening wore on. Then they realized that wasn't going to happen so they hunkered down for the night. There was considerable frost on the ground and on the cold, white marble.

A few had questions; some focused on the queuing system, so I walked them over to the queuing area and explained the system to them. One individual constantly interrupted, but the group eventually silenced him to listen intently. They asked about the people inside and what was really happening to them. I assured them, the people inside had food and blankets. They asked if the folks inside would be arrested and I informed them that before that occurred, they would be given ample opportunity to avoid being arrested.

The sleepers inside the building had dropped from 153 to 107. Inside the Interior Branch, the Rotunda Community population sign was changed to 107 and re-hung on the wall in 400 NE right next to the retirement sign of *"Freedom date T+10."*

For whatever reason, the Command Post wanted to talk to me at 7:00 a.m. today, earlier than usual. The Assembly meeting room, where the CP video conferencing had been, returned to normal

Dodge County Sheriff deputies team with other law enforcement outside the Capitol's King Street entrance. (March 1, 2011)
(Photo by Mark Golbach)

UW Police Sergeant Aaron Chapin directs the queues, while UW Police Sergeant Anita Kichefski stands by. (March 2, 2011)
(Photo by Jim Escalante)

Assembly operations, so I was just using a phone. Chief Tubbs was participating by phone as well. The CP wanted to discuss what the "new normal" would look like in a few days. I was glad the CP wanted to take the lead on that plan.

In the meantime, today was going to be really busy and I wanted to keep my focus on the Governor's Joint Address regarding the budget and all the energy around it. We all agreed we really needed the queues to work. With that, we ended the briefing and I headed for the 7:45 am briefing in COS Keith Gilkes' office. Colonel (ret) Tim Donavan, acting as the Public Information Officer (PIO) for the Interior Branch, also joined us.

We turned our attention to the Joint Address. The plans were solid and we had plenty of officers for whatever we would need. I reminded everyone that we were going to block vehicular traffic to the entrances closest to the Capitol wing that housed the Assembly. We returned to access for the day and prioritized the queues: hearings, constituent visits, and then "everything else."

There were three potential flashpoints we needed to consider: one was about what would happen when the Democratic senators returned; two was when the Budget Repair Bill passed and was signed by the Governor; and three was March 13, the day the Bill called for the union contracts to end, triggering the possibility of a general strike.

There was another interesting development. Because the Bill contained fiscal provisions, a vote would need a quorum, meaning that at least some of the Democratic senators would need to return. However, the Bill could pass without the larger quorum if the fiscal provisions were removed. It would then have to go a conference committee for the Assembly and the Senate to iron out the differences. If this occurred, the Governor could sign a bill stripping collective bargaining rights without repairing the budget. The likelihood of this occurring was increasing every minute that the

Democratic senators stayed away. The reaction of the protesters to this type of political maneuvering after such a long hard fight would not be positive.

At 8:30 a.m., the daily organizational meeting began in the Interior Branch.

Today at the Capitol: Tuesday, March 1

8:00-11:15: Listening Session, 225 NW, 30 people.
            Sgt at Arms staff to provide escorts
9:30: Forestry committee in 300 NE
9:30: Senate Committee on Natural Resources, Senate Parlor, 20 people
9:45: TV to begin set-up for the Joint Address
9:45: Supreme Court Hearing, Hearing Chamber
9:45: Supreme Court Student Group
10:30: Joint Committee for Administrative Rules
10:30: Senate going into Session
10:45: Supreme Court group
11:00: Senate Committee on Workforce Development and Small
            Business, 330 SW 40 people
12 noon: Explosive Ordnance Detection (EOD) sweeps to begin
12 noon: GOP Caucus, NO public access, 411 S
12 noon: WEAC rally at State Street entrance
1:30: Supreme Court Student Group
2:00: WPEC Rally for Rights
2:00 – 6:00: Defend Wisconsin to march and rally
3:00: Senate organization meeting in the Parlor
3:00 – 7:00: Wisconsin Public Employees Against
            Walker's Attack on Workers
3:30: Senate Session in Senate Chambers
3:45: Senate Procession to the Assembly Chambers
3:45: Supreme Court Procession to the Assembly Chambers
4:00: Governor's Speech in Assembly Chambers (ticketed event)
6:00: Joint Finance Committee Session, 412 E
7:30 (approx.): Candlelight vigil from campus to Capitol

All the division commanders needed to know what hearings or events were in their areas and communicate their plans effectively to the staff. Keeping a tight perimeter of the building was a must. Because we knew access was becoming more of an issue, we wanted to increase the security on all the tunnel entrances to the Capitol, not just the main tunnel we used regularly.

Chief Warden Randy Stark mentioned that he had conversations with several of the protesters who had worked in the Capitol in the past and knew of the tunnels leading into the building. Several spoke of knowing the utilities and how the power sources worked. CPD Lieutenant Marc Schmidt would reassess the tunnel and keep a heavier police presence throughout.

Within the Interior Branch, the Wisconsin State Patrol (WSP) had been staffing the Assembly and Senate chamber and galleries. For this afternoon's Joint Address, they wanted to quickly be able to deal with any disruption. WSP Lieutenant Brad Altman was concerned about the removal of people from confined space in the galleries. It was not a skill that troopers practice, nor did they have a need. He asked Deputy Branch Director University Police Assistant Chief Brian Bridges if the UW Police officers would run a short training session, since UW Police remove people from seats in Camp Randall football stadium and Kohl Center (a 17,000 seat arena used for basketball and hockey, among other events) on a regular basis. Brian agreed and set up the training.

Ten different escort teams were established to handle the processions and movement for today's address. CPD Lieutenant Marc Schmidt was responsible for coordinating all the escorts. He sent all of them into the building to review the routes, emergency plans, and alternative routes.

Chief Warden Randy Stark reported that the negotiations were going well, as the protesters were now accepting their move from the first floor. Food deliveries ended at 8:00 a.m., given that everyone (including protesters) agreed there was plenty of food already inside. The protesters agreed to stop texting that they were being starved because it simply was not true. I made it clear that we would allow more food in as supplies were exhausted as I was not going to be cutting off food.

Meanwhile, University Police Assistant Chief (ret) Dale Burke and crew were working the queues and people were getting access for listening sessions and constituent visits. The communication would be faster once the Interior Branch one-way blog was established. We would create signs with the blog address so that people could keep track of new information.

The 10:00 morning briefing with the Command Post covered a lot of ground, but none of it new. Everybody knew we had to make the queues work and we had to ensure safety for the Joint Address.

At 11:00, I had a meeting with both sergeants-at-arms regarding the Joint Finance Committee 100th Anniversary celebration scheduled for March 2.

Back to the Interior Branch Operations Room, I sat down and ate a quick lunch while reading up on the number of arrests and crowd data from the last two weeks. We began to blog information to the public—finally. While I was doing this, Dane County District Attorney Ismael Ozanne and Dane County Sheriff Dave Mahoney were holding a press conference on the steps of the Dane County Courthouse. DA Ozanne was talking about opening an investigation into matters at the Capitol, and the Sheriff stated he would not allow his deputies to act as "palace guards."

As I was scheduled to be in court at some point this afternoon, Kevin and I headed to the Governor's suite to meet with DOA attorney Cari Anne Renlund, who was to prepare me. The meeting went well, although there wasn't much preparation. It was more about general directions and an explanation of the state's strategy, which was that Administrative Code, Chapter 2, trumped all else. I wasn't sure that was true, but at least I understood the strategy.

Kevin had arranged for us to ride with the Capitol Police to the courthouse, but first we headed to the Policy Group meeting in the basement.[17] The COS started the meeting with news of the injunction against the closing of the Capitol and the news that the appeal had been filed. He announced to the group that I would be testifying. Keith said things would remain status quo for now.

Dan Blackdeer then followed with a situation update. The unions wanted more people inside than the one-to-one Rotunda Community protesters exchange going right now. I thought we should eliminate the one-to-one exchange, as reducing the number of people staying inside overnight would eventually return us to normal. The DOA Secretary had made it clear to Charles and me the night before he wanted things back to normal as soon as possible. The majority of the Policy Group stated there would be no change in the one-to-one policy.

In anticipation of the Joint Address, the streets around the Capitol Square were now closed to traffic. Concrete barriers were in place. The outside crowd size was only about 2,000 but was expected to grow.

I reported that the queuing was going well right up until the crowd received a copy of the signed injunction. The crowd had charged the doors and did not want to abide by the queues, making it tough to facilitate those wanting access to hearings and meetings. As far as I was concerned, it was now up to the court to rule on the appeal.

---

[17] Governor's Chief of Staff (COS) Keith Gilkes, Chief Charles Tubbs, Dave Matthews DCI, Administrator Ed Wall DCI, General Dunbar, Incident Commander D/C Dan Blackdeer, WSP Major Darren Price, Anne Tonnon Byers Assembly Sergeant at Arms, Patrick Fuller Assembly Clerk, Ted Blazel Senate Sergeant at Arms, Deputy Branch Director Chief Warden Randy Stark, Chief Noble Wray MPD, Sheriff Dave Mahoney, Kevin Wernet and me.

The Incident Command structure had broken down in a way I was unwilling to ignore. Until the court ruled, I was not willing to make major changes.

The group thought we had to get through the Joint Address safely. The Interior Branch had plans in place for various possibilities, including a major breach during the Joint Address. The Interior Branch was prepared to use reasonable and necessary force to ensure the Joint Address would occur without interruption.

My readiness to use order maintenance or crowd control tactics was, like it or not, to leave politics out of the playbook. The 5.5 million citizens of the state deserved a functioning government, even if they disagreed with the current Governor. The Governor had been duly elected three months earlier, sworn into office in January, and was fulfilling his responsibilities as chief executive of the state.

The speech had been postponed once; to have it postponed again was a precarious direction for a democratic society to pursue. I was done with voluntary compliance as the only method to move forward. I now had Adm 2, Use of State Buildings and Facilities. I had given my word to the DOA Secretary that I would enforce it unless I was told otherwise. I went over the Joint Address plan in its entirety. Even Charles, usually positive, said he thought we should plan for the worst.

I received a text at 2:00 p.m. that it was time for me to head to court. We went through the screening process at the Courthouse and found the correct courtroom. Waiting for me outside the courtroom was John Dowling from UW Legal Services. I was pleased he was there. I had no idea what or where this process would take me and it was comforting to have a lawyer with me whom I knew and trusted.

Upon entry to the court room, I immediately recognized opposing counsel, former Attorney General Peg Lautenschlager. In yet another strange twist of events, I thought it ironic that I knew opposing counsel better than the state's counsel.

> *Peg Lautenschlager served in the Wisconsin Assembly from 1989 to 1993. I met her when she was appointed United States Attorney for the Western District of Wisconsin in 1993. She served in that post from 1993 to 2001. Following her service, she was elected Attorney General of the State of Wisconsin in 2002 and was sworn in in January of 2003. She was the first woman to hold this office in Wisconsin, and served until January of 2007.*
>
> *When I was vice President for three years, and then President of the Wisconsin Chiefs of Police Association (2000-2004), I had occasion to work with Peg as U.S. Attorney and then Attorney General. Peg's husband and stepson are both in law enforcement and she always went out of her way to be available to and assist law enforcement throughout the state. I also admired her for the manner in which she dealt with her diagnosis and treatment of breast cancer in 2004. Like so many, I was saddened by the manner in which she handled her drunken driving arrest, which resulted in her political downfall.*

For now, she was opposing counsel and as I took my seat behind Assistant Attorney General Steve Means, Peg glanced over. Surprise registered on her face. She acknowledged me and again looked puzzled. It was obvious she had no idea of my role at the Capitol and was confused by my presence. DOA Secretary Michael Huebsch, DCI Administrator Ed Wall, and DCI Agent Tina Virgil were also present. Ed handed me a three-page overview of the DCI's position on the matter before the court.

Judge John C. Albert was presiding. It appeared there was going to be testimony from several people to illustrate how the access to the Capitol yesterday and today were problematic. Time was ticking away, which was troubling to me because the Joint Address was fast approaching. Assistant Attorney General Steve Means asked the Court if it was all right if those of us with operational responsibilities could be excused since we were not going to be testifying today due to the presumed length of the union's case. The judge agreed that those of us with operational responsibilities could leave.

I bolted from the court room, with Kevin Wernet and John Dowling right behind me, and quickly returned to the Capitol. There were a substantial number of protesters already there with others walking up the side streets. The snow fencing and troopers were in place.

Many of the Rotunda Community knew I had gone to court and so upon my return, wanted to know what the court had ruled. I explained that the proceeding had just gotten started and I hadn't testified yet. Tomorrow afternoon was probably the soonest I would testify. I didn't expect a ruling until tomorrow night at the earliest. That, I thought, might be ambitious.

The group of about twenty had gathered around and thanked me. Janie spotted me and asked if she could give me a hug. I nodded and she wrapped her arms around me. I then inquired if Janie was getting her blood pressure checked as we had arranged. She was very pleased to report she was receiving the BP checks and they had been good. She was cold again, and so I fetched a cup of hot water for her as I had the day before. Kevin was standing off to the side and I could tell he was anxious to get me upstairs to the Operations Room. I said good-bye to Janie and headed up.

With the queues came security checkpoints and metal wands. (March 4, 2011) (Photo by Joe Lynde)

Firefighter unions showed up en mass with the color guard and bagpipes in the lead. (February 18, 2011) (Photo by Kevin Wernet)

University Police AC Dale Burke, who was responsible for the queuing operation that day, had received twenty general public tickets to the Joint Address that he was to distribute. Dale went outside and walked up to people who were in the queues and quickly the tickets were distributed. The people receiving them were happy to be headed inside. They had been standing in line for quite some time.

Inside the Operations Room, the Interior Branch was humming. The dispatcher informed me UW Chancellor Biddy Martin was inside the Assembly gallery attending the speech. Other dignitaries and ticketed guests were arriving as well. Everyone entering the galleries were screened for weapons. All our preparations had worked perfectly so far.

The Senate went into session, as did the Assembly. The escorts were in place and people were moving to where they should be, right on cue. We turned the television to Wisconsin Public Television to see the address. The Governor took the podium right on time.

Outside the Assembly wing, state troopers held the balustrade. In the planning, we had overlooked an outside staircase that went from the ground floor to the first floor. People trying to get a view and simultaneously make even greater noise packed the staircase. The crowds, now swollen to several thousand, were attempting to make enough noise to disturb the Assembly proceedings. But with the microphone the media was using, the Governor was able to overpower the crowd noise to be heard by the television audience. However, inside the chamber, it was not as quiet as it appeared on television. His address was relatively short for a budget speech and was delivered without incident.

The Assembly Democrats did not attempt to verbally or physically interrupt. The sergeant-at-arms did not need to take any official action against any member. Remaining neutral on the content, the delivery of the speech had been a success from a policing point of view.

When the Governor was safely returned to his office and as the other members of the Legislature and Supreme Court exited, we shared a round of high fives in the Interior Branch. Everyone was tired. We had been at this a long time now. Today was an important day for democracy. The public who supported the Governor were able to see him give his budget speech and the public who opposed the Governor had been able to have their voices heard, (literally) in opposition.

DAY 17: WEDNESDAY, MARCH 2, 2011

ACCORDING TO UNIVERSITY POLICE LIEUTENANT MARK SILBERNAGEL, THE Interior Branch had 36 law enforcement staff overnight, in addition to the twelve Division of Criminal Investigation (DCI) agents, and 35 troopers. While we needed the assistance overnight, I did not want to use DCI staff in this way. It wasn't about the staff; they were all fine individuals. Their normal responsibilities centered on investigations, not crowd management or order maintenance. In addition, they didn't wear a standard police uniform; instead they wore more tactical emergency response outfits with "raid" jackets and cargo pants. Seeing DCI dressed in this manner caused some in the crowd to think we were changing tactics and preparing to use more force.

A few protesters following the event on their iPads, laptops, and phones saw pictures of the DCI staff guarding the exterior of the tunnel thought we had hired "Blackwater" security from Iraq. No matter how much we attempted to dissuade people from that belief, it hung in the air. The change in staffing patterns and the closure of the building to the general public occurred simultaneously. This combination was troublesome for the public image we wanted to maintain. The need to change was driven by the cost of keeping Emergency Police Services active. It was less expensive for DOA to use state resources, as it had no intention of reimbursing state organizations for the basic salary costs of state staff.

Overnight, the medical needs of some of the protesters were becoming more serious. We had protesters inside, like Janie, who were undergoing chemotherapy, suffering from mental illness, had colostomy bags they were cleaning and caring for in the bathrooms, had heart conditions, and were physically challenged in a variety of other ways. While we had been aware of this before, the protesters' own first aid and medical caregivers had handled the situations and issues as they arose.

We now had a medical challenge. We had dismantled the first aid function on Sunday, yet had not removed everyone from the building. The Interior Branch division commanders wondered if the Madison Fire Department would take on the challenge. Most doubted MFD would do this because they had stopped providing the police wellness checks a few days earlier. We had switched to having a local HMO provide the checks. We decided to ask the Command Post to sort through the issue with MFD.

Last evening, the Interior Branch had been in touch with a medical doctor who wanted access to the Capitol to recover prescription medication that had been left behind by one of the protesters. Over the course of the past two weeks, we had met and dealt with a small number of people on medication for mental illness. With the change in environment, schedule, sleeping patterns, and the level of noise, some of them were not coping well.

Earlier, the volunteer first aid providers had kept a watchful eye on helping them to remember their meds. Now law enforcement needed to step into the service gap. The doctor wanted to see if he could find the medicine and talk to another of his patients. The

Capitol Police facilitated his entry and reunited him with his patient. Later, the doctor left feeling confident his patient was fine.

The latest count of people staying inside the Rotunda was 107. The Rotunda Community contained no homeless people. Some days earlier, the homeless had grown weary of the protests and the noise—especially the ever-present drumming. By the time DOA announced what turned out to be the false closing of the building on Sunday, the homeless were long gone. Everyone here now understood the issues, understood how government worked, and in their minds, how government had failed. They understood at some level that their days in the building were coming to an end, and they believed their presence would slow the legislative process.

While the Rotunda Community was not one united group, it did have consensus on most issues. They held meetings where every-one was able to make his or her points and be heard with respect. In some ways, watching them operate their meetings with a certain level of maturity was refreshing, given the way the full-time, elected politicians from both sides had behaved over the past two weeks.

I had again checked in with Janie. She looked extremely tired and I suggested she try to find a quiet corner and get some more sleep. I was concerned about her. We sat together briefly after I had found her another cup of hot water.

It was soon time to have our daily organizational meeting. I made sure our mascot, Snoopy, had his glasses on, his tie straight, and was once again ready for business. The morning offsite briefings had gone very well. There were 233 officers in the building. With the problems we had encountered outside on the balustrade yesterday, I was glad to have plenty of officers in reserve. We had a one-way blog established and continued to use it to communicate directly to the crowd. The queuing was in place and the King Street doors were ready to be opened at 8:00 a.m.

Capitol Police Department Lieutenant Marc Schmidt informed us that the first Wednesday of the month was fire alarm testing day. We all laughed at the thought of alarms blaring and he said he figured he would reschedule it. Just what the current situation needed—the fire alarms sounding—employees heading out every door, when we were queuing all others. We knew the protesters would think it was a ruse to get them to leave and they wouldn't move. Lieutenant Schmidt successfully stopped the testing.

Today at the Capitol: Tuesday, March 2, 2011

8:00: Fiscal Bureau – all-day meeting in 412 East
8:00: Rep. Barca – all-day listening session, 328 West
              Actual hearing to begin at 11:00 a.m.
9:00 – 2:00: Assembly Committee on Natural Resources, G.A.R.
9:30: Committee on Labor/Public Safety/Urban Affairs
9:45: Supreme Court
10:00 – noon: Committee on Rural Economic Development
              & Rural Affairs, 225 NW
11:00: Senate to go into Session – galleries to be open
Noon – 2:00: Caterers for the Joint Finance event to be delivering food
Noon: Senate session in the Senate Parlor
1:00: Rally at Bascom Hall on UW Campus
5:00: Rally at Bascom Hall on UW Campus
Evening: Anniversary of Joint Finance – celebration on 4th floor

We established the room capacity for each of the rooms in use. The applicable number of badges and corresponding queues were ready to go and were already at the doors.

Randy had a request from the protesters to receive a change of clothes. Randy was working through the negotiations of the exchange. The final note of the Branch meeting was that I would be headed to court to testify at 10:00 a.m. With that, we were off to handle our responsibilities.

The queues were up and running. CPD Lieutenant Marc Schmidt, who was the division commander responsible for escort teams, was having a hard time keeping up with the demand. He was making adjustments on the fly. The limitation of eight constituent visitors to one representative's or senator's office at a time was frustrating to many Democrats. Many more people wanted to visit their representative or senator. While we had the queuing system established and the queues were now often empty, the Democrats and their constituents had a vested interest in thwarting the queuing system so it would not work.

To further resist the queue system and to be able to meet with more people at one time than the eight authorized, some Democrats on the ground floor opened their windows and let people climb into their offices. When that was stopped by the police, some representatives passed their desk and chairs outside the windows and set up their offices on the lawn. One had even placed an American and Wisconsin flag on either side of his meeting area. There he sat, meeting with his constituents. I had to admit, it was a clever idea.

The movement of furniture outside the building via the windows upset representatives from DOA. The furniture was placed directly on the grassy/muddy area outside the offices and they argued that this wasn't good for these antiques. DOA requested our assistance in returning the furniture to the building, as well as getting the practice stopped. I declined to assist as I didn't see how that was a law enforcement issue. I instead referred them to the sergeant-at-arms for the Assembly. It seemed to me the sergeant was in a better position of authority to command that the representatives stop moving their furniture.

We held our customary meeting with the Command Post. DC Dan Blackdeer started the briefing by saying the aim on Sunday,

March 6, was to close the Command Post and return the space back to the use of the Madison Fire Department. Dan would then be stationed in 400 NE, the current Interior Branch.

Once that change was made, I would be able to relinquish command and return to campus. We had a list of equipment in 400 NE that belonged to the University that we would return to campus when we departed the Interior Branch. I gave Dan a list of those items so he knew what he needed to replace to keep 400 NE operational as the on-site Command Post.

The Interior Branch was happy to report all the queues had worked and were now empty, except for the queue to join the Rotunda Community. The Community was still on a one-in, one-out, exchange. However, the population had somehow dropped to 98 and they hadn't replaced the last nine people who left. We were not sure why that happened. For the moment, no one was leaving the Rotunda Community, so no one would be going in.

Dan then informed us the airport wanted its tensor barrier returned right away. We knew we couldn't do that until we had it replaced. We needed CP Logistics to find replacement barrier—bike racks, different tensor barrier, or something else that could work.

At 12:00 noon, we held another situation briefing in 400 NE of the Interior Branch. Things were in good shape. The queues were operating well. Again, the only queue not moving was for the Rotunda Community.

Once again, the tighter restriction on Capitol building access came as a result of a strangely "liberal" enforcement policy turned on its head. Chief Tubbs' insistence that we maintain voluntary compliance, along with a hands-off approach, meant the doors remained closed to the general public. This liberal enforcement tactic denied more people access and kept the rights of the few (now 98) ahead of all the others. Had the Interior Branch been allowed to use capacity management, information sharing, education, police presence, police dialogue, and some stronger tactics of enforcing the building hours, we could have opened the Capitol to the general public and avoided the queues, which had led to the Capitol essentially having been shut down.

Chief Tubbs and DC Blackdeer couldn't see how their efforts to keep the police from becoming the "spark" were actually resulting in access rights of more people being restricted or denied. The fact that 9,000 people at one time could have legally accessed the Capitol during business hours would have been a greater exercise of democracy than allowing 98 people to be inside the Capitol, exercising their objections to the building hours. I understood the protesters inside felt the building hours and their enforcement were political and not operational. However, for the business of government to function regardless of what laws are passed or cases are ruled upon, closing and maintaining a building was a legitimate action.

Randy reported that the negotiation with the protest leaders was going well. I wasn't sure what that meant at this point. He hoped to meet with them at 3:00 p.m. to discuss a swap of people so that some could go home to shower and change, and then come back and resume their positions. The storage area we had given the protesters for extra bedding and laundry left behind was getting to be quite odiferous. We had two more days to go before the standard five-day grace period expired in the DOA policy that allowed folks to claim their belongings. Everyone wanted to do something about the smell—now. Randy talked to the protesters about the odor issue, got their ideas, and gained their cooperation.

The Rotunda Community wanted to stay. They had no idea that we had no approved plans to force them to leave. They were negotiating for something they already had and were not about to lose. Meanwhile, the protesters outside believed it was the police and not their fellow protesters who were preventing them freer access to the building. There was a bit of truth in each vantage point. It had been a rough three days.

Watching the crowds from the Capitol bridge. (Photo by Joe Lynde)

Protesters come in all shapes and sizes. Chief Riseling with some of the crowd outside the Capitol. (Photo by Kevin Wernet)

Chief Riseling in action (March 3, 2011) (Photo by Kevin Wernet)

CHAPTER SEVEN
TRIALS AND TRIBULATIONS

AT THIS POINT, IT SEEMED THAT NO ONE FROM THE REPUBLICAN Party trusted the Democratic Party or vice versa. Many in the larger crowd and certainly several in the smaller Rotunda Community did not trust the administration. Everything that was occurring was viewed with cynicism. The thought that the police were acting on the public's behalf or purely for safety had started to erode with significant doubt that our actions were independent of the administration. The queues were seen as stifling free speech and symbolic of that view were the locked doors of the Capitol.

It would take a different branch of the government—the judiciary—to decide between the protesters and the Administration. The drama was unfolding in a Dane County courtroom. All testimony was available for public viewing around the world through Wisconsin Eye. *Without my realizing it, my testimony would be a missed opportunity to set the record straight regarding access to the Capitol.*

I had been to court several times in my career, but this time, the public nature of my testimony would be vastly different. While I had been very busy for the past two weeks, my work had been behind the scenes running the Interior Branch. Chief Charles Tubbs was the public face of law enforcement, and many believed he was the commander of the operation. It is what we wanted the public to believe. So aside from University of Wisconsin–Madison Chancellor Martin and a handful of people at the University, few people outside of law enforcement knew of my role. Today, as I raised my right hand, swore to tell the truth, and explained how things were actually working, much of that public understanding of the operation would all change.

On the first and second day of the proceedings, Peg Lautenschlager had called witnesses who testified about the difficulties entering into the Capitol over the past several days. The witnesses were largely Democrats, staff to Democrats, or union leaders. There were a lot of restrictions in place this week that had never been in place for the Capitol. Each witness' testimony was very similar; there was only a slight variation on the theme of access being "too restricted."

The most significant witness for the state was Department of Administration (DOA) Secretary Michael Huebsch. When the protests began, he had been in his job for about a month. His testimony focused on his authority, as DOA Secretary, to implement Administrative Code 2, which regulates how state buildings are operated. He talked about why the current situation of having people "live" in the Capitol was not sustainable. He made five points:

1. The cost of the operation was staggering. The number of police officers needed per day (160 to as many as 400) to sustain "voluntary compliance" was costing tens of thousands of dollars each day.

2. The inability to clean and maintain the Capitol, a historic landmark.

3. The general safety of the people working and staying in the Capitol was compromised. The unregulated nature of the

occupation was exceedingly disruptive to those not engaged in the demonstrations. For example, 41 tours had been cancelled over the previous two weeks and many other events postponed.

4. The noise was deafening at times and made it very hard for staff to be productive.

5. The amount and type of prohibited items being brought into the building created fire, health, and evacuation hazards.

I agreed with his five points. He testified about trying to strike a balance between allowing people to protest, and constituents who may or may not be protesting, to meet with their legislators. With the crowd size and sheer noise levels, constituents who were not part of the protest were finding navigating the Capitol very difficult. It was time, in his view, that the prime use of the Capitol building be restored. It was not a hotel and could not offer shelter for people endlessly. The measures put in place were needed to regain control of the daily operation of the Capitol. He referred to the Rotunda and ground floor as occupied territory.

The Secretary made it clear that he had not authorized a first aid center, family center, or an overnight campground. He stated he had never ordered the windows barred, nor had he denied access to the Legislature or visitors with scheduled appointments. This was, in fact, true but we had certainly changed the nature of how people were gaining access.

As his testimony continued, he predicted the size of the crowd was not going to diminish. The inability to clean thoroughly and the amount of food within the building being served and possibly left out for hours, coupled with having people camped out, was beginning to make the facility unusable. He wanted the protesters to respect the closing times of the building by leaving at that designated time.

Secretary Huebsch stated he had authorized a press release on February 25, which stated the building would be closed on Sunday, February 27 at 4:00 p.m. (regular closing hours). The building would be cleaned and reopened Monday, February 28. However, he testified that when the time came on Sunday to close the building, others had shown up to thwart the closing.

That statement was troubling to me. Other people had not shown up on Sunday to thwart the closing. In fact, we had carefully decreased the number of people in the Capitol on Sunday. Something wasn't correct. The decision not to remove people had been made on Friday during the Policy Group meeting in my absence. The Governor's chief of staff told me on Sunday morning that we were not to remove people on Sunday at 4:00p.m. I did not believe the Secretary was lying under oath. Instead, I believed someone hadn't told him the truth. This would explain why he had been so angry with me the night we first met. He must have been told I was unwilling or unable to remove people from the Rotunda on Sunday, and neither was true.

He continued, noting that the protesters who remained had instructions for civil disobedience and had tips for such activity furnished by the American Civil Liberties Union. This was true; however, he and I had never spoken about this or the fact that I wasn't at all troubled by the instructions. He testified that, from the beginning, law enforcement was policing via voluntary compliance and that the primary strategy was to avoid physical contact by the police toward the protesters. This, too, was a troubling statement.

Chief Charles Tubbs hadn't been preaching voluntary compliance when he had ordered me to close the Capitol on February 18 at 6:00 p.m. Had I followed that instruction, force would have been needed and lots of it. It was an unreasonable order in my judgment and I did not carry it out. Then again on February 20, Chief Tubbs ordered the Command Post to close the Capitol at the end of building hours for that day (4:00 p.m.) That order also would have required a high degree of force to carry out against a non-violent crowd. Had I received that order, I would not have followed it. There were fundamental principles I practice regarding giving notice. I also believe in allowing peaceful demonstrators to have choices free of hastily made threats. This is especially true when there had been a number of days of demonstrations followed by nights in which the building was kept open.

In this segment of Secretary Huebsch's testimony, he had not mentioned giving the orders the week before to close the Capitol.[18] In fact, early on he hadn't realized his responsibilities as DOA Secretary involved such decisions.

Claiming law enforcement had used voluntary compliance as the only strategy from the beginning was also misleading in that we set a capacity management number of 9,000 on February 19 and we held people outside, against their wishes when the capacity was reached. We had changed to voluntary compliance as *THE* only strategy after a week of on-again, off-again "orders." Over the past week, we had used negotiating teams to move people down from floors 4, 3, and 2 and held those floors over and over again.

The Secretary's testimony pointed out that because people chose to stay past 4:00 p.m. on Sunday, February 27, and did not leave voluntarily, he had kept the building largely closed on Monday to deal with the noncompliance of approximately 200 people. This portion of his testimony did coalesce with my experience and understanding. The fact that we were keeping people out of the Capitol is what I figured would happen if we did not remove people on Sunday, February 27 as we announced we would do.

The Secretary continued his testimony that he was now working to establish a ratio of a manageable number of people,

---

[18] Wisconsin Eye, March 2, 2011, AFSCME vs. Huebsch

with the sustainable number of law enforcement personnel needed to ensure the safety and functioning of the Capitol. (Randy and I had already calculated a decision matrix for occupancy management a week earlier. Clearly, no one had shared it with the Secretary.) He went on to say that he was working toward allowing protesters, the general public, constituents, and lobbyists back in the building, based on the ability to manage those various groups of people and activities. But first, he said, those staying in the building overnight had to leave. [19]

It was now obvious to me that no one accurately briefed him on what actually was happening or had happened before he became directly involved. In addition, it seemed no one shared with him or received his permission to only allow 354 people in, which was the number the Policy Group had established. Also, since the Capitol did not have an official capacity number, the Secretary testified how many people were allowed in was a judgment call on his part. He did not testify to the number of 9,000 I had established for the building capacity. I wondered if anyone had ever told him that we had established a capacity number.

Secretary Huebsch was continuing on the witness stand as I met with Assistant Attorney General Maria Lazar in a small room at the back of the courtroom gallery. She asked me some basic questions about my experience, my training—all the usual stuff. She told me a little about the state's line of questioning for me. Ms. Lazar explained the plaintiff strategy was to show all the ways access had been blocked over the past several days. With that, we entered the court room together.

Secretary Huebsch was still testifying and I was surprised to hear him say that he had discussed issues of access and police strategy on a daily basis with the Capitol Police Department. Up

---

[19] Wisconsin Eye, March 2, 2011, AFSCME vs. Huebsch

Officers stand outside the Capitol's King Street entrance to stop
protesters from rushing the doors (March 2, 2013)
(Photos by Joe Lynde)

Chief Riseling and the Interior Branch in full swing. Note the cola and emergency chocolate bar. (March 2, 2011) (Photo by Kevin Wernet)

until Monday night February 28, the 15th day of the operation when I first met the Secretary, I had no idea of his involvement. I shook my head in frustration at the ridiculous manner in which this situation had developed.

Half-listening to the Secretary, I thought back on a few of my other court appearances. The contrast in preparation was significant. Months and months of preparation, depositions, documents, studying, and discussion had gone into those former cases. There was none of that here. In fact, this court hearing was indicative of what I had been experiencing in the actual event. Here too, there was little preplanning, things were quickly thrown together, and nobody was sure where it would all lead. In the scheme of things, I thought this case could be precedent-setting—albeit the least thoroughly argued. This isn't to say either side hadn't been professional and hadn't done an outstanding job representing its position. It was just being done at warp speed.

The questioning of Secretary Michael Huebsch had been going on for some time. He was being cross-examined and even the judge stopped to ask him questions. Judge John Albert was getting to the heart of the matter and I appreciated his style in doing so. The lead attorneys from both sides looked as tired as I felt. When the Secretary stepped down, it was my turn.

My direct testimony was perfunctory. Through a series of questions, AAG Steve Means established how I came to be in charge of the police operations. We also covered the basic command structure—at least the standard incident command structure that was on paper. Over the past two weeks, it had not been particularly clear who was really in charge. But I answered technically and honestly.

I was tired and didn't feel sharp in my testimony. I was asked a key question and while I answered honestly, I missed the opportunity to answer the question more fully. It wouldn't be until days later when I would realize my mistake.

The question was, "How did access to the Capitol change over the last several days?" I answered the question narrowly, talking about just the past few days, February 28 through March 2. I spoke of the plans in place for managing behavior and then managing access with queues and badges.

I should have answered the question more fully, returning to the actual beginning of the operation, February 14. I should have talked about the fact that when I took over the Interior Branch on February 17, there was no stated building capacity. It would have been valuable to describe the significant concerns of the over-crowding from February 15 to 18. It would have been beneficial for me to explain how those concerns and my experience led me to develop the capacity number of 9,000 on the evening of February 18 and why I implemented capacity management on February 19. Instead, none of that was in the record, which meant the judge had no way of knowing, nor did the public, about why access rules had changed from February 18 to February 19. The change had nothing to do with politics or restricting free speech. It was based on safety and the ability to evacuate if the need arose due to a fire or other disaster.

I did, however, manage to testify about how unprecedented the events over the past 17 days had been. When asked if I thought the demonstrations had been relatively peaceful, I answered, "Yes. I never—I've never experienced anything like this in my life. This has been exceptional. I mean, to have this many people, with this much emotion, be part of something historical and, as it stands today, eleven arrests from the Interior Branch, which means eleven from the inside, none since Sunday night, I just think is unprecedented." (Actually, the number of arrests was 13. I had unintentionally been given the wrong number when I was briefed prior to testifying.)

My testimony continued: "I don't think there's another place in the country that could say that they've gone through what we've gone through with this. The crowds have been exceptional. They've been polite. They've been respectful. They've been grateful. They've been appreciative. I've never been thanked so many times in my career as I have in the last two weeks."[20]

When asked if the presence of a well-trained, visible body of law enforcement officers contributed to the success of the last two weeks, I answered unequivocally that there was no doubt in my mind that it was a key to our success.

Then we moved on to cross-examination. Cross-examination in comparison to direct questioning is usually more exciting. Attorney Peg Lautenschlager began by asking me about the number of police on any given day. It has been a long-standing policy of mine that I never give out the actual number of police during an operation. One never knows who may be out there planning something that might disrupt or harm people participating in an event. When asked about the exact numbers, my lawyer objected and the judge asked me directly to explain, which I did. I wasn't trying to be coy or deceptive; I just had no way of knowing how long we were going to have to maintain operations. The judge sustained the state's objection.

Ms. Lautenschlager probed the police and policy leadership structure. The structure on paper was not exactly clear and it was even less clear in operation. I answered about the various groups that met and how the groups attempted to go about making decisions. Evidently, it was far murkier on my end than the Secretary had stated. From his perspective, he was in charge and had dealt with the Capitol Police Department. On my end, I didn't know when he became involved and the communication and direction were not consistent or particularly illuminating.

---

[20] Riseling court testimony, March 2, 2011, in AFSCME vs. DOA Secretary Huebsch

I testified about the group still in the Capitol and for the first time publicly explained how we had begun to refer to them as the "Rotunda Community." The group referred to themselves as the "Capitol City." I explained that the Rotunda Community remaining overnight since the beginning of the protests had established its own culture with rules, responsibilities, tasks, customs, procedures for dealing with debate and decision-making by giving everyone a voice. Their methods were not always the most efficient, but their methods certainly were an extension of democracy. They had shown patience with us and we had shown patience with them.

More questions came about the queues. During the entire event, the communications with the public by law enforcement left much to be desired. Our communication with staff within the Capitol was equally lacking. In both testimony and in general, the government failed to adequately explain why the plan was needed, what its implementation was intended to accomplish, and how it would operate.

When law enforcement did communicate, we sent confusing directions and then updated directions, which just added to the confusion. There were those who embraced the plan—mainly Republicans, and then there were those who made little effort to use the plan as intended, mainly Democrats. Regardless of political affiliation or beliefs, the queue never worked well.

I finished my testimony wondering about all the questions I hadn't been asked and all the information I knew, but didn't have the opportunity to share. Little did I know I would be back twice before the proceeding ended the next day.

After I stepped down, the State called Republican Senator Glenn Grothman of the 20th Senate District to testify. Following Senator Grothman, Ed Wall, Administrator of the Division of Criminal Investigation (DCI) with the state Department of Justice, took the stand. I was curious to hear his testimony. A year earlier, I had served on the selection committee tasked with interviewing and culling all the candidates for the DCI Administrator's position. I was familiar with Ed's background and prior experience.

> *Just prior to becoming the Administrator of DCI, Ed had served as Director of Wisconsin Emergency Management. Throughout the current events, Ed had seemed to be close to the Governor's staff and had been a tougher voice for how to respond to the circumstances than other law enforcement leaders.*
>
> *A former New Hampshire state trooper, his exposure to community policing tactics was far less than his exposure and experience with traditional police tactics and strategies. When it came to the threat of harm, disasters, or terrorism, Ed had significant experience that was widely respected.*

Ed testified about the lack of fire safety and capacity standards for the building, his concerns about crowding, and the unfettered access of the early days of the demonstrations. He testified about vulnerability and crowd demeanor. He was concerned that large crowds would draw attention seekers or simply lone wolves looking for an opportunity to harm others. The idea of "planting troublemakers" in the crowd had come up publicly during the hoax phone call between Governor Walker and the pseudo-Koch brother, actually Ian Murphy of the *Buffalo Beast* blog, pretending to be Dave Koch.

Planted or not, individuals with ill intent could easily enter the crowd and use the masses as "cover" to carry out horrific acts. It was one of the reasons we staffed law enforcement so heavily to deter violence, and if necessary, react quickly.

When asked, Ed described the fifty threats that had been investigated to date. He was asked about the open carrying of weapons that had occurred during some of the demonstrations. The plaintiff wanted to establish that if Ed believed the open carrying of firearms wasn't threatening, why he believed the presence of people staying in the Rotunda was threatening. It was not an exact comparison, but the plaintiff's attorney made her point.

Once Ed finished, I returned to the Capitol while the state continued to call more witnesses to testify. Most were asked to explain how their ability to work and move about the building had improved since the queuing was put into place. Some talked about the fear they had experienced when the Capitol had been so crowded the first week. Some staff members and legislators had been confronted verbally by protesters screaming at them or entering their offices and disrupting their operations. Many of these witnesses were called to counter the plaintiff's initial witnesses, who wanted unfettered access.[21]

At the end of the day's proceeding, Judge Albert stated he was thinking of issuing a court order to Secretary Huebsch that would require the people still remaining in the Rotunda Community to leave the Capitol building that night, March 2. At this point, neither side was in favor of such an order.

The plaintiff stated the Rotunda Community was not her client, therefore, she couldn't speak for its members. The state surprisingly argued against the order because the Rotunda Community wasn't represented and so, in Assistant AG Means' view, the order would not be valid. The state's argument surprised many, as most people thought this was exactly what the state was seeking—a removal of the remaining protesters. The judge stated they would reconvene at 1:00 p.m. the next day.

---

[21] Court testimony, March 2, 2011, in AFSCME vs. Huebsch

As far as the state arguing against the judge's proposed order to remove the people remaining in the Capitol—I just shook my head. For me, it highlighted even more that throughout the process the "State" had no clear idea of what its goal should be or how to achieve it.

Back in the Interior Branch, the day had run rather smoothly. The queues were beginning to work and people were lining up to be screened. They seemed more likely to return the badges and make an effort to obey directions. Not surprisingly, the one-in, one-out queue of the Rotunda Community had been the slowest of all the queues.

Word had come to the Interior Branch while I was in court that a letter had been received by Secretary Huebsch from a credible source pricing the alleged damage to the Capitol at $7.5 million. I thought that had to be wrong and unreliable. $7,500,000 maybe should have been $75,000 or at most $750,000. I thought $750,000 was too high, so ten times that amount was laughable. General Dunbar asked for my reaction and I told him that I thought it had to be a typo; there was no way there was that much damage. In fact, I told him that I wasn't sure what had actually been damaged except possibly the Capitol lawn.

Secretary Huebsch called me and attempted to explain the state's reasoning behind the fact that no one was representing the Rotunda Community because no one knew who they were. I chuckled to myself and thought this would be news to the Rotunda Community, who believed AFSCME was fighting for the right to occupy the Capitol. The Secretary wondered if I knew for certain whether the Rotunda Community was planning to stay tonight or if they would leave voluntarily if asked. I said I could not know for certain. He asked me to approach the Rotunda Community and ask.

So with Deputy Branch Director AC Brian Bridges and my assistant Kevin Wernet in tow, I went down to the ground floor of the Rotunda, where I proceeded to approach small groups of people and asked them if they were ready to leave. All of the groups or individuals I approached were friendly. The sight of me in uniform was no concern to them; they had seen me around in the crowd and many I had talked to daily.

I found Janie and asked if she and her husband, who was in a wheelchair, were ready to leave tonight. She responded they were tired and cold, but they would stay as long as they physically could, or until they were arrested. Person after person said they were not willing to leave without being arrested. They intended to live in the "people's house" for the foreseeable future.

One young man told me he intended to die in a beautiful place and the Capitol fit that description. He explained that he had a heart condition and had a limited life expectancy of 15 years. When I asked if he thought he might live here for 15 years, he answered, "Why not?" Others said they intended to stay until the 14 Democratic senators returned to the state. They felt it was important to maintain a presence here in the senators' absence.

Some said they would leave, shower, get a change of clothes, and then come back as long as they could—indefinitely. A few said they planned to leave on Friday, Saturday, or Sunday. Still others noted that their medical situations might cause them to leave via ambulance. Of the remaining protesters, only a few said they were going to leave in the morning to get back to work and to their families. Not one person said yes to my inquiry about leaving voluntarily that night.

I was informed by Kevin that a meeting was being organized by Secretary Huebsch in the Attorney General's office on the Capitol's first floor. The Secretary was requesting I attend. With my informal survey complete, I headed for the meeting.

Participants at this meeting were similar to the state Policy Group.[22] As I entered the room, General Dunbar informed me that the Capitol damage estimate of $7.5 million was accurate and the number was not a typo. I still couldn't believe it.

DOA Secretary Huebsch was seated at the far end of the room at the head of the table. Across from him was the Governor's Chief of Staff, Keith Gilkes. Over the ten days I had worked with Keith, I had grown very comfortable with him. He had promised me that when this was all over, we would meet at the lakefront Union Terrace at UW–Madison to teach me how to play the popular card game, Euker.

I pulled up a chair next to Keith and without thinking, said, "Keith, would you like to go into business with me cleaning marble? It could be called Keith and Sue Marble Cleaners—giving you top billing."

Then I added, "You take $4 million and I'd take $3.5 million, because I am such a generous business partner."

He laughed out loud, said "DEAL!" and we shook hands. He added, "I'll complete the paperwork in the morning for the LLC." We were cracking each other up.

Oblivious to the rest of the group's reaction, we kept on going with this back and forth until the Secretary boomed, "I've heard enough."

Whoops. I got serious quickly and said, "Mr. Secretary, I apologize. Mr. Secretary, please don't use those estimates or numbers. You will be a laughing stock, sir. There is no way those numbers are accurate."

He studied me for a minute and said, "I never like it when you start out by saying 'Mr. Secretary.'" Everyone chuckled. He went on,

---

[22] Keith Gilkes, Dan Blackdeer, WSP Major Darren Price, Ed Wall, General Don Dunbar, Kevin Wernet, and me. We were joined by Dave Mahoney, Secretary Huebsch, DOA Attorney Cari Anne Renlund, and eventually Charles Tubbs.

"Whenever you start with 'Mr. Secretary', I know I am in trouble and I'm not going to like what I hear." And then he smiled. More quiet laughter.

He passed two sheets of paper around the table to show me the written estimates. A company had placed the estimates in writing without ever inspecting the building. I just shook my head and whispered to Keith that we might be too late in forming our LLC.

Again I tried, "Mr. Secretary, I really believe you have been given bad information and just because it is written down, doesn't make it correct."

He nodded and said, "Let's move on. Have you had a chance to speak to the people staying overnight?"

I then summarized the responses I had received.

The group talked about how Judge Albert had essentially stated he was willing to order everyone out of the Capitol and allow the reinstitution and enforcement of Administrative Code 2. Secretary Huebsch asked Sheriff Dave Mahoney if he would honor the court order. I knew the Sheriff would not go against a court order, but that didn't mean he would assist us in clearing the building if it came down to that. I was not sure the Secretary understood the difference.

The court was set to reconvene at 1:00 in the afternoon on Day 18, Thursday, March 3, and the judge was insistent that the proceeding be completed and he would make his ruling. If the judge's demeanor today was any indication, he would be ordering the Rotunda Community out.

I immediately knew I wanted the removal plan briefed that we had put in place for last Sunday, but were not allowed to use. Depending on the timing, we could have a sufficient number of officers present to enforce the court ruling. Or if the proceeding went too late into the evening, we would need to bolster our evening staffing numbers.

Of course, Charles Tubbs hoped that if the predicted order came down, we would still use voluntary compliance. I agreed we would start there as we always did. If the order stated the building needed to be emptied, and if we had to carry people out or arrest them, we would do so by using only reasonable and necessary force. I was not going to disregard a court order and I was not going to await any further appeals. I assured Secretary Huebsch we had sufficient plans in place in the Interior Branch to move forward if the court ordered us to do so.

Charles shared that the union leaders he had worked with all along would abide by the court order. He again noted that some of the members of the Rotunda Community were not affiliated with the unions. With that, the meeting ended.

The Overnight Commander had instructions from the Incident Commander that he was not to allow anyone in the building after the 6:00 p.m. building closing hours. He held to that standard when he turned away a small group. Shortly after his denial, his decision was overridden by Chief Tubbs. When the Commander tried to maintain the agreed-upon standards, the Rotunda Community responded that they didn't have to listen to the Commander or follow the agreement; they would just call Chief Tubbs instead.

DAY 18: THURSDAY, MARCH 3, 2011

As I headed in the Wisconsin Avenue entrance door, I ran into Representative Mark Pocan in the hallway. He explained he was going to the Martin Luther King Jr. entrance this morning between 9:00 and 9:30 without his identification and attempt entry. He was doing this to prove a point that some folks were being let in without having to show identification, often at the direction of Chief Tubbs. We knew, and I had to acknowledge, Chief Tubbs was making exceptions to the rules and I could understand Representative Pocan's frustration. Representative Pocan stated strongly that if he couldn't gain entrance, then he was going to get arrested for trying to make his point that not everyone was being treated equally.

I made it clear to Mark that this type of stunt wasn't helpful and would only serve to raise tensions. However, if he insisted on knowingly and willfully disregarding the entrance protocol, I informed him I would facilitate his arrest. I headed up the stairs to the Branch.

We jumped right into the early morning briefing. There were now 98 people in the Rotunda Community. Chief Warden Randy Stark was joking that he and Chief Tubbs would soon be running as co-mayors of the Rotunda Community. An additional 25 people slept outside the building overnight without the benefit of tents. Again, we marveled at their devotion to their cause and we spent a minute asking ourselves what would get us to sleep outside in March in Madison. We couldn't think of anything. "Hunting," some of the guys joked, but "causes," none.

Getting back to the briefing, we learned there were no sheriff's deputies outside overnight. Sheriff Dave Mahoney had been told by the Command Post he wasn't needed after Tuesday night. Of course, this further stretched the Interior Branch's overnight resources.

Because of my earlier conversation with Representative Pocan, I asked CPD Lieutenant Marc Schmidt to contact Chief Tubbs regarding Representative Pocan's plan and to ask Chief Tubbs to go to the MLK entrance. I felt that since Charles was making exceptions, he should have to deal with Pocan, not the officers staffing the door.

Court was to resume at 1:00 today. We needed contingencies for all possible rulings. The Interior Branch assignments were divided up and in addition to running their divisions; the staff was given a few hours to think through and draft preliminary plans. At

11:00, they were to outline their plans and identify any big issues that might keep them from finishing or otherwise thwart their efforts. As Assistant Chief Dale Burke joked, we want NBI (no big issues) to stop us from succeeding.

We then received a report that a citizen stopped a police officer outside on the balustrade and gave him a live round of .22-caliber ammunition he had found. Upon searching the balustrade, more .22-caliber rounds were found. Then more rounds were discovered at other entrances.

The grounds were then thoroughly searched. Eleven rounds were found near the State Street entrance, 29 rounds by the King Street entrance, and one round by the North Hamilton entrance. All told, 41 rounds were found. Given that a box of .22s usually contains 50 rounds, we were missing nine. All the ammunition found was of the same type and same brand. Later in the afternoon, I learned that nine of the same type of round had been found in the stairwell of the City-County Building, a block from the Capitol.

At the 10:00 a.m. Command Post briefing, we discussed the phase-out of the Emergency Police Service. I stated that the University would like to have our last day be Sunday, March 6. This coincided with COS Keith Gilkes' and Dan Blackdeer's assessment at an earlier Policy Group meeting. The Capitol Police, DNR wardens, and the State Patrol would then need to do some future planning.

The plan for how to handle the return of the 14 Democratic senators was a Command Post responsibility and I requested an update on the status of their plan. There was no update. The CP had been comfortable without the sheriff's folks outside overnight. I was not. In light of the fact we had found ammunition outside and the court was going to make a ruling today, I felt we could have a mess on our hands tonight.

The Command Post group brought up the issue of when or if the police should be allowed to go "hands-on" with people regardless of what the court order may contain. With all the political maneuvering swirling about, it was hard for me to fathom what they were really saying "regardless of what the court order may contain." I was lost.

I understood the number of police should decline due to cost and sheer fatigue. The need to support enforcement directives by the use of some hands-on tactics needed to be clear. We could have reduced law enforcement numbers significantly if we allowed law enforcement to take reasonable action earlier. If it were my decision, we would have closed the Capitol on Sunday, moved the people out gently, cleaned the building, and re-opened Monday, and avoided court altogether. The time for talking ended when the court ruled this evening. It had been the Command Post and Chief Tubbs who preached voluntary compliance at all times and at any cost. And I was confident they would bring it up yet again at the Policy Group meeting.

> *There hasn't been a time in my entire career that I believed in treating people roughly or with more force than was reasonable and necessary to achieve safety, order maintenance, or other legitimate enforcement goals. I did believe that a reasonable amount of force used at the right time and in the correct manner, combined with intelligent capacity management and crowd redirection, could reduce tension and stabilize a crowd. Throughout this event, the idea that no touching was allowed to enforce the disregard or violation of verbal directives from the police continued to be troubling.*
>
> *I do not support placing police in lines to act as human barriers to then have the lines disregarded. If that is the policy, then don't have the damn line in the*

first place. Any time I place police in a line, as we did in
front of the doors or at the queues, they were instructed
to warn people verbally, then to act physically if their
warning was not heeded. I trusted that the commanders
understood how to preserve the balance.

We moved down the agenda to the menu for feeding the police—once again. My assistant, Kevin Wernet, continued to lead the charge on this topic. We teased him about his obsession with our food; however, truth was that his desire for variety and healthy alternatives was because of his experience in the fire service.

It was a standing joke between fire and police that fire got paid to sleep and eat. Cops, on the other hand, got in trouble if they slept on their shift and no one ever fed us. We even have to pay for our own doughnuts—that line always brings a laugh. Of course we had been feeding the police for the past 18 days—largely because they couldn't leave to find food and many were staying in hotels. They were captive on their posts or assignments for each 12-hour shift.

I attempted to close the briefing with a listing of all the contingency plans the Interior Branch commanders were drafting on the fly. I informed the Command Post that the first drafts of those plans were due by 11:00, roughly 22 minutes away. I explained the second drafts were due by 3:00 p.m. I would then share those plans with the CP at the 4:00 briefing and they could give me feedback by 5:30, so we would be ready to go by 6:00. This was a very aggressive time frame, but I knew the division commanders would meet it.

The Command Post wanted the plans sooner. I told them it was impossible to quicken this process. I really had it with these CP guys. There was no consistent leadership coming from the CP, nor was there an exit strategy. The Interior Branch had no planning support, and although logistics support had improved, it was now

Day 18 and we are still talking about food for the officers. Incident Commander Blackdeer, Operations Chief Captain Teasdale, or Capitol Police Chief Tubbs—all who were supposedly "above" me in the Incident Command Chart— weren't being sent to court to testify and speak for law enforcement. I was the one who was sent and would be testifying two more times before this was over. I was happy to do it to get the information out, but what was the Command Post's role in all this? What were these guys doing all day?

I then pointed out that several days ago, the Command Post had taken responsibility for developing the plan for the 14 senators returning to the senate floor, and no one had seen a draft yet. I went on to say that the Interior Branch, on the other hand, had implemented queuing, dealt with the occupation, dealt with large crowds on the balustrade, designed and successfully implemented plans for the budget address, and created and continued the scale-down plan. We handled all the events inside the Capitol, I had been to court and the Branch was now drafting several plans for a 6:00 p.m. implementation deadline. The CP would get the plans at 4:00 p.m. and they should be grateful. End of story and end of briefing.

As we walked back to the Operations Room, DCI Special Agent Tina Virgil said to me that she understood why people liked working for me. She explained that I was incredibly strong when standing up to those of "higher authority," was very demanding, but would fight long and hard for the people who worked for me. I responded that I was a police chief, not "Miss Congeniality." We had a good laugh. She teased that there was no worry of my winning that title.

March 6, 2011 had better be my last day. My deference to anyone short of DOA Secretary Huebsch was gone—and my deference to him was limited. At our 11:00 a.m. meeting, each commander reviewed his first-draft plan and identified the big issues with implementation. Each big issue was discussed by the group and we settled on a way forward. By noon, we had reviewed all the plans. The commanders knew they had three hours before presenting final plans to me.

The ammunition rounds found outside the Capitol this morning made me think twice about not having deputies out there overnight. So I called Sheriff Mahoney and asked if his deputies would come back and staff the balustrade again tonight. I realized the CP had told him to stop, but I felt I needed him. David said, "Anything for you, Sue." That night the deputies were back.

The attorneys for DOA and for the state from the AG's office had heard about the rounds of ammunition we had found outside on the balustrade. They wanted me to return to court and to testify about the matter. I wasn't sure what if anything this had to do with access issues but I began to prepare. Lieutenant Marc Schmidt furnished a copy of the police report from the morning. I had staff in the Interior Branch quickly develop one large map of the Capitol Square that I could use as a display in court.

At 1:00 p.m., Kevin Wernet and I headed back to court, where I testified about the ammunition found outside the Capitol.[23] This meant that I missed the Policy Group meeting.[24] It was one of the least attended policy meetings. Sarah Pfatteicher went in place of Kevin and took thorough notes.

Upon my return from court, Sarah briefed me. The topic of staffing daytime hours with just eighty officers by March 7 was a goal that all felt could be met. Captain Teasdale raised the issue that eighty police would not be sufficient if they were not empowered to actually enforce the rules using reasonable force to do so, a point I

[23] Riseling testimony, AFSCME vs. DOA Secretary Huebsch, March 3, 2011
[24] In attendance were Incident Commander Dan Blackdeer, Operations Chief Teasdale, General Don Dunbar, Chief of Staff Keith Gilkes, DCI Ed Wall, Assembly Sergeant-at-Arms Anne Tonnon Byers, Capitol Police Chief Charles Tubbs, MPD AC Davenport, and a newcomer, Rachel Veum, assistant to the Chief Clerk of the Senate.

completely agreed with. Staffing would have to be adjusted if metal screening was going to continue.

Sarah stated that Chief Tubbs felt the remaining people inside the Capitol were no longer being represented by the unions. He stated that the group still inside were independent of the Budget Repair Bill and would be resistant to leaving.

The Policy Group discussed moving the Command Post to DNR headquarters instead of using the Madison Fire Department facility. Also, by Monday, DOA wanted to re-institute the permitting process for demonstrations and activities inside the Capitol.

The group discussed two upcoming potential flashpoints: the court ruling and the return of the 14 senators. They speculated on how things would evolve. They thought the court decision would be made before 4:00 p.m. that afternoon and likely would be "tweeted" from the court room. Some hoped it would direct DOA to clear the building. There were those who suggested that we remove people at midnight or 2:00 a.m. with or without arresting them, because the outside crowd would be smaller. Others made their pitch for not permitting demonstrations inside the building from here on out, again citing the U.S. Capitol as a model.

When the building was eventually cleared, the Wisconsin State Historical Society, a few of the protesters, and even the Smithsonian, had expressed an interest in retrieving and preserving various posted signs, banners, and materials. It was agreed the materials would be collected and people would be allowed to retrieve them at some point after the building had re-opened.

The weekend was two days away and while no one had any specific information, everyone believed the large crowds would return again to the Capitol and to the Square. The Policy Group agreed to meet again when the court decision was announced.

Meanwhile, as the afternoon progressed, I went to court, and several thousand people began to gather on the Capitol grounds in anticipation of the court's ruling. As the afternoon turned to early evening, the crowd grew to approximately 14,000. Most were interested in having the freedom to enter the Capitol unimpeded, and had no interest, and in fact resisted, the idea of queues and other restrictions.

After I left the courtroom, the state continued its case with several witnesses testifying about safety concerns around crowding and electrical overloads. There were several witnesses, mainly from Republican legislators' offices, the Governor's office, and the Attorney General's office, who testified about the level of noise and disruption to their work day. Several spoke of angry confrontations with protesters yelling and getting into the staff's personal space. Many were particularly concerned because of the shooting in Arizona of U.S. Congresswoman Gabby Giffords two months earlier.[25]

Secretary Huebsch was recalled to the stand to talk about damages. He testified to the estimated damages of $6 million to restore the interior, $1 million to restore the exterior, and $500,000 to supervise the project.[26] I had offered my best advice to him earlier, which was not to use those quotes. I recognized that the grounds outside near many of the entrances had sustained lawn damage from the large crowds walking all over the soggy grass. Yet I couldn't imagine that re-sodding the Capitol Square lawn would cost a million dollars. Inside, I figured the cleanup and removal of tape—duct, electrical, masking, adhesive or most commonly blue painter's tape—might cost $250,000. His estimates hit the media

---

[25] Testimony in AFSCME vs. Huebsch, March 3, 2011
[26] Huebsch testimony in AFSCME vs. Huebsch, March 3, 2011

like lightning. Over the coming days, the Secretary would have to retreat from those inflated numbers. [27]

The commanders had done a great job in a short amount of time. As each of them summarized their work, they all ended the same way by saying "NBI, Chief." (No big issues). We were all smiles.

The phone rang and I was recalled to testify yet again, so the scheduled 4:00 p.m. Command Post briefing would have to wait. Kevin and I went back in the courtroom and I walked straight to the stand. The judge wanted to hear what I had found out last night about the people's desire to stay in the building.

I testified to what I was told the night before. I described some of the challenges we had faced with mental health and other medical issues. On cross-examination, I was asked about whether I had posed a question or gave an order. I explained that because I had talked to almost everyone in the Rotunda Community before that night, I started the conversation fitting my previous relationship or lack of relationship with the person. I posed questions; I did not order anyone to do anything. Nor had I been asked by the Secretary to issue any orders. From what most of the people had told me, they were going to stay, sleep and live in the Capitol for as long as they could. Many were ready to be arrested if it came to that.[28] With that bit of testimony completed, I returned to the Capitol once more.

The plaintiff called some rebuttal witnesses who testified to more access difficulties. Eventually, the testimony ended and the court was ready to move to closing arguments. While the closing

---

[27] One year after the protests, the administration paid just under $200,000 to clean up and re-seed the lawn. Stein/Marley, *More Than They Bargained For*, University of Wisconsin Press, 2013, p. 200.
[28] Riseling testimony, AFSCME vs. DOA Secretary Huebsch, March 3, 2011

arguments were being made, the Interior Branch was finalizing plans to respond to the court ruling. [29]

During the eventual Command Post briefing, around 4:30 p.m., I went through all the plans as I had promised to do earlier in the day. The only assistance we would need beyond what I had available in the Branch was some transportation for a few protesters who were frail. We hoped the Madison Fire Department would transport them out of the Capitol if they would not leave on their own. We felt this was the most humane way to move them, if it came to that. MFD asked if those protesters would go to a hospital and I said I didn't think that was the case. Because they didn't need to go to a hospital, MFD declined to assist. We requested the Command Post to find us some stair chairs, lightweight lifting chairs to move patients up and down stairs, that could be used by law enforcement to remove protesters with medical issues.

To ensure we had enough staffing to deal with the outcome of the court ruling and the reaction from the crowd, we were ready to hold over the day shift. I informed them that I had spoken to Sheriff Mahoney, who said his deputies would be back outside tonight.

The Command Post informed me that in the Policy Group meeting, which I had missed because I was in court, the idea was raised of moving the protesters out by 6:30 p.m. or waiting until 3:00 in the morning. Given the way Charles had dealt with the crowds and negotiated his way along the week on our behalf, I thought a 6:30 exit would be too quick, especially given that the court hadn't yet ruled. As far as the 3:00 a.m. removal time suggestion, I recalled a middle-of-the-night tactic I had used successfully in 2000.

---

[29] Testimony, AFSCME vs. DOA Secretary Huebsch, March 3, 2011

Back in 2000, after using a ruse to gain entry to the Chancellor's office, several protesters decided to make a point by staying put. They then locked bicycle U-locks around their necks and to each other. When police arrived to escort the clerical and administrative assistants from the office, a larger group of protesters attacked the police with 2 x 4s and fire extinguishers.

The group had been consistently uncooperative and talked openly about resisting the police. While many of their demands had been met as conditions for them leaving peacefully, they still wouldn't leave and instead would establish new conditions. This group did not sleep and they came and went throughout the day and night. We used a 4:00 a.m. forced removal of the protesters and found it to be the safest course of action for all.

In the current set of events, the 3:00 a.m. removal was a non-starter for me for a number of reasons. All we had used for weeks were negotiation, dialog, and voluntary compliance, so there was no evidence these protesters would actively resist police. While occasionally, a few had been aggressive, they had not been violent or used tactics like bike locks. The number of police available at 3:00 a.m. was too small to ensure safety or success. Additionally, to rouse people from sleeping in the middle of the night would anger everyone. To place them outside in the cold in the wee hours of the morning when transportation may be an issue was unsafe.

After all the rapport Charles had established with these folks, this tactic was just disrespectful and counterproductive. Finally, the building would be reopening at 8:00 a.m. when they could all return and when they did, we would have made them our enemies.

Instead, I wanted to use the two hours after the court ruling to allow Charles to talk with the people, hopefully gaining the Rotunda Community's cooperation. They would then have time to gather their belongings, say their goodbyes, and march out into a waiting crowd. Last Sunday, the march-out had worked well for us and for the unions. I hoped it would work again. If they wouldn't go at that point, we would remove them.

Information now had arrived that approximately 2,000 additional people were marching up State Street. They would join the thousands who were already on the Square. It was 4:45 p.m.

Back in the court room, Assistant AG Means gave the state's closing argument and he addressed the extraordinary nature of the times we all were facing. The main thrust of the state's argument was that the Capitol was not a public forum in the traditional sense, like parks or streets. Because large segments of the building were offices, there was limited space that could be designated public forum. The argument was that certain parts of the building are open to the public, while other parts are not. The state, through time, place, and manner may regulate space within the building.

The state cannot regulate content and while the state was screening for those who wanted to occupy the Capitol, it was due to the "manner" of occupation, not the content of the argument being made. He argued correctly, in my judgment, that the state can set and maintain reasonable building hours and enact other rules addressing safety, health, maintaining a workplace, cost, averting violence or damage, and for appearance and preservation of this historical landmark. The measures the state had in place this week were to transition from the large crowds of the last few weeks and return to normal building operations. In essence, the state reasserted its responsibilities and authority granted under Administrative Code 2 of the Wisconsin Statutes .[30]

The plaintiff's argument given by Attorney Lautenschlager focused on the ever-changing rules of the week and the premise

---

[30] AFSCME v Huebsch, March 3, 2011. AAG Steve Means closing argument

that the rules were content-based. The plaintiff acknowledged the state had rules for operating the building and that the state was disregarding its own rules. In the plaintiff's most cogent moment, she argued, "In extraordinary times comes our biggest challenge not to diminish our Constitutional rights because the Constitution doesn't diminish during extraordinary times. And the Constitution doesn't diminish when we face new challenges. Instead, it is then that we need to recognize the Constitutional protections that are guaranteed all citizens."[31]

Both Steve Means and Peg Lautenschlager were correct. What was happening wasn't Constitutional, yet what needed to happen to return the Capitol to "normal" was not allowing the unfettered access of the earliest days. The judge would rule quickly as he had promised to do.

Judge Albert asked for people from all sides to remain peaceful as he made his ruling. He then ruled that the queues as established were overly restrictive and while they were a good faith effort, the restrictions were unconstitutional. He praised the crowds and the police for the successful exercise of the First Amendment. He ordered the access be returned to an "open state." The distinct queues should no longer be used, and he ordered the Rotunda Community to leave the building. The ruling reaffirmed the state's ability to use Administrative Code 2 to regulate the opening and closing of the building and establish reasonable regulations regarding the access of the public to the Capitol.[32] As he spoke, what he was saying was being tweeted.

At the Capitol, the crowds continued to grow outside. Fed by Twitter, there were some who were determined to get the doors of

---

[31] AFSCME v Huebsch, March 3, 2011. Peg Lautenschlager closing argument
[32] AFSCME v Huebsch, March 3, 2011. Judge John C. Albert ruling

the Capitol opened as the queuing operation ended for the day. At the State Street entrance, one of the doors was breached and opened. Some of the crowd rushed in and the battle between the crowd and the police was in full swing. Democratic lawmakers whose offices were on the first floor opened their windows and people rushed to climb in. The other entrances were holding for the moment—but we knew once the demonstrators were inside, they could open more doors to others outside.

I sprinted out of the Operations Rooms and ran down the steps, taking two or more at a time, pausing at the second-floor landing to look over the side into the Rotunda where people were gathering. I radioed the Command Post and requested a team of state troopers be placed into hard gear. The CP agreed and my Deputy Branch Director Brian Bridges consulted with Division Commander WSP Lieutenant Brad Altman, and the selected troopers began to change into their hard gear. Hard gear is equipment worn by the police in crowd control situations. Police refer to it as "turtle gear;" the public thinks of it as "riot gear." It includes a helmet, shin, knee and thigh guards, forearm pads, chest pads, and back pads.

I then continued to sprint down the steps until I reached the ground floor and headed to the State Street entrance, where there were three sets of doors. The center revolving door had been re-secured. The police were actively pushing and shoving with the crowd, trying hard not to give up access to the double doors to the left and right of the center revolving doors. The crowd was pushing into the vestibule area and the interior doors could not be secured. The scrum of police pushing to maintain the security of these antique doors was four to five officers deep in places. The crowd outside now comprised thousands of agitated protesters. The officers, deputies, and troopers were fast becoming fatigued.

I pulled out my handcuffs and crawled beneath the outstretched arms and legs of the officers and troopers until I reached the door handles. I hooked one cuff to each door knob. Standing up, I told the cops to take one step backward. When they did, the handcuffs caught, the door knobs held, and the crowds realized they were in fact "locked" out. The crowd stood in the vestibule frustrated.

The officers and troopers stepped further back to disengage physically and visibly. I went over to the third pair of doors at the State Street entrance, where the same scene was being acted out. I asked if anyone had a pair of handcuffs. The cops were fighting to hold their position, they were stressed out, and growing very tired.

One of them looked at me incredulously and said, "We are cops. We all have handcuffs, stupid." I had to laugh. I reached up to his duty belt and took his handcuffs and repeated what I had done at the other door. I ordered the cops back and again the cuffs and knobs held. Within moments, the tension de-escalated.

Handcuffing the doors to the Capitol. (Photo by Tony Barnes)

A Capitol Police officer approached me and challenged the use of the handcuffs on the doors. He insisted the use was against the fire code. I had to smile. The building wasn't covered by the fire code, but his safety concern was valid. Not wanting to repeat my same silly handcuff question with yet another silly question of whether anyone had handcuffs keys, I asked a couple of officers if they would take responsibility to staff the doors with handcuff keys in case there was an emergency that required exiting. Several officers said they would.

Meanwhile, one of the officers had placed his cuffs on the door where mine hung and then removed mine and returned them to me. I headed to the Rotunda, where 200 to 300 people had gathered. The Rotunda Community had grown, but the mass arrest plan would still work. I really didn't want to have to use it, but for now, the situation was still well within its parameters.

While the other doors held, the first-floor windows leading to the Democrats' offices had been breached and dozens of people climbed in. In response, we sent law enforcement into offices and bathrooms on the ground floor to close and lock the windows. The tension in the crowd outside remained very high.

Word came that the court had determined that all those in the Capitol should leave or be removed. No one believed us when we told them. Attorney Lautenschlager came into the building and we talked briefly. She confirmed the court ruling for me. She said it would be a while before anything was sent in writing. I knew that without a document, folks would not believe us, so I asked her if she would address the crowd.

Dog-tired from working to represent her union clients and suffering from a bad head cold, Peg had won her portion of the case and now wanted to head home and rest. She reluctantly agreed. She explained to the group in the Rotunda that they won. The restrictions that were in place at the Capitol did not stand. However, they did need to leave the Capitol and respect its hours of operation. With that, she left, and the group decided it was going to have to fully discuss the issue before anyone would go anywhere. With 90-some principal members of the Rotunda Community and the 200 or so who had recently joined them, this discussion was going to take a while.

I headed upstairs to the first floor to survey the crowd and decide whether any of the tactics in the mass arrest plan would need to be changed in light of the current circumstances.

Shortly thereafter, a radio transmission was made about an altercation at the Wisconsin Street entrance. The officers were acting on my orders to secure the perimeter and not to allow any access at this point. Without showing any credentials, a man had attempted to gain access to the building. After several attempts by Officer Kirchner of the Two Rivers Police Department to turn him away, he tried to push past Kirchner and the other officers on the post. The officers took the man to the ground.

While on the ground and again as the officers were bringing the individual to his feet, the man insisted he was State Representative Milroy. A lieutenant from Two Rivers and Sergeant Ruth Ewing from the University Police approached the subject. Representative Milroy then produced his state identification. The lieutenant and sergeant walked the representative away from the area and into the building. About ten minutes later, Representative Milroy returned, looking for Officer Kirchner and apologized for his behavior.[33] It came as no surprise that within minutes, a video of the incident would be on the Internet with the crowd able to watch it on their smartphones.

Meanwhile, as I watched the crowd from my vantage point, Chief Tubbs and my Branch Deputy, Chief Warden Randy Stark,

---

[33] Incident 2011-00000885, Two Rivers Police Department ORI Number WI03600200

continued to talk with various members of the Rotunda Community. Randy would later tell me he had thought back to last Sunday and recalled the arrangement with the unions that had them march out the State Street entrance. However, he knew the State Street entrance was a problem for us tonight and due to the tension in the crowd and the earlier breach, he thought using that same door would be a challenge.

He said that he approached this group with a similar idea, this time with the group leaving through the Martin Luther King Jr. exit, treating this exit march like their version of the famous civil rights march on the Selma Bridge. He hustled around to the various groups of the media and he spread the word about the use of the MLK exit.

I circulated among the various groups in the building. I talked to several reporters and elected officials. Everyone wanted to know what the police were going to do with the group. Of course, we were hoping the group would abide by the court order and leave, but we were preparing for the opposite reaction. Meanwhile, the Secretary of DOA and the collection of folks who usually met as part of the state Policy Group were upstairs in the Attorney General's conference room, trying to decide what their reaction should be to the court order. We were all awaiting a written copy for some formal and official direction.

Secretary Huebsch wanted me to join them but I respectfully declined and said I was not going to leave the Rotunda until this matter was resolved peacefully—or the group was removed. Now the talking needed to come to an end. I didn't want Charles Tubbs to have to stand alone and face this group while presenting its members with an ultimatum. If there was going to be an ultimatum, I felt I should issue it. Even though this phase of the operation was winding down, the debate was sure to continue. If I issued the removal order, then the relationship Charles had built with the group could be preserved.

Kevin Wernet knew he had to get me a copy of the order. As soon as it was available, he made two copies and brought them down to me in the Rotunda. The order wasn't long and I didn't know exactly what it said. I gathered everyone together in the Rotunda, with Charles at my side. I handed a copy of the order to a random member of the crowd and asked him to follow along so that everyone would be assured I was reading exactly what the order stated. I then read the order in its entirety.

> *Based upon the hearings before the Court on March 1, 2011 through March 3, 2011, and the Court having concluded that the current DOA policy regarding access to the State Capitol violates the State Constitution and that unauthorized materials and people remaining in the State Capitol beyond closing each day are there in violation of State law, NOW THEREFORE IT IS ORDERED that the defendant DOA shall do the following:*
>
> 1. *DOA shall immediately enforce its inherent authority pursuant to Admin Chapter 2, including but not limited to, taking such action as allowed under law to remove unauthorized materials and people remaining in the State Capitol after 6:00 p.m. today.*
>
> 2. *By 8:00 a.m. March 8, 2011 DOA shall open the State Capitol to all members of the public and rescind the access policies put in place February 28, 2011 and replace them with the access policies in effect on January 28, 2011.*

This order shall remain in effect until further order of the Court consistent with the Court's Decision of March 3, 2011.

Dated this 3rd day of March, 2011
By the Court:
John C, Albert Circuit Court Judge Branch 3 [34]

I took my copy of the order and gave it to Janie to keep. Afterward, I took questions from the Rotunda Community and some of the people who had joined them. The perimeter at the entrances was holding. It was now time for these folks to go. Many of them simply got up, said their goodbyes, and left. Others continued to talk about the situation, wondering if being arrested was an option they wished to explore. Charles and I made it clear that we didn't have all the answers to their questions about what would happen going forward, but I gave them my word I would do everything in my power to maintain their First Amendment rights to speak out, without violating Capitol building hours or rules.

They did not, in my opinion or the court's judgment, have a First Amendment right to sleep in the Capitol after closing hours when the government was not in session. Charles was asked by a crowd member about the signs that plastered the walls. He said the signs would remain for a few days to give time for the proper removal and the Historical Society to take photos to document the event. More protesters began to leave. Charles and Randy kept the dialog going.

Throughout this time, I was receiving text messages from people sitting with the DOA Secretary. Kevin kept at me that I was

---

[34] Judge John C. Albert Order in Case No. 11CV 990 Dane County Circuit Court Branch 3 AFSCME v Huebsch, March 3, 2011

needed in the AG's conference room to meet with the Secretary and the group he had assembled. The most frantic text came from my aide, Sarah Pfatteicher, who was in the meeting room. Sarah felt the discussion in the room was headed in a bad direction. Finally, with the majority of the protesters gone and the media outnumbering the demonstrators, I left the Rotunda and went upstairs to the AG's office. Charles stayed behind to talk the remaining few protesters out of the Capitol. While on my way, I communicated with AC Brian Bridges to begin the demobilization of the day shift police.

Upstairs in the AG's office, the same group from the night before[35] minus the sheriff, Chief Tubbs, and me, had been meeting for some time to discuss the court order. Kevin Wernet and I joined the group around 8:00 p.m. The written court order had, what they believed to be, an error in it. Judge Albert had verbally said in court that the Capitol could reopen Monday, but the order had a date of March 8, 2011 which was actually a Tuesday. The group was discussing keeping the Capitol closed until Tuesday. From my perspective this was not a good turn of events. It was precisely this discussion and tactic that Sarah was worried about and why she and others had repeatedly texted me to get to the meeting.

Most felt the court had given a transition time that should be used as a cooling-off period. Having the Capitol closed Friday through Monday would allow for a thorough cleaning and removal of all the signs, banners, and posters in a manner that didn't damage the Capitol walls. The extra time would also give DOA the ability to develop a permit process and establish areas within the building that would be designated for protests. They revisited the

---

[35] In attendance were DOA Secretary Mike Huebsch, Chief of Staff Kevin Gilkes, Deputy Chief of the Capitol Police Dan Blackdeer, Wisconsin State Patrol Captain Chuck Teasdale, DOJ Division of Criminal Investigation Ed Wall, DOA's Jodi Jenson, DOA attorney Cari Anne Renlund, WI National Guard General Don Dunbar, DOJ-DCI assistant administrator Dave Matthews, and my aide, Sarah Pfatteicher.

fact that the U.S. Capitol did not allow protests inside the building. The group seemed to be in agreement to keep the building closed as long as the court allowed, and to establish new rules before it was reopened. All of the authority they needed to make this decision was contained in Administrative Code 2 and the court had reaffirmed that.

I began with a question of law. I asked if my assumption was correct that the Wisconsin State Constitution was of greater weight than Administrative Code 2 or this court's order. Establishing that my assumption was correct, I reminded the group that the Senate was in session tomorrow; therefore, the building would need to be open to the public, according to the State Constitution.

Keith Gilkes left to call the Senate leaders to ask them not to meet in session on Friday. He returned moments later with the information the Senate would not be in session tomorrow, and the building could remain closed.

I summarized how the reading of the order had gone and the fact that most people were out of the building. Chief Charles Tubbs was still dealing with a few stragglers. It was important to the crowd that had remained for days in the Rotunda that the signs, banners, and posters be treated with respect so that the State Historical Society and others be allowed to photograph them before they were removed. Charles had committed to that request. The protesters also wanted the items removed in such a way that they could be retrieved by those who wished to claim their signs. This group agreed to an off-site location for retrieval, but was not enthusiastic about delaying the removal.

Then it was time for me to make the case for opening the building the next morning, Day 19, March 4, Friday, which I felt was the right thing to do and I believed was within the spirit of the court's decision. I proposed the Capitol open at 8:00 a.m. without any restriction beyond the capacity management number I had established two weeks ago. Secretary Huebsch responded quickly that, "Eight thousand who whisper are equal to one hundred who drum."[36] We all laughed and I told him I was going to write that quote down and use it in my book.

I continued on with the plan that we would close at 6:00 p.m. Friday and be ready to clear out those folks who would not leave. I noted that Admin 2 and the reaffirmation of the court order gave us the authority to close the building on time each day the legislative houses are not active. Opening at 8 o'clock in the morning would show good faith on our part.

Chief Tubbs and Sheriff Dave Mahoney joined us. Tubbs reported there were still about 15 people who were not leaving. I continued to state that the issue that had gotten us into trouble with the court was not enforcing the closing last Sunday after the scale-down plan had worked and the majority of the people had left. Our answer to not removing people had been to establish queues, which were now ruled as being too restrictive. To not open tomorrow because of the 15 who remained was ceding the power to those 15 non-compliant people.

I would not go along with this inconsistent enforcement. If the 15 needed to be removed, I would have them removed. No one was staying overnight in the Capitol tonight. I wanted Secretary Huebsch to place his faith in the vast majority of the people who had complied last Sunday and again tonight. Voluntary compliance had been tried again and again.

The court had spoken—politics was not a consideration for me. The "spark" everyone was so concerned about law enforcement

---

[36] The capacity management number I had established on Day 5, February 18, 2011, was 9,000. Secretary Huebsch was trying to make a general point, using the 8,000 reference, not the actual number.

creating if we "touched" people had been extinguished by the court and by the majority of citizens who made it clear they wanted the building reopened and access restored. We needed to rebuild some trust we had lost with the queues.

Secretary Huebsch listened carefully. Others around the table were still holding on to their position of the Capitol remaining closed. Eventually, Keith Gilkes stated he was inclined to open the building, making sure prohibited items stayed out of the Capitol, as described in Admin 2 and were a part of our previous scale-down plan. He suggested we keep everything above the ground floor somewhat restricted from protests, although access should be able to flow throughout the building's common areas.

Deputy Chief Blackdeer thought it would be good to rebuild the trust but he was worried about Friday night. The implications would be serious if the group was uncooperative. Knowing the level of staffing I had scheduled to arrive in the morning, I felt we were ready to deal with enforcing the 6:00 p.m. closing Friday night. I would ensure that we managed capacity all day long to the 9,000 visitors at any one time and that we maintain, through Charles, Randy, and negotiation teams, a constant communication with the visitors and protesters.

There were more questions and discussion, but I held firm. The Secretary then stated that on Friday, the Capitol would open at 8:00 a.m. and close at 6:00 p.m. If anyone remained after 6:00 p.m. and there was any kind of trouble, the building would not open on Saturday.

He further instructed that I was to enforce the closing hours by the tactics I thought were appropriate to the circumstances. Finally, I thought, a clear directive. I reaffirmed my understanding that no one be allowed to stay in the building tonight. Charles acknowledged he understood that he was running out of time to get the remaining 15 out by voluntary compliance. He headed out to the Rotunda to talk to the stragglers.

I had to marvel at Charles. He had certainly frustrated me on many occasions over the past three weeks—and I him. But with few exceptions, he and I had held to the principles to which we had pledged when we met with the union marshals back on February 15, 2011 at the Masonic Center. Charles had maintained a constant schedule throughout this period, he had dealt with serious personal issues in his family, and he had little sleep. I wanted the remaining 15 to leave by voluntary compliance, for Charles' sake, and through his efforts, they finally did leave.

We left the Attorney General's conference table and I walked out with Secretary Huebsch, Sheriff Mahoney, and Deputy Chief Blackdeer. We walked to the first floor Rotunda. There was little sound in the building. The posters, banners, and signs all hung in place. The people were gone; only a few working staff remained. We stood at the railing, looking all around and reminding each other that we would never see anything like this again in our lifetimes. This is what non-violent democracy looked like.

Everything had been managed to date without mass arrests or injuries. There had been only slight damage to the grounds and facility. I wished the Secretary a good night. He wished me good luck for Friday. We shook hands. I thanked him for his leadership and the trust he had placed in me. With that, he left the building.

Sheriff Mahoney and I remained at the railing for a while, standing in silence. We watched as representatives from the State Historical Society began their work photographing the signs and banners. We also had our picture taken.

Kevin Wernet, Sarah Pfatteicher, and I returned to the Interior Branch Operations Room in 400 NE to review the morning briefing materials. We worked to adapt the new rules of engagement so that the officers arriving at 6:00 a.m. could be briefed accordingly.

Just after midnight, Sarah, Kevin, and I walked out of the Interior Branch Operations Room, knowing the remainder of the night would be quiet. As we went down the steps, I thought it would be nice to take one last look at all the banners and signs up throughout the Rotunda with no people present. As we got to the first floor and headed to the Rotunda, I sensed something was wrong. Much to my shock, the cleaning crew had already taken down all of the signs and banners from every floor except the ground floor.

"*Oh, my God,*" I thought. Charles had given his word that the main banners and signs would not be removed before the State Historical Society had photographed them. I believed at that moment, it was Charles' intention to have the materials up through Saturday. I could hear a floor cleaner somewhere in the building. I called down to a police officer on the ground floor of the Rotunda and asked him where the lead custodian was. He started a search

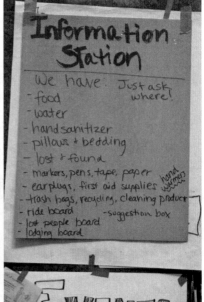

Banners and protesters in the Capitol. (Photos by Mark Golbach)

and I called out for the custodians. The building was so quiet my voice and his echoed off the marble.

Before long, a lead custodian supervisor came to the Rotunda. I asked her where the banner and signs had gone and I insisted she stop taking them down. She agreed.

She took Kevin, Sarah, and me to the Capitol basement and there, stacked neatly on flat dollies, were all the banners and signs. Kevin and I went through the banners and signs, pulling from the pile the major pieces. We took them back upstairs. Sarah had photos available of the Rotunda that had been taken earlier in the day. From the photos, we figured out where the banners had been hung.

In yet another bizarre twist to this event, Kevin and I went to those locations and we re-hung the banners, so that Charles' credibility would remain intact. Part of me couldn't believe I was hanging protest banners in the Capitol at 12:40 a.m. Another part of me knew these banners were a symbol of our word and a necessary step to rebuild the public's trust.

Kevin Wernet and Chief Riseling rehang protest banners at 12:40 a.m. on March 4, 2011.

To preserve Chief Tubbs' word, Kevin and I rehung some protest banners at 12:40 a.m. on March 4, 2011. Just one lone officer remains in the Rotunda. (Photo by Sarah Pfatteicher)

The Interior Branch remained a bustling place. L-R: Brandi Schaffer, Kevin Wernet, Bill Curtis, Chief Riseling, Johnnie Diamante. Standing: Michael Newton. Seated: Brian Bridges, Dale Burke, Brad Altman, Marc Schmidt and Dave Zebro. (Photos by David LaWall)

Conferring with Secretary Huebsch in a quiet hearing room, March 4, 2011. Someone thought I could use a friend and set Snoopy next to me. (Photo by Kevin Wernet)

CHAPTER EIGHT
TRANSITIONS

THE COURT ORDER SEEMED TO REMOVE THE POLITICS FROM THE issue of access to the Capitol for the moment. The fact that the remaining protesters left the Capitol without being arrested or carried out preserved the overall positive feeling between the protesters and the police. Circumstances were now shifting.

While the 14 Democratic Senators were still out of state, the Assembly had passed the Budget Repair Bill. The Interior Branch would close, only to reopen in a swirl of activity. Political maneuvering was far from over between the three branches of government and the people they were there to serve.

DAY 19: FRIDAY, MARCH 4, 2011

MY HOROSCOPE OF THE DAY WAS INTRIGUING. "THERE'S SOMETHING IN THE air pushing you toward change and renewal. Is it time to change your wardrobe? If so, today is the day."

I had a laugh as I once again put on my navy blue uniform. It was 6:00 a.m. and time to head to the Capitol. This time, entering the Capitol felt different; it was as if I were entering a cathedral. Gone were the people asleep in the Rotunda and hallways. Gone were the sleeping bags and tables of food. Gone was the earthy human smell. The custodians had made tremendous progress. The police officers whispered when they spoke. You could feel the silence.

My emotions began to surface. Then I looked up and saw the banners hanging right where Kevin and I had left them— unbelievable. It was critical for the Capitol to reopen at its 8:00 a.m. scheduled time. We could not be a minute late.

The officers were briefed offsite with the new instructions we had crafted at midnight. As a result of the court decision, the rules of engagement had changed. I thought it would be appropriate for me to address the specifics of the ruling with each busload of officers as they arrived. We hustled them into the basement room where the public tours normally gather, so I could address forty at a time.

As the officers came in, we asked for a show of hands of those who had worked the event before and almost all hands shot up. We distributed Administrative Code 2 to the supervisors and quickly reviewed it verbally for the officers. Capacity management would still be in effect and we would restrict items allowed in the building. Although we had enough police for just about any eventuality, we were concerned about how tense things might get with the new "protest instructions" decided upon by the Secretary of DOA:

- A Protest Area has been established on the Ground Floor Rotunda.
- The area is signed as such.
- All protesters are to be directed to this area.
- Protest activity at any other location is prohibited and persons doing so must be directed to the Rotunda.
- Officers will educate people on the protest location or (people must) cease the activity.
- Officers will escort people from the area and outside the building if necessary.

- If those escorted from the building return and exhibit disruptive behavior, they should be arrested.

When the doors opened at 8:00 that morning, those entering would have no idea there were new rules. I wanted to ensure the officers knew that "Job One" was education and facilitation. Today, like the past 18 days, we would start with voluntary compliance. However, we would be prepared to increase our response as enforcement requirements dictated. High tolerance was still needed but noncompliance by the public would need to be addressed.

If the numbers of people not complying with the new rules was significant and dialog wasn't working to move them along, we would begin to peel people from the railings and reposition police to control the spaces. Education, followed by one verbal warning, was the word of the day. If the warning wasn't heeded, then ejection would occur. Every group of officers cheered the new instructions, as if to say, "Finally!"

Chief Warden Randy Stark and Chief Riseling on March 4, 2011, in the basement of the Capitol brief officers on the new rules of engagement following the court's ruling. (Photo by Kevin Wernet)

The doors opened at 8:00 a.m. Few people entered and those who did, came into the building and were much quieter and subdued then on previous days. There now seemed to be an atmosphere of reverence. They looked at the signs and whispered.

We moved our negotiating teams to the first floor so that those teams could address protesters with the new rules. If people attempted to protest in undesignated areas and needed to be moved along, we would have our best folks on the assignment. All visitors would be screened for weapons as they entered.

With the Assembly and Senate not in session today, the next concern was making sure everyone left at 6:00 p.m. when the building closed. No matter the number of people, we would need to ensure they were out of the building tonight. I had several brief conversations with DOA Secretary Huebsch throughout the day and we both knew closing the Capitol could be a major task. It was still my belief that people would respect the building hours now that they knew the court had ruled.

As the day went along, few problems arose. We had an arrest at the weapons screening post when a woman refused to pass through the metal detector and was escorted out two times. On her third try, she attempted to run by the checkpoint and was arrested. After her arrest, she returned, went through the metal detector, and was admitted. Even though the Family Center space on the first floor was turned back into a regular hallway, the woman who had operated the Family Center still wanted Chief Tubbs to stop by at 4:00 for their traditional "story time."

At the Policy Group meeting, Secretary Huebsch joined us for the first time. If things went well at closing, it was agreed that the law enforcement numbers would drop to the 80-officer level as of Monday. I thought that was too soon so I suggested not reducing the number of officers significantly until the "Fabulous 14," the Democratic senators, returned to the Capitol. I believed levels should stay at about 120 officers. I was overruled.

General Dunbar told us he was going to staff an after-action review by Wisconsin Emergency Management when things settled down. He also was going to have Military Affairs complete an assessment of the Capitol for a "new normal" going forward. Some might have thought it odd that the military would make such an assessment. The military knows security from many angles. I thought it was a good idea and I offered the two men a place to work in the Interior Branch Operations Room. Their adaptation to a civilian setting might prove challenging but as far as assessment, there are few government institutions better.

We turned our attention to the two permits for Saturday, March 5, with an estimated crowd of 30,000 for the AFL/CIO and another 30,000 for Wisconsin Wave. Once again, I asked in the meeting about the plan to deal with what would happen when the Democratic senators returned. Again, there was no response.

Randy and I had thought about and had been quietly planning for the senators' return, voluntarily or involuntarily, for more than ten days now. We had been present when the sergeant-at-arms requested trooper assistance to go to the senators' residences. We knew we needed to be ready to deal with the political and public circus that a forced return could have caused.

We were now guessing the senators might return tomorrow because the Capitol was no longer occupied. Randy started the discussion with the scenario of an "arrest" by the sergeant-at-arms, compelling the return of a senator. Randy sketched out scenarios that included the senators being at their homes when the arrests occurred, and contingencies in case the senator(s) surrendered in front of television cameras at a media outlet. I sensed Keith Gilkes and DOA Secretary Huebsch were pleased we had thought this through.

After the meeting, I focused on the Capitol closing time and what needed to be done between now and then to be successful. As of 4:00 p.m. we would carefully watch the volume of people entering the building. The Interior Branch distributed leaflets to folks, reminding them of the 6:00 p.m. closing. We re-crafted the closing announcements and changed the times those announcements would be used via the public address system.

At 5:30 p.m. as planned, I ordered the closing announcement broadcast throughout the building by the Capitol Police Department. I ordered another reminder announcement at 5:45 p.m. At 6:00 p.m., I ordered the final closing announcement and we found a small group of folks who were not leaving. We had anticipated this would occur as we were sure some people would test the new procedures. Chief Charles Tubbs was on the scene and continued talking to those who had not left. As he had done day in and day out, Charles patiently talked and discussed matters with the group. At 6:15 p.m., another announcement was broadcast and included wording about noncompliance.

I would give Charles about 15 more minutes before I ordered removal. Sure enough, Charles was once again successful and the group walked out. The Capitol was closed and no arrests were necessary. The total entering the Capitol for the day had been approximately 4,653. I texted the news to DOA Secretary Huebsch and he congratulated us on our success.

Last night in the AG's conference room, I had argued we needed to open today and we would get the building closed at 6:00 p.m. The only one who stood with me initially in my position last night was Charles. There were those who felt we were risking too much and that we should just keep the building closed today. Eventually, we convinced the Secretary. We were all glad the protesters had left on their own accord within a reasonable amount of time, and began demobilizing the day-shift police early.

DAY 20: SATURDAY, MARCH 5, 2011

THE REMAINING BANNERS HAD BEEN REMOVED OVERNIGHT WHEN I MET with all of the day-shift police officers as they entered the Capitol basement for the morning briefing. Many of them were returning to Capitol duty, but had not worked since the change in the rules of engagement. Education and facilitation were the starting points again. Enforcement, if needed, was the correct course of action.

The Capitol opened right on time at 8:00 a.m. Since we anticipated the large crowds outside, capacity management would be needed today.

The news of the day was the shift of focus from rallies and occupying the Capitol to forming committees to hold recall elections for six Republican senators. A conservative-backed group also began to lay the groundwork for holding recall elections for six of the fourteen Democratic senators.

As the rally began, some big names were on hand: film maker Michael Moore, Reverend Jesse Jackson, and Wisconsin Congressional Representative Tammy Baldwin (Democrat). There were no big issues (NBI) in the Branch and approximately 7,380 people entered the building. Now that the signs and banners were gone from the walls, there was less to see.

Outside activities went well and the day passed quickly as we prepared for the transition of command. The Capitol closed at its normal weekend hour of 4:00 p.m. without incident. We had re-established the operating hours of the Capitol. I again sent a text message to DOA Secretary Huebsch with the news. He again congratulated us.

Day 21: Sunday, March 6, 2011

Things were shifting as the Capitol was almost back to normal operations. Today would be the last day of operations for the Interior Branch. The command was being reduced and the Command Post (CP) would officially move to this room, 400 NE.

Having a Command Post inside a venue is generally not a wise site selection, so the CP would be moved to the Department of Natural Resources building two blocks from the Capitol when space there was ready later in the week.

By Monday, the University Police would head back to the University. To aid in the transition, we prepared two complete sets of all the plans we had created, whether they had been used or were just there for contingencies. We left two matching thumb drives with all our documents and forms. There was no sense in having the commanders start from scratch.

I gave CPD Deputy Chief Blackdeer a tour of the Operations Room he would inherit and walked him through the plans, the set-up, and the daily routine of meetings and briefings. Most of the DNR, WSP, and CPD staff were staying. I had gotten to know these folks well over the past three weeks, including their strengths and capabilities. Dan would have a solid team to support him with a can-do attitude and a passion for getting things done.

Thousands of demonstrators gathered outside the Capitol again on Sunday to protest the Governor's move to strip state employees of collective bargaining rights. Meanwhile, a pro-Governor Walker rally organized by the Americans for Prosperity was held at Madison's Alliant Energy Center, 2.5 miles from the Capitol. About 100 supporters of the Governor attended, while the counter-rally nearby drew about 1,000 people. Only 4,600 people visited the Capitol interior all day.

At 4:00 p.m., the Capitol closed again without incident. As the day drew to a close, Randy and I talked about the fact that he was staying in his Capitol assignment and I was going back to the UW. We had really bonded over the past three weeks.

The commanders and staff had gotten together and made a small picture album for me of various photos taken over the past three weeks. It meant the world to me that they had each signed the book. In addition, while staff had ordered items, they had also purchased an "EASY" button. They presented me with a gift box with one inside. When pressed, it says "That was easy." I teased them as to why the button hadn't been ordered weeks ago.

We posed for some pictures. Folks were having a good time today, as our end date was near. The group then presented Randy with a gift. He unwrapped a children's book and we all laughed, telling him he would be ready for "story time." Randy, not missing a beat, opened the book and began to read aloud.

Randy decided it was time to play a joke on Deputy Chief Blackdeer over at the Command Post. Randy called over to the CP, demanding to speak to the man in charge, and in an accent any southerner would be proud of, he tore into Dan. Claiming to be an angry father, he wove a story that his son from Oklahoma had come to the Capitol to support the Governor. Because the place was so filthy, his son had gotten very ill with an infection and had to seek medical attention. He was so mad, he was driving up to Madison from Oklahoma to get his son and to "whoop somebody's ass" when he got here. Randy was carrying on so well for so long we were all muffling our laughter, trying not to make any background noise. Finally Randy, having fully ranted, slammed down the phone. He proclaimed he had Dan going at first, but he thought Dan caught on at the end.

As we shared a few memories of the last 21 days, I shook each commander and staff member's hand and gave each a "Chief"'s

Challenge Coin." The coin is a special medallion I had made a few years back to recognize strong leadership. The coins are metal, covered with enamel. On the front is the logo of the University Police, with our four values of Respect, Integrity, Compassion, and Honor. There is a quote by Dr. Martin Luther King Jr., "Injustice anywhere is a threat to justice everywhere." On the back of the coin is an eagle flying over top of an American flag, with the phrases: "The Courage to Act, Leadership, and Service to Others."

At various times over the past few weeks, I had done pseudo "field promotions" for most of the commanders in the Branch. There was CPD Lieutenant Marc Schmidt, who I "promoted" to Captain. I had also promoted WSP Sergeant Craig Lindgren to Sergeant/Lieutenant and WSP Sergeant Les Mlsna to Lieutenant-Lieutenant.

However, I had not promoted WSP Lieutenant Brad Altman. Folks told me over the weeks that Brad had brought this up several times. So I cleared my throat and reminded everyone that the Superintendent of the State Patrol wears one star insignia to denote his rank. One star in the army is a Brigadier General. Brad was just a Lieutenant. So I "field promoted" Brad to Lieutenant General, which has three stars and outranks a Brigadier General. I gave Brad the collar brass with three stars. He smiled ear to ear.

At 7:00 that night, I picked up Snoopy, turned over command to the night shift, decommissioned the Interior Branch, and with a few hugs, and some more handshakes, I headed home.

DAY 22: MONDAY, MARCH 7, 2011
DAY 23: TUESDAY, MARCH 8, 2011

I RETURNED TO ROOM 400 NE FOR ABOUT AN HOUR AND A HALF ON Monday afternoon to complete some paperwork and file my last reports. It was strange to be back in the room. It had already taken on a very different feel. I finished my work as quickly as I could and left. Unlike the quiet of 400 N.E., politics were in full swing. The Governor rejected offers to meet with the Democratic senators who were still out of state.

The Democratic Party of Wisconsin filed an ethics complaint against Governor Walker for statements he made referencing a possible trip out of state at the invitation of the "Koch" brothers.

Meanwhile, I was "sleeping in" these days, arriving at my office at 8:00 a.m. Captain Steve Rogers had done an outstanding job of running the show in my absence. Yet my work had really piled up while I was away. The police officers who worked in shift mode just fell back into routine coverage.

Most of the University Police staff who worked at the Capitol were supervisors and did not have coverage or shift jobs. They, too, had jobs in which their work piled up and waited for them to return. Backlogged tasks included security surveys, building occupation plans, continuity of operation plans, inspections, training, case follow-up, investigations, inventories, audits, crime prevention surveys, crime analysis, and emergency management planning. As an organization, we were three weeks behind in what was a busy spring semester and we were already tired. For some things that were pressing, we used overtime to bolster our response and cut through the backlog. Other items we had to re-prioritize, delay, or not do at all.

I checked in with Deputy Chief Dan Blackdeer every day to see how things were going and if he needed anything. He took a picture each day of my "Time plus X days to my Freedom date" and sent it to me. It was nice they were keeping it up on my behalf. Dan was continuing to use the one-way blog to communicate with the public. We discussed such things as where an operational plan might be located in the binder and whether plans should be readjusted.

Some "normalcy" seemed to be returning to the building. The Capitol was closing on time and without much fuss. Capacity management hadn't been a factor as the crowds had thinned considerably. The number of law enforcement needed was being reduced each day. He asked if we could send some computers back to 400 NE for them to use. I had the equipment delivered right away.

News outlets reported that Senate Majority Leader Steve Fitzgerald (Republican) believed the continued delay by the Democrats to return to the state was linked to President Obama and the recall effort. Meanwhile, a coalition of progressive groups claimed to have raised a half million dollars to aid in the recall effort of Republican senators. Conservative groups were working on recalling Democratic senators as well. The conservative groups had not made their fundraising efforts public to date.

DAY 24: WEDNESDAY, MARCH 9, 2011

WHEN I CHECKED WITH DAN A LITTLE BEFORE NOON, HE SAID THAT everything was quiet and he thought maybe they had about 400 or so visitors in total for the day. When I checked in around 3:00 p.m., he thought maybe a total of 600 had come through. There were no problems to speak of and he was sounding quite relaxed. We shared a few laughs. I was just two days now from my freedom date.

When 4:00 p.m. arrived at University Police, our day shift and evening shift went into their routine of debriefing and briefing. The campus had been relatively quiet and those whose scheduled day ended at 4:30 p.m. didn't waste a single minute lingering around headquarters after the shift had ended.

I was still trying to dig out of my backlog when my cell phone rang at 5:30. It was Dan Blackdeer. I knew instantly by the sound of his voice something was seriously wrong. He asked me to grab all the police I had on hand and head to the Capitol right away. He said the Capitol perimeter was being overrun. Because the building was still open, I assumed he was referring to the metal screening operation, but I wasn't sure.

I wouldn't learn until much later in the evening that the Republicans had quickly convened a session to strip the Budget Repair Bill of its fiscal components, thus allowing the modified Bill to go before the Senate and be voted upon without needing the 14 Democratic senators to return from Illinois.

I went into my dispatch center to have every available unit return to headquarters and retrieve their hard gear so we could go to the Capitol. I headed up the stairs to retrieve my gear from our equipment room and ran into some officers who were headed home for the day and no longer in uniform. I yelled for them to turn around and change, grab their hard gear, and meet by the back door.

Only six of us were available, as other units were handling calls on campus. We met within ten minutes, piled into a vehicle, and sped to the Capitol. En route, I called Dan to give him our numbers and receive our assignment. This is when Dan explained he had begun demobilization hours earlier because the last two days the Capitol had closed without incident. So the numbers of officers on duty were dramatically lower than what he needed to stop or even slow the volume of people entering the Capitol. In addition, Dan said the crowd was aggressive and angry. I asked where he wanted us to head. The King Street entrance was in the worst shape, so he told us to head there.

When we arrived and got inside the King Street entrance, only two troopers were there. The crowd was streaming in through the three sets of double doors. We managed to cut off one set of doors and secured the big outer wooden doors.

University Police Lieutenant Pete Ystenes started to shout instructions to the crowd. He told them they could all come in; we just needed them to slow down, take a deep breath, and go through a quick metal screening. He repeated his message that everyone would eventually get in. The crowd stopped shoving and formed a line for a more orderly access. I organized the troopers and asked them to do a very quick search of backpacks.

"Remember," I told them, "we don't care about anything besides weapons and explosives."

With things now running more smoothly, I ran up five flights to the former Interior Branch Operation room, now serving as the Command Post 400 N.E. Winded, I entered the room and reported in. What was next? Where did they want me to go?

Deputy Chief Blackdeer looked stunned. He was standing and had the "thousand-yard stare." I asked him again what was going on and where did he want me to head next. He then told me he had requested the assistance of the Madison Police because the officers in the building had been overrun and the crowd had breached the building's perimeter. Dan informed me that MPD had declined to assist. No more law enforcement was coming to help us.

Of all the plans and contingencies we had developed, being overrun with fewer than fifty cops available, doors and windows being actively breached by a very angry crowd, was a twist.

I asked if he wanted my advice. He did. I told him to have all the police not actively screening people fall back and regroup on the third floor. I would head to another entrance to see how the officers were doing there. Then, I would go to the third floor and direct the police who had assembled there.

Dan agreed with that plan. I ran down the five flights of steps to the ground floor and found a group of DNR wardens at another entrance screening the incoming crowd. They, too, had managed to limit the entrance to just one set of doors and were actively screening and also communicating with the crowd.

People were loud and angry but they were complying with the metal screening. The wardens were stressed but were doing a terrific job interacting with the crowd.

I was standing about 20 feet back from the metal detectors, when I noticed a man approaching the screening area. Something about him didn't look right. He was dressed appropriately for the weather, was unshaven, and looked a bit disheveled. He locked on to my eyes, as mine locked onto his. He stared at me and did not break his line of sight. He cleared the metal detectors and started running right at me. Because he had just finished screening, I knew it was unlikely that he had a gun, but he was quickly coming right for me. As he got close, I raised my arms to shoulder height and stepped aside as he fell right into my arms. I immediately lowered him to the ground and rolled him onto his back as he began to seize.

The look in his eyes was now complete fear and panic. I radioed for a paramedic. He was grabbing at his pocket. I opened his jacket, reached into his pocket, and found his nitroglycerin pills. I opened the container and placed one in his mouth. His eyes looked relieved and grateful. A paramedic arrived and I explained what happened; he took over from there.

I walked down another hallway and people were coming out of representatives' offices in groups of 15 or more. I became suspicious so I entered the office suite and found staff sitting at their desks while people were climbing in the open windows. Once I stopped the protesters who hadn't quite made it in, I closed and locked the windows. Then I went back to where the staff members were stationed and told them with great clarity not to reopen those windows. They stared at me unresponsively.

With that short intermission, it was back up the stairs to the Senate. I entered the second-floor offices directly off the Senate floor and there in the interior hallway were the Republican senators. Unlike past days, where we had secured the staircases so we could move the senators safely and securely, the hallways and staircases had not been secured and were now filled with very agitated crowds. Their rage was targeted at the senators for removing the fiscal components of the Bill to circumvent the need for a larger quorum.

I huddled up with the troopers who were available, and told them how I wanted them to form a wedge line across the top of the staircase landing. Then two other troopers were placed in front of the group of senators, with Chief Tubbs and two other troopers alongside the group. I would be with the last of the senatorial group and behind me would be two additional troopers.

I greeted the senators cordially. Most of them knew my face and recognized me from the previous weeks of activity. They looked genuinely scared. Some were emotional and others very somber. I made sure they all knew the plan and understood their role. We would head out as a unit, down the steps, through the tunnel, and then send off the senators via secured transportation. I explained that the crowd was directly next to us and there was little to no stand-off area.

I started to queue everyone up when Senate Sergeant-at-Arms Ted Blazel turned to me and asked, "Where did you come from? I'm glad to see you here." The door was opened and the noise and jeering of the crowd rang out. This was not the cooperative, peaceful crowd we had seen for the three previous weeks. The troopers held their ground even as the crowd surged and attempted to come over the railings toward the senators.

The plan worked and we hustled the senators out of the building. For weeks afterward, I would receive criticism from some in the public that I protected those senators that night. It was criticism that was easy to live with. Not to protect democratically elected officials from legislating and doing what they believed to be right would have been wrong on my part. Would anyone really think it appropriate for me to step back and let the crowd come into closer contact with the senators?

After the escort of the senators was completed, I walked back to the second floor with Senate Sergeant-at-Arms Ted Blazel.

The "Fabulous 14" were, in some ways, heroes to the crowd and the Republicans had cut out the heroes! As Ted and I parted ways, I ran into Madison Mayor Dave Cieslewicz (Democrat) on a staircase. He asked me what was going to happen to the crowd now. It was well past closing hours and the Senate had finished its business. Technically, the Capitol should now be closed and cleared. I assumed people would stay for quite a while to chant, yell, and talk. The crowding outside the Senate Chambers and in that whole wing of the building was problematic. They had really wedged themselves in there. As angry as they were, there was no getting them out of there right now.

The majority of the police had retreated as ordered to the third floor to await further instructions. I went back to the Command Post in 400 NE. Dan thought he had 50 to 56 police on hand. I probed for what he was thinking and hoped he wasn't going to try to force people out. I explained to him that there was no longer a leader for the protesters to talk with or volunteer marshals to assist. Instead of a friendly, peaceful crowd, this group was angry and frustrated.

The latest political maneuver had ignited a firestorm. Dan didn't have enough police in place, besides which, there was no point in taking on a very angry crowd at this time. All of the elected officials he was responsible for protecting were, for the most part, out of the facility. He thought for a few minutes and said he didn't believe forcing people out would work.

I went to a vantage point to watch the crowd of approximately 10,000 without trying to mix with them. I made phone calls and though hard to hear, I set in motion the return to the Capitol of about 20 University Police officers for the morning. After watching the chanting crowd for a while, I returned to 400 NE.

When I entered the room Dan waved me over. I told Dan I had ordered up our return and could re-establish the Interior Branch in the morning at 6:00 a.m., bringing back our equipment and support staff. He quickly concurred. I suggested I go down to the Capitol Police headquarters and use the public address system to make some announcements to see if people would leave the building tonight on their own. He agreed.

When I reached the basement and headed into the Capitol Police dispatch center, there awaiting assistance was Representative Mark Pocan. He wanted a handful of people with him to have their photos taken for staff identification. Because of the new rule that only staffers and representatives could sleep in their offices, Mark was going to make a lot of people his staff so they could stay in the building overnight. He told me he was going to keep bringing more and more people down for staff identification cards. This was more game-playing for which I didn't have time or patience. I told him he would have to work it out with Chief Tubbs and left it at that.

I worked out a series of scripts for the dispatcher and she and I tried several times to make the announcements, but the crowd noise was so loud no one in the Rotunda could hear the announcements. Our repeated efforts failed to get anyone's attention. Our efforts a couple of hours later met with the same unsuccessful results.

The night went on from there. All doors and windows were eventually secured. The crowd lingered and was not leaving anytime soon. The evening shift was not large enough to take any enforcement action and those who had worked all day were very tired, now going on sixteen straight hours. I explained to the wardens and troopers that unless the behavior of the crowd was deliberately damaging to the contents of the building or was physically assaultive, they should not attempt arrests overnight. They nodded their agreement. It was time I went home. Tomorrow would be a busy day.

DAY 25: THURSDAY, MARCH 10, 2011

JUST LIKE BILL MURRAY'S CHARACTER IN THE MOVIE *GROUNDHOG DAY*, I returned to the Capitol again, this time without Snoopy. Just as on February 17, Job One was to establish the Interior Branch—in this case, re-establish. Our equipment was back and the room was arranged as if we had never left. We put all the commanders we had used before back into their places, and the chaos was quickly converted to order. We re-established the rhythm we had for our schedule of briefings and meetings. We reviewed the Interior Branch mission statement we had written weeks ago. A reminder and review of the rules of engagement was underway as high tolerance was expected, but enforcement action would occur if voluntary compliance did not work after one warning.

Over the preceding three weeks, we had never lost control of the Senate Chamber or Parlor, nor the Assembly Chamber or Anteroom. Overnight, the security of the Assembly Anteroom had been breached and protesters had taken over the space. They did this hoping to slow down the scheduled Assembly vote.

The priority would be to reopen the Assembly so that government could function. I went to the Risser Justice Building across the street to meet with the DOA Secretary Mike Huebsch and a smaller Policy Group. Chief Tubbs was present. The current situation was thoroughly discussed. We talked over various options—from moving the Assembly to another location to removing the protesters by force. Tactically, we had to control the perimeter of the building, especially the office windows. It was clear from last night that the Democrats were doing everything they could to thwart our efforts to secure the building. Secretary Huebsch outlined three objectives to meet before opening the building:

1. Clear the Assembly Anteroom
2. Secure the West Wing
3. Secure the perimeter

I returned to the Branch with Captain Teasdale, the Command Post Operations Chief, in tow. I asked him if he was going to head to the CP and he said he would rather stay in the Branch. Moments later, the Superintendent of the State Patrol, Steve Fitzgerald, and his aide, Major Darren Price, entered the room. *Wonderful,* I thought, *we're going to have an audience.*

The Interior Branch started to develop a plan for the removal of the crowd from the Assembly Anteroom; so far, the Assembly Chamber remained secured. We laid out the floor plans and the Capitol Police representative in the room showed us the ins and outs of the space. The officer told us about the antique furniture pieces that the protesters were placing in front of the doors. Of course, none of us wanted those antiques damaged. We then revived a plan we had used several times in the last three weeks to secure the West Wing. I ordered both plans to be implemented.

The night-shift police had been talking to the protesters about coming out of the Anteroom. Those discussions broke down at about 3:00 a.m. Since that time, little had been communicated until this morning.

Wisconsin State Patrol (WSP) Lieutenant Brad Altman, Division Commander for the second floor, left 400 NE to supervise the removal personally. The message I wanted delivered to the group inside the Anteroom was that they could remain in the Capitol, but until they left the Anteroom, the Capitol would stay closed to all others. Brad would make sure my message was delivered.

People were queuing up outside the building wanting to get in. "Déjà vu—all over again," Yogi Berra. The Anteroom occupiers needed to think about the fact that they were holding up public access to the Capitol, while we moved forward to secure the West Wing. The response came that the protesters in the Anteroom weren't going to budge. Protesters in the hallways around the Senate were somewhat cooperative, but others stayed put. We needed to move them in order to get the wing secured. The troopers began the operation in earnest.

Secretary Huebsch wanted a status update and we met in an office within the Attorney General's suite on the first floor of the Capitol. A much smaller group was there. In fact, I was the only law enforcement person present who was directly involved with the day's activities. Chief Tubbs was not present. Secretary Huebsch was under tremendous pressure to get the building opened. I received an update from my staff about the West Wing and I told the Secretary the wing was secured and removal from the Anteroom was about to begin. He was tense and told me he understood, but also wanted me to be clear that the building must be opened and opened soon. I assured him I understood completely.

Meanwhile, Brad wanted to be ready to fully carry out my order. While I was meeting with the Secretary, he called WSP Captain Teasdale and requested that a squad of troopers be placed into hard crowd control gear. Teasdale approved of this. I was never asked or told about the troopers being placed into gear until a year after the fact. Fortunately, those dressed in hard gear were never needed.

I returned to the Interior Branch and ordered the removal from the Anteroom to the center Rotunda to begin after a formal warning was given. Once the formal warning to leave or be re-moved was given, Brad gave the protesters some time to consider their options. They didn't move.

The troopers began to implement the plan, picking up one protester at a time and carrying each to the Rotunda. When the troopers reached the Rotunda, they set the protester down and returned for another. Things were going well because most protesters simply went limp.

We were halfway through the removal process when Chief Tubbs arrived at the Assembly Anteroom and told the troopers to stop. He was going to talk the remaining people out of the Anteroom. When informed by WSP Lieutenant Brad Altman that Charles had overridden my directive, I was incredulous.

Secretary Huebsch had given me three objectives in two different meetings that morning. One was complete; I was halfway through the second and still trying to get resources to carry out the third. I called the DOA Secretary and asked if he had changed the objectives. He had not changed anything and had not ordered Chief Tubbs to re-engage. I turned to Captain Teasdale who, on paper, was technically my boss. He was at a loss. The Major and the Superintendent just shook their heads. I ordered Lieutenant Altman to restart the removal process as quickly as possible.

I called the Command Post to see if they had, by chance, sent Chief Tubbs in, and if we were going to be aided by more officers to control the exterior of the building. The answer to both questions was no. So I ordered that we redeploy the officers we had in the building to the entrance doors, established a team of officers to patrol outside on the balustrade to prevent people from climbing in the windows. The perimeter was as secure as it could be given the limitation in resources.

As that exterior plan was going into place, word arrived that the Anteroom was clear and, along with the Assembly Chamber, was now secure. Brad then redeployed those troopers who had been in the hard gear to change uniforms and head outside to the balustrade to assist on the perimeter. With our objectives met, we opened the outside doors to the public.

Fifteen minutes after the doors were ordered open to people who were flowing into the building after being screened, Chief Tubbs ordered the doors closed. No one knew why. The division commander for the perimeter came directly to me in room 400 NE to tell me his lieutenant staffing the door was receiving orders directly from Chief Tubbs to stop all access. I overrode the order and told the lieutenant to open the doors and keep them open. I sent the division commander to the scene to deal with Chief Tubbs and the lieutenant.

Moments later, CPD Lieutenant Marc Schmidt turned to me and said Chief Tubbs was on the phone and wanted all doors secured. Chief Tubbs wanted to speak to me. I took the phone. I was seething. Charles thought the doors should remain closed for reasons that were unclear to me. I told Charles that DOA Secretary Huebsch had given me three objectives to meet, after which I was to immediately open the Capitol.

Charles had not been at the second meeting earlier when the Secretary directly gave me my orders, nor had he heard the sense of urgency the Secretary possessed. I told Charles he was to get out of the way and hung up the phone. He called back. He told me I shouldn't hang up on him. I told him he needed to stay out of the tactical command of this operation. This conversation ended almost as abruptly as the last.

Within minutes, Secretary Huebsch and Chief Tubbs entered the Interior Branch Operations Room. I firmly reminded Secretary Huebsch that he had given me three objectives to meet before opening the building. We had met those objectives. I reminded him he wanted the building open as soon as possible and I did just that. Twice, Chief Tubbs had interfered with that mandate. I did, indeed, hang up the phone on Chief Tubbs and I wasn't about to apologize. Chief Tubbs had missed the second policy meeting that morning where the Secretary had expressed urgency. It wasn't my job to worry about who was and wasn't attending meetings.

Secretary Huebsch said he thought we would see more police deployed before the building reopened, but according to the Command Post, no more police were available for deployment. Whatever police we had on hand was what we had to work with. With discussion aired, the tension fell, we all shook hands. They left the room and it was time to move on. The Assembly would be voting soon and that was sure to be another crowd flashpoint.

My division commanders seemed confused and out of sorts. At 11:00 a.m., we were scheduled for a check-in, which couldn't come soon enough. Each division had "Big Issues." Commanders couldn't account for their people, the index card system we had used for post assignments had been discontinued by DC Blackdeer, and people were confused as to their assignments and post expectations. The objectives we had been given had been twice overruled by Chief Tubbs. He had given permission to the protesters to store their "stuff," as it was described, in the circular "rooms" on the 1st floor East and West. DOA had rescinded that permission and DOA wanted the "stuff" removed. I directed the division commander from DNR in charge of that area to remove the materials.

We worked to establish new objectives, to plan for the Assembly vote, and the end of the day closing. We would be enforcing closing hours. We identified what could possibly go wrong in the next three hours and what our answer would be to those scenarios.

The team of division commanders who had worked so well together for three weeks was once again gelling. I put Captain Teasdale to work planning the afternoon deployment of troopers. He became a *de facto* division commander. I had to chuckle at this turn of events, given our prior argumentative relations. Then I asked him to make the plan to shore up the exterior with another deployment of incoming troopers at 5:30 p.m. He seemed to enjoy his time in the Branch.

By the time 2:00 p.m. rolled around, we did another check-in. This time, as we went around the table, I heard over and over from the division commanders, "NBI" (no big issues). Each one made me smile. We were on top of things now. We were set again for the possibility the protesters would not leave at 6:00 p.m. We were ready to remove them if it came to that. I hoped it would not, but Secretary Huebsch and the court had been clear.

The Capitol building hours of operation should be respected and staying after closure was not considered a protected First Amendment right. I placed a call to the DOA Secretary because I was concerned that tactical plans had been countermanded twice today. In addition, I let the Secretary know that Chief Tubb's permission for storage of protesters "stuff" had been rescinded. I wanted to know from the Secretary exactly what he expected at the 6:00 p.m. closing. He stated he wanted the building closed and cleared if necessary, no later than 7:00 p.m. unless there was some major overriding safety issue that did not allow for it. I thought what he was asking for was within our ability to deliver.

I assigned University Police Captain Johnnie Diamante and Capitol Police Lieutenant Marc Schmidt to plan for Governor Walker's signing of the Bill, scheduled for 10:00 a.m. tomorrow in his office in the Capitol. We would need some of the same reinforcements as we had used before at "The Rock." We had established a plan to defend the Governor's office before, so at least we were not starting from scratch.

In a bit of a role reversal, Captain Teasdale briefed me on his plan and I approved it. I wanted him to implement it, beginning at 3:00 p.m. He was on top of it. It turned out Captain Teasdale was a good planner and I was glad I had gotten to work with him for the day.

The Assembly voted and passed the Bill as expected. The Representatives were escorted from the building. Governor Walker announced he would sign the Bill into law the next day.

As the end of the day approached, we had very good perimeter control. Placing the UW Police, troopers, and wardens outside on the balustrade controlled the windows, and the doors were secured on time at 6:00p.m. We went with the multiple closing announcements as we had earlier in the week. It all worked very well. Chief Tubbs once again was on hand to talk any closing issues over with anyone who was reluctant. The Capitol closed without trouble.

I spoke to Secretary Huebsch and he was heartened to hear the Capitol closed without any problems. I then explained that we had built the Interior Branch on February 17 and it was dismantled after we left. While we had rebuilt it for today, I would not continue to lead an operation if there was interference with carrying out his orders, such as I had experienced today. I told him respectfully that I would not be returning tomorrow. He was very complimentary and understanding.

DAY 26: FRIDAY, MARCH 11, 2011

THE INTERIOR BRANCH WAS AGAIN DEACTIVATED AND THE COMMAND POST moved once more. I returned to the University and this time we left behind the computers and other equipment for the CPD to use until they could properly transition. Without any protester interference, the Governor signed the Bill into law greatly restricting collective bargaining by the unions that represented many public employees. The Governor's signing of the Bill ended the legislative action on the matter; however, the debate was far from over. The battle lines between Democrats and Republicans were clearly drawn and both sides were working hard to shore up reinforcements.

The hastily passed Bill led Representative Peter Barca to file a complaint, arguing the Bill's passage had violated the Open Meetings Law because insufficient notice was provided prior to the vote. On March 11, Dane County Executive Kathleen Falk (Democrat) also filed a complaint indicating that the signed Bill still contained many fiscal items, and therefore required a larger quorum for passage.

It was my Freedom Day. March 11, 2011 marked the 20th anniversary of my employment as the University of Wisconsin Police Chief. I was 50 years old and eligible for retirement. The freedom date sign was changed in room 400 NE to say T (ime) + 0. When I called to check in with Dan, we shared a well-deserved laugh and he congratulated me on "making it." Of course, I had no plan to actually retire.

In fact, my department was going to become nationally accredited on March 26 by CALEA, the Commission on Accreditation for Law Enforcement Agencies. When the accreditation was bestowed, the University of Wisconsin Police Department would be the third nationally accredited law enforcement agency in the State of Wisconsin, joining the City of Beloit and the City of Oshkosh Police departments. As far as I was concerned, I still had much I wanted to accomplish before retirement.

The day went well at the Capitol from a public safety perspective. The Capitol closed without much fuss. It was rumored that the next day, Saturday, March 12, was when the Democratic senators would return to the state. If that were true, it was likely to be another busy day.

DAY 27: SATURDAY, MARCH 12, 2011

THE LARGEST RALLY TO DATE WAS UNFOLDING ON SATURDAY MORNING. Demonstrators came by the tens of thousands to welcome the fourteen Democratic senators to the Capitol Square, along with numerous farm tractors! The Fabulous 14 were greeted like a mix of heroes and rock stars. They made speeches, led chants and cheers, and walked among the people. Talk among the protesters had turned to recall petitions for the Governor, Lieutenant Governor, and eight Republican senators. Off the Square, conservative groups were organizing the recall of six Democratic senators.

At its peak, the crowd on the Capitol Square comprised approximately 125,000 people. As with the preceding month, there were few issues and virtually no problems with the event.

Following the rally, the Command Post closed once again.

CHAPTER NINE
THE LINGERING END

After March 12, 2011, the focus shifted away from protests and rallies to the politics of recalling office holders and court battles. A group of regular and frequent protesters came to develop "Walkerville," a tent colony permitted by the City of Madison for the city side of the Capitol Square. A group of about forty people continued to show up inside the Capitol to disrupt meetings, hearings, and legislative sessions and were promptly and repeatedly arrested. The CPD and a small contingent of state troopers were all that were left of the once massive law enforcement presence. This group of protesters bore little resemblance to the people who once made up the large crowds of February and March.

Signatures were collected in the attempt to recall Republican and Democratic senators. It was back to court as the union proceeded with its lawsuit, and the Dane County District Attorney filed charges alleging that the Legislature had acted contrary to the state's Open Meeting law.

The race for Supreme Court Justice became a referendum of sorts by the populace to show their unhappiness with the Governor. Conservative incumbent Justice David Prosser, who originally was thought would win re-election easily, almost fell to JoAnne Kloppenberg, a virtual unknown at the time.

The actual money spent on damage repair totaled less than $200,000, a far cry from the $7.5 million projected. Most of that money was spent to restore the Capitol Square lawn.

The Legislative and Executive branches of the government were clearly continuing the political battle. Judge Albert's orders issued in early March intended to clarify building hours and access policies. Confusion remained.

The Department of Administration (DOA) continued to argue that restricting access to the Capitol was both necessary and prudent to ensure the work of the government could continue without undue disruption. Yet the small group of protesters believed the work conducted within the Capitol was work of and for the people of Wisconsin. According to this small group, if they wanted to witness government in action or even disrupt it, it was their belief that this is their right. The protesters argued that the Capitol is not just any office building—it is, in an important way, their "house." The fundamental conflict and arrests continued.

Protesters sleeping in the Capitol had been stopped. A permitting system was being established by DOA for groups wanting to access and demonstrate in the Capitol. Weapons screening at the entrances continued. The CPD and WSP resources maintained security measures with far fewer personnel than were present at the height of the protests.

Voluntary compliance, which Chief Tubbs clung to with the large groups of protesters, gave way to arrests and citations almost every day there were committee meetings, hearings, or legislative sessions. Eventually, the weapon screening upon entry would end.

Governor Walker eventually signed into law a measure allowing for the concealed carrying of weapons by citizens throughout the state, including inside the Capitol.

Meanwhile the arguments between the two sides went to court. On March 16, Dane County District Attorney Ismael Ozanne (Democrat) filed a complaint, claiming the actions of the Legislature in hastily stripping the Budget Repair Bill of fiscal implications violated the Open Meetings law of the state.

Two days later, Dane County Judge Maryann Sumi issued a stay on the collective bargaining bill. Her action, however, did not prevent the Legislature from convening again, clearly following the Open Meeting law of the state, and voting a second time on the measure. Few Republicans had the desire to go through the contentious voting process again. Judge Sumi ordered the Bill not be published by the Secretary of State until its legality could be determined. She noted delaying implementation would cause less trouble than having to de-implement the Bill if it were later found to be illegally passed.

To allow the courts time to act, Secretary of State Doug LaFollette (of the famous Wisconsin political family) announced his intent to delay publication of the law until the last possible moment. Republican leaders disagreed and announced their intent to begin implementing the Bill.

On March 25, after a meeting with Senate Republicans, the Legislative Reference Bureau attempted to circumvent the delay and went ahead and "published" the Bill, although it claimed its "publication" was not the same as the Secretary of State's official "publication." On March 29, Judge Sumi issued a clarifying order, which insisted that implementation of the Bill halt until further notice. The Republicans decided to heed the Court's ruling this time.

Politics and the debate over how government was functioning in the state focused next on the Wisconsin Supreme Court. The State Supreme Court race between David Prosser and JoAnne Kloppenburg didn't start out as a referendum on the state's leadership. The primaries on February 15 drew little attention. But by the time of the general election on April 5, it was being described as a proxy for a vote on Governor Walker.

Under ordinary circumstances, the results of the vote would have come in late in the evening on the April 5, but these were no ordinary times in Wisconsin. The lead flip-flopped all evening, with Kloppenburg declaring victory on April 6 with a margin of just over 200 votes. In the coming days, however, new votes appeared from a Republican stronghold in Waukesha County that had been left out of the original count. Justice Prosser was declared the winner on April 15. Ms. Kloppenburg requested a recount on April 20. The recount was officially to take place between April 27 and May 9, but Waukesha County, where most of the "lost" votes had been found, received an extension until May 26. In the end, Justice Prosser retained his seat on the court.

On June 6, the Wisconsin Supreme Court heard arguments from attorneys representing Governor Walker and Dane County District Attorney Ozanne. In the courtroom on the second floor of the Capitol building, the case turned on legal fine points about the intent of the state's Open Meeting law and the circumstances in which it applies to the business of the Legislature. In the Rotunda below, protesters were concerned about government transparency.

The Supreme Court focused on whether a judge could halt the publishing of a bill. The answer the court eventually gave was "no" and the Bill was published and went into effect. Other court cases continued on and will likely continue for years to come.[37]

By June of 2011, when the Supreme Court ruled on the publishing of the Bill, Governor Walker had been in office just six months.

---

[37] Wisconsin Supreme Court Cases 2001AP613LV, 2011AP765W. State of Wisconsin ex rel Ismael R. Ozanne, Jeff Fitzgerald, Scott Fitzgerald, Michael Ellis, Scott Suder, and Douglas LaFollette

Also in June, in yet another bizarre twist of the soap opera that was Wisconsin politics, some of the justices were meeting in Justice Ann Walsh-Bradley's office. During the encounter, allegations arose that newly re-elected Justice David Prosser placed his hands around Justice Bradley's throat. Investigations followed, and versions of what occurred took a decidedly partisan tone. It was a damaging blow to the Supreme Court's otherwise high standing in the state.

THE NEW BADGER PARTNERSHIP
WITHOUT STEROIDS AND WITHOUT BIDDY

THE STATE BUDGET THAT EVENTUALLY PASSED CONTAINED ALMOST ALL THE New Badger Partnership flexibilities Chancellor Biddy Martin had envisioned. The new flexibilities of purchasing authority, pay plans, personnel systems, and some small autonomy from the Board of Regents, was now in place. The UW system's efforts to ensure that UW–Madison, the flagship, did not attain public authority status and move out of the UW system, were successful and UW–Madison remains a part of the system today.

The relationship between the regents, President Reilly, and Chancellor Martin were severely strained. The tension between UW–Madison and the UW system was at an all-time high. Among the students and most of the faculty and staff, Chancellor Biddy Martin was highly regarded and in some circles had attained an almost rock-star quality. Her leadership with the Madison Initiative for Undergraduates, her efforts to solidify relationships with legislators, alumni, and with several key universities in China, plus her seemingly boundless spirit and her vision for the New Badger Partnership, had gained her national attention.

Other universities and colleges came calling. On June 14, 2011, Chancellor Martin accepted the invitation to become the 19th

President of Amherst College in Amherst, Massachusetts. The first woman to hold the post, she began her duties there in September 2011.

RECALLS

THE FERVOR FOR RECALLS CONTINUED AT THE SENATE LEVEL AND FOR THE Governor. An elected official cannot be subject to recall until the individual has served at least one year. The recall of the Governor would take over a year; the Senate recalls would occur much faster. Eight Republican and eight Democratic members of the Senate were considered for recall.

Ultimately, the required numbers of petition signatures were successfully gathered against six Republicans and three Democrats. The special election took place in June for the primaries and then on July 12, 2011. The results changed the dynamic of power in the Senate as Democrats gained two seats, but the Republicans still held a slim majority, 17-16.

Eventually, the first year's anniversary of the Capitol events passed. Over one million signatures were collected to recall Governor Scott Walker. In May 2012, the Democrats held a primary to select their candidate. Mayor Tom Barrett of Milwaukee, who had unsuccessfully run against Scott Walker in 2010, was picked to face him again.

Massive amounts of money flowed into the state in support of Governor Walker. The rhetoric was at a fever pitch. It seemed the citizens had strong opinions for or against the Governor. We at University Police were contacted about a month in advance by Capitol Police and asked to assist with the recall election coverage at the Capitol.

Shortly before the recall election, Chief Charles Tubbs resigned his position to become the Dane County Emergency Management

Director. Deputy Chief Dan Blackdeer became Interim Capitol Police Chief.

The differences were striking in the planning and execution of the event from the previous year. The entire event would be staffed with just state law enforcement within and on the grounds of the Capitol; we wouldn't use emergency police services from around the state. In every meeting, lawyers and representatives of DOA were present.

Debate ensued regarding capacity numbers and I watched as the Madison Fire Department weighed in with their opinions over and over again. For many of these meetings, I had to chuckle to myself, thinking *"Nice of you to show up this time."* The stated capacity number for the Capitol dropped to under 3,000. Permits were required for four or more people. Demonstrations would only be allowed on the ground floor. I believed the harsh application of the rules by the DOA would someday be ruled unconstitutional.

All sorts of questions occurred to me that once again no one wanted to see answered. The worst scenario from a law enforcement perspective would be that the Governor lost by a small margin, likely triggering more court battles and recalls. And what would happen if the Governor would not cede power? Would the people turn out in hundreds of thousands again, perhaps with greater fervor and less patience?

The Governor, through his cabinet, would control the Capitol Police Department and the rules of demonstrations. The Governor would still be in charge of the National Guard. What possible ramifications would this have? No one wanted to even discuss this possibility. From law enforcement's perspective, if either Governor Walker or Mayor Barrett won handily, it was my belief that people would accept the outcome peacefully and continue with the status quo or transition to a new administration.

As we approached the recall election date of June 5, Dan had a firm grasp on command. He was in charge and all of us were ready to support him. This time, he opened the state Command Post in the Department of Natural Resources.

I visited the Square and Command Post several times. My staff was assigned to various locations with various responsibilities. All was well organized and running smoothly. There were so many differences between this operation and the operations during the protests more than a year and a half prior. Command was clear, the Command Post was not going to be moved multiple times. Staging and briefings were set and well planned and logistics was running smoothly. Most impressive was a Joint Information Center that was well-staffed and highly organized to communicate at every turn. There was no void or vacuum of leadership. I wasn't needed anywhere in particular and was proud to watch Dan shine.

In the end, the voters did not recall Governor Scott Walker. The Governor won the election with a wider margin than in 2010. Dan, Randy, and I walked the perimeter of the Square swapping stories of the previous year. The small crowd of people who had gathered on the Square in opposition to the Governor left quickly after his victory was announced. The state Command Post closed early, I hugged Dan goodbye and headed for bed knowing I would be back at the University in the morning.

THIS IS WHAT DEMOCRACY LOOKS LIKE

THE U.S. CONSTITUTION AND ITS AMENDMENTS SHOW REPEATEDLY HOW intelligent and forward-thinking our founders were. All those checks and balances built in. Funny thing is some Americans seem to lose patience when other Americans take to the streets to try to exercise their rights. Yet we are so willing to embrace movements in other countries who strive for the rights we possess.

The Arab Spring was in full swing when Governor Walker introduced his version of "dropping a bomb" called the Budget Repair Bill. People across the Middle East were finding the courage to stand up to leaders and take to the streets. Americans seemed eager to support such actions by the people of Tunisia, Egypt, and Libya. Yet when large groups of Midwesterners showed up at their state capitols in Wisconsin, Ohio, and Indiana, some people grew weary and apathetic.

For 30 days in February and March of 2011, it is estimated 1.5 million people cycled through the Capitol grounds.[38] There were 13 arrests and some of those had nothing to do with the protests. There were no acts of violence. Some grass had to be reseeded. Democracy worked as it was designed.

The protection of civil rights is easy when everyone agrees. It is in moments of disagreement, debate, and discord that our beliefs and principles are tested. It is these moments when women and men of law enforcement must be the thin blue line between groups and with the Bill of Rights as the guide, with a respect of the Rule of Law, not political gain or favoritism or personal bias influencing our actions.

In my view, the police must act as facilitators, safeguarding the exercise of Constitutional rights. It is in moments of turmoil that law enforcement leaders must take a stand and resist using force unless absolutely necessary. At times, they must speak the truth to those in power, knowing it may require some level of personal sacrifice.

After all, courts can rule, politicians can legislate, but it is the police who take those results to the street, to the home, to the school and enforce the rule of law. It is a complex role, a role few outside law enforcement leadership ever understand. Without a

---

[38] This is an estimate based on the crowd sizes taken each day by the Interior Branch for visitors to the Capitol and Capitol Square.

strong sense of principle, of understanding the importance of free expression, exercising Constitutional rights and the police protecting those rights using only reasonable force, we as people will not succeed.

Democracy is intentionally messy. If it were efficient, it wouldn't be a democracy. The ability to redress one's grievances with the government can take many forms. Large crowds marching to surround the seat of government is but one way. This form of democracy is expensive and cost Wisconsin approximately $8 million in wages and expenses. The thing is, to live in a nation where protests take this form without violence, without destruction —well, that's priceless.

Democracy at work (Photo by Mark Golbach)

INDEX

Page references in italics indicate illustrations or photographs.
Titles, positions, political offices, and party affiliations have been omitted.

A

Ackeret, Brian, 26
Administrative Code 2 (Use of State Buildings and Facilities), 283, 285, 293–94, 310, 326, 339–40, 349–50, 358
Albert, John, 317, 322–23, 326, 340, 346–48, 386
Allerman, Steve, 80
Altman, Brad, 59, *64*, 102, *356*, 366
 as camera monitor, 65–66, 83
 as division commander, 61
 on lack of support, 56–57
 on measuring Capitol floor space, 88–89
 as Operations Chief, 41, 45
 on removal of people from galleries, 292
Amesqua, Debra, 87
Archer, Cynthia, 187

B

Bablitch, Bill, 50
Baldwin, Tammy, *85*, 363
banners/signs by protesters. *See* signs/ banners by protesters
Barca, Peter, 126, 383
Barica, Sue, 270–71
Barrett, Tom, 151, 390–91
Bazzell, Darrell, 60
Blackdeer, Dan, 59, 61–62, 84–85, 149, 351
 on Capitol building capacity, 87
 on closing/clearing the Capitol at night, 104, 140, 210, 252
 on EPS, 57–58
 following protesters' breaching of perimeter, 368–70, 373–74
 frustrations of, 38–40
 on inadequate police coverage, 57
 as Incident Commander, 61
 as Interim Capitol Police Chief, 391
 lack of authority, 86, 95, 121, 140, 252, 275
 on officer safety, 209
 in the Operations Room, 364

 at planning meetings, 19–20, 31–32, 36, 38–40
 on workers' compensation claims, 186
Blair, Ron, 105, *169*
Blatter, Tom, 277, 288
Blazel, Ted, 67–68, 78, 89, 198, 273, 277
Bloody Sunday (Selma Bridge, Ala., 1965), 8
Breit, Fran, 230
Bridges, Brian, 57, 74, *169*, *356*
 assesses the crowd, 50, 55
 assists Riseling in interior operations, 59
 at the Capitol, 30, 32, 40–41, 45–46
 on the civil disturbance plan, 134, 142, 147
 crowd management by, 96
 on food deliveries, 80
 as Interior Branch deputy, 61, *64*, 74
 on Planning and Logistics, 84
 at planning meetings, 17, 32, 39
 police dispatching by, 116
 police training sessions by, 292
 Riseling supported by, 233–34
 visitor queuing handled by, 227–28
Brooks, Karl, 178, 218
Brunner, Clark, *30*
Burke, Dale, 33, 46, 75, 84–86, 121, 269, 271, 293, 299, 329, 356
 background, 24
 as EOC leader, 38
 on the escort system, 269
 leadership skills, 24–25
 personality/reputation, 24
 queuing visitors, planning for, 226–27, 231
Bush (George W.) administration, 12
Byers, Ann Tonnon, 66–67, 71, 93, 273, 281–82

C

Capitol
 capacity, 86–87, 105–9, 133, 187, 220, 314, 391
 damage to, 323, 325–26, 335–36, 386

dome, *236*
entrances, 40, 91
evacuation plans, 81
firearms in, 114
fire code inapplicable to, 87
floor plans/layout, 43, 84
floor space, 88–89, 105–6
government branches in, 106–7
Governor's conference room, 283
history, 106
Joint Finance Committee Hearing
    Room, 76
marble staircases and floors, 43, 106,
    108, 137
normal hours of operation, 30, 189, 381
(*see also* Administrative Code 2)
public use space, 106, 339
tours, 213
tunnels, 89–91, 138–39, 164, 292
views of, *6, 12*
War Memorial, 225
Carpenter, Tim, 123
Chapin, Aaron, *289*
Chief's Challenge Coin, 365–66
Cieslewicz, Dave, 373
Clark, Jim, 8
Connor, Theophilus Eugene ("Bull"), 7–8
Constitution (U.S.)
    checks and balances in, 392
    on free speech, 219
    not diminished during extraordinary
        times, 340
    police as safeguarding rights in, 393–94.
    See also First Amendment
Constitution (Wisconsin), 349
Cullen, Tim, 50
Curtis, Bill, 178, *356*

D

Dane County reporting structure, *101*
Davidoff, Judith, 175
democracy
    and the Constitution, 393–94
    forms of, 394
    meaning of, 171
Diamante, Johnnie, *30, 64,* 74, 112, *356,* 382
Dixon, Phil, 42
Donovan, Tim, 273, 290
Dowling, John, 295
Doyle, James ("Jim") E., 11

Dunbar, Donald
    after-action review proposed, 361
    on closing/clearing the Capitol at night,
        211–12
    on health issues, 211
    meets with law enforcement leaders,
        140–42
    on the National Guard, 119
    reputation/leadership skills, 86

E

Ellis, Mike, 50, 89–90
Erpenbach, Jon, 123, 138
Evans, Nancy, 71–72
Ewing, Ruth, 226–27, 231, 235, 344

F

Fadness, Joseph, 281–82
Falk, Kathleen, 147, 383
Finkelmeyer, Corey, 278
First Amendment, 340
    meaning of, 171
    protecting/upholding, 3, 5, 79, 147, 191
    scope of rights, 347, 381
    tenets of, 28
Fitzgerald, Jeff, 96
Fitzgerald, Scott, 89–90, 96, 116
Fitzgerald, Stephen ("Papa Fitz"), 96–99,
    368, 376
Flynn, Ed, 206–7
Folsom, Jim, 8
Fuller, Patrick, 67, 99, 152, 172

G

Giffords, Gabby, 123, 335
Gilkes, Keith, 102, 104, 152, 154–56, 186
    on the Capitol's return to normalcy, 188,
        275, 276
    on closing/clearing the Capitol at night,
        212–13, 220–21, 232
    directions to officers, 40
    policy meetings, 157, 254
Goetsch, Byron, 37, 61, *64*
Goldstein, Herman, 28
Gosenheimer, Carol, 139, 167, 181, 205
Governor's Mansion (Madison), 18
Groppi, James, 135–36
Grothman, Glenn, 320

H

Hanson, Doris, 97–99
Hefty, Thomas R., 18
Hintz, Gordon, 99–100
Hogan, John, 152, 172
Hooker, Jim, 1, 3
Huebsch, Michael, 186, 351
  background, 283–84
  on clearing the Capitol, 284–86
  on damage to the Capitol, 325–26,
    335–36
  pre-Assembly vote objectives,
    376–77, 379–80
  testimony on Capitol access, 310–14, 317

J

Jackson, Jesse, 84–85, *85*, 104, 363
Jansen, Jerry, 33, 104, 133, 185–86
Jauch, Bob, 34
Jensen, Jodi, 171, 173, 186, 189, 210,
  212–13, 220, 276
Joe the Plumber, 142

K

Kennedy, Robert, 8
Kichefski, Anita, *289*
King, Martin Luther, Jr., 8, 28, 366
King, Rodney, 16
Kirchner, Officer, 344
Kloppenberg, JoAnne, 385, 387–88
Klu Klux Klan, 7–8
Koch brothers, 175, 194–95, 197
Kuschel, Todd, 19–20, 31, 39, 80, 84–86,
  121, 134, 140

L

LaFollette, Douglas, 387
LaFollette, "Fighting" Bob, 11
Langner, Sue, 83
Lautenschlager, Peg, 295–96, 310, 319,
  339–40, 343
LaWall, Dave, 178, 185
Lazar, Maria, 314
Lind, John, 37–38, *64*
Lindgren, Craig, 366
Lyall, Katharine, 149

M

Mahoney, David, 154, 173, 333
  background, 50–51
  on closing/clearing the Capitol at night,
    100, 102, 104
  press conference held by, 293
  sheriffs called in by, 57
Mansky, Ben, 204
Marchant, Rob, 68, 89
  on office sleepovers by protesters, 172
  security measures by, 123
  on threats to senators, 116, 123, 133
Martin, Carolyn A. ("Biddy"), 49, 59–60, 75,
  221, 223
  as Amherst College president, 389–90
  birthday celebrated by, 111, 130–31
  Chinese universities visited by, 150–51
  Madison Initiative for Undergraduates
    (MIU) proposed by, 150
  meeting with Walker, 48
  New Badger Partnership (NBP) proposal,
    148, 151, 184–85, 193, 389
  reputation, 389
  Riseling supported by, 237, 286–87
  at staff meeting re TAs and TAA, 22
Matysik, Jerry, 221–23
Maurer, Jude, 131
McCarthy, "Tailgunner" Joe, 11
Means, Steve, 278–79, 317, 322, 339
Merdler, Scott, 135
Miller, Mark, 78
Milroy, Representative, 344
Mlsna, Les, 142, 366
Moore, Michael, 363
Murphy, Ian, 321

N

national anthem, 170–71
Nelson, Don, 129
New Badger Partnership (NBP), 148, 151,
  184–85, 193, 389
Newman, Ben, 40, 84
Newton, Michael, 63, *64*, 282, 356
  background, 56, 267
  as division commander, 61
  as EMT, 267–68
  at planning meeting, 37–38
  resourcefulness, 56

O

Obama, Barack, 139, 368
Olin House, 130
Open Meeting Law, 383, 385, 387–88
Ozanne, Ismael, 118–19, 293, 387–88

P

pepper spray, 77–78
Pfatteicher, Sarah, 177, 333–34, 348
Pickerel, Kurt, 143
Pocan, Mark, 258, 327–28, 374
President's Commission on Law
 Enforcement and the Administration of
 Justice (1967), 9
Price, Darren, 171, 210, 376
Prosser, David, 385, 387–89

R

Ray, Gina, 263, 266
recall elections/petitions, 363, 368, 384–85,
 390–92
Reilly, Kevin, 48–49, 149, 389
Renlund, Cari Anne, 186–87, 293–94
Riseling, Susan, 307–8, 316, 356, 359
 attire, 74
 on Capitol building capacity, 87, 105–9,
  391
 on clearing the Assembly Anteroom and
  Chamber, 376–82
 on closing/clearing the Capitol at night,
  145–46, 156, 190–91, 208, 210,
  212–15, 225–26, 230–32, 245–
  47, 284–85, 312–13
 Command Post, frustrations with, 229,
  232–35, 331–32
 on Constitutional rights, 182 (see also
 First Amendment)
 on court-ordered removal of protesters,
  327, 346–47, 350–51
 crowd estimation by, 122, 125, 230
 on evacuation plans, 81
 following protesters' breaching of
  perimeter, 369–75
 on health issues, 213–14
 ICS model used, 60–61
 as Interior Branch Director, 61, 64, 102,
  229
 Interior Branch established, 59
 Interior Branch re-established, 375, 382

parting gifts to, 365
 police dispatching by, 374
 on queuing visitors to the Capitol,
  226–27, 244, 250–51, 260, 263,
  268–69, 294, 304
 at Regents' meeting, 150, 221
 resumes normal police duties, 367
 on retirement, 109, 368, 383
 senators protected by, 372–73
 on the senators' return, 361
 testimony on ammunition found at
  Capitol, 333
 testimony on Capitol access, 310, 317–20
 testimony on protesters' desire to stay
  in Capitol, 336
 on Wisconsin State Constitution, 349
Rogers, Steve, 32, 148, 367
rules of engagement, 76–77, 358–60, 359,
 362
Rutherford, Lisa, 129, 278

S

Sasso, Kari, 30, 279–80
Schaffer, Brandi, 37–38, 356
Schmidt, Marc, 59, 63, 64, 356, 366
 bill-signing planning by, 382
 on Capitol building capacity, 86–87
 as division commander, 61
 escort teams handled by, 292, 304
 evacuation plans obtained, 81
 on fire alarm testing, 303
 frustrations of, 57
 knowledge of the Capitol, 116
 on measuring Capitol floor space, 89
 on mobilization/demobilization of
  police, 133
 police dispatching by, 116
 on portable toilets, 263
Schmitt, Ursula, 97
signs/banners by protesters, 347, 349,
 352–54, 353–55, 363
Silbernagel, Mark, 32, 159, 175, 300
Simms, Pat, 257
Soley, Karen, 74, 84
 explosive ordnance plan of, 147
 as ICS branch commander, 150, 203
 leadership/planning skills, 184–85
 on transportation of officers, 203–4
Stark, Randy, 359
 assists Riseling in interior
  operations, 59
 belongings flyers made by, 232
 on Capitol building capacity, 108–9

on the Capitol's return to normalcy, 276
communications handled by, 115
contact teams formed by, 218
food arrangements by, 272
as Interior Branch deputy, 61, *64*, 74, 76, 78
on leadership, 56
on mobilization/demobilization of police, 132, 194
as negotiator, 276
on officer briefing process, 107, 114, 124, 58
on radio communications, 80
Riseling supported by, 234–35
on the senators' return, 361
staff shortages handled by, 177
transportation of officers handled by, 164
St. John, Kevin, 117–18
Stults, Gary, 105–6
Sumi, Maryann, 387
Sweeney, Jack, 278

T

Taylor, Lena C., 277
Teasdale, Charles ("Chuck"), 59, 270, 274–75
background, 39
as CP commander, 39
on the ICS, 228
as Operations Chief, 61
on police staffing, 333–34
troop deployment by, 381–82
on the Winter Festival, 66
Thompson, Tommy G.
as a moderate, 11–12
Pursuit Bill signed by, 98
as Secretary of Health and Human Services, 12
Tubbs, Charles ("Charlie"), 25, 38
addresses AFSCME, 27–28
on AFSCME permits, 21
on the alcohol ban, 172
background, 14
on the Capitol's return to normalcy, 192, 204, 265
on Capitol tours, 213
on closing/clearing the Capitol at night, 102–4, 140, 145, 206, 212, 219–20, 247, 258, 274, 312–13
on court-ordered removal of protesters, 327
as Dane County Emergency Management Director, 390–91

frustrations of, 40, 53
inaccessibility of, 52–53, 85–86, 121, 183
Jackson assisted by, 85
leadership skills, 155
as negotiator, 243–45, 259, 261–62, 264–65, 269, 273, 275–76, 282
no-arrest, no hands-on policy of, 180–81, 248, 275, 305, 352
personality/appearance, 14, 163
at planning meetings, 19–21, 25, 33–34, 36
policing style, 28–29
protesters, exception made for, 327–28
relationship with unions and protesters, 156, 172, 190, 192, 212, 215, 243, 247–48, 345–46, 351–52, 362
Riseling's removal directive overridden by, 378–81
on signs/posters by protesters, 347
tasks assigned to Blackdeer, 61–62
on the Winter Festival, 66

V

Vinehout, Kathleen, 216
Virgil, Tina, 87, 123, 125–26, 196, 207, 296–97, 332
Vos, Robin, 34
Vukmir, Leah, 123

W

Walker, Scott
budget speech by, 299–300
Budget Repair Bill announced by, 14–15, 393
Budget Repair Bill signed by, 382–83
on calling in National Guard, 15, 17, 35
campaign contributions to, 175
on closing/clearing the Capitol at night, 102–3
concealed carrying of weapons bill signed by, 386
election of, 11
ethics complaint against, 367
and Martin, 151
press conference held, 74
recall of, efforts toward, 390–92
threats against, 123, 197
on UW–Madison's becoming a Public Authority, 148, 151
Wauwatosa residence of, 18–19

Wall, Ed, 88, 117–18, 189, 209–11, 279
  background, 321
  testimony on Capitol access, 320–22
Walsh-Bradley, Ann, 389
Wernet, Kevin, *356*
  background, 48
  at the Capitol Operations Room, 48
  on fire-scene management, 60
  food arrangements by, 80, 158, 181, 331
  on ICS organizational structure, 55–56
  parking/transportation arrangements
      by, 68
  as Riseling's aide, 63, *64*, 74, 104
  on SW-IMT, 62
  task templates created by, 178
Wisconsin Supreme Court, 387–89
Wray, Noble, 100, 102, 104, 196

Ystenes, Pete, 49, 370

ABOUT THE AUTHOR

Associate Vice Chancellor/Chief Susan Riseling currently leads the Police Department at the University of Wisconsin-Madison. She is a past president of the Dane County Chiefs of Police, the Wisconsin Chiefs of Police Association, and the first woman and first University Police Chief to hold that particular position.

She is also a past president of the National Association of Women Law Enforcement Executives. In addition, Chief Riseling is a former Vice President at Large of the International Association of Chiefs of Police (IACP), the world's largest police organization with over 20,000 members from over 100 countries. In August 2003, Chief Riseling was awarded the Motorola NAWLEE (National Association of Women Law Enforcement Executives) Law Enforcement Executive of the year.

Susan Riseling's email: decisionmaker10@gmail.com
Please contact the author via www.mysterytomebooks.com